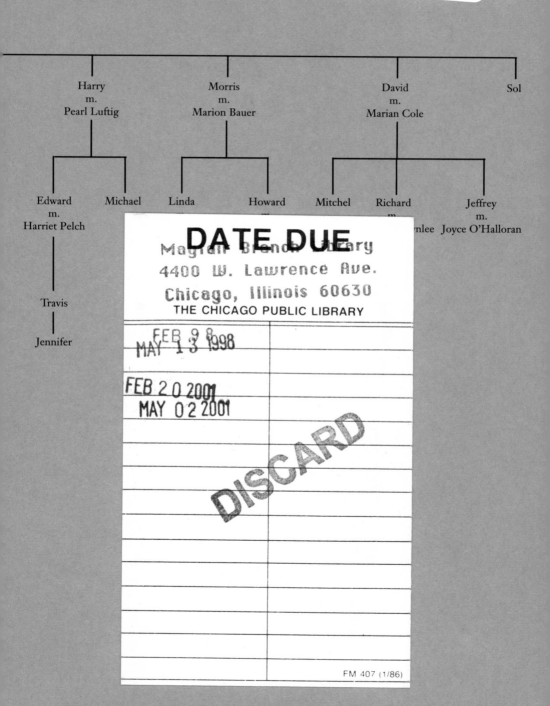

Harry
m.
Pearl Luftig

Morris
m.
Marion Bauer

David
m.
Marian Cole

Sol

Edward
m.
Harriet Pelch

Michael

Linda

Howard

Mitchel

Richard

Jeffrey
m.
Joyce O'Halloran

Travis

Jennifer

I BOUGHT IT AT POLK BROS

The Story of an
American Retailing Phenomenon

Ann Paden

Bonus Books, Inc., Chicago

00   99   98   97   96   5   4   3   2   1

Library of Congress Cataloging-in-Publication Data

Paden, Ann.
    I bought it at Polk Bros : the story of an American retailing phenomenon / Ann Paden.
        p.   cm.
    Includes index.
    ISBN 1-56625-073-0
    1. Polk Bros (Firm)—History.   2. Electric household appliances industry—Illinois—Chicago—History.   3. Stores, Retail—Illinois—Chicago—History.   I. Title.
    HD9971.U64P657   1996
    381'.456838'0977311—DC20   96-41398

International Standard Book Number: 1-56625-073-0

Bonus Books, Inc.
160 East Illinois Street
Chicago, Illinois 60611

Printed in the United States of America

Table of Contents

Preface

In the spring of 1992 a *Chicago Tribune* front-page banner headline announced, "End of an era: Polk Bros. to close doors." Except for the prominence of the headline, this might have been just another business story. It was not. The word spread fast: "Polk Bros. is closing!" The news kindled a surge of nostalgia throughout the Chicago area, and, in fact, across the nation. Polk Bros. was not just a business. The fabulous old appliance and furniture chain was a retailing legend, a Chicago institution, a household word. In the coming months people would realize how deeply the passing of Polk Bros. would be mourned.

The words "I bought it at Polk Bros." had been spoken so often over the fifty-seven-year history of the company that the idiom was virtually woven into the Chicago vocabulary. For millions, the very name — Polk Bros. — evoked the excitement that surrounded the purchase of the family's first television set, first automatic washing machine, first dishwasher. It stirred memories of Polk's colorful army of "let's make a deal" salesmen; of promotions that included carloads of Georgia watermelons, Hawaiian pineapples, Washington apples; of live television and midnight movies, circus tents and Santa Clauses.

* * *

The memories reached back to the 1930s when an eighteen-year-old entrepreneur named Sol Pokovitz opened a bare-bones appliance outlet in a northwest Chicago working-class neighborhood. Driven by a single-minded idea — offering the best for less — and propelled by the buoyant optimism and material plenty of the postwar period, the five Polk brothers and their sister built this small family business into a magnificent merchandising machine that, along the way, became the archetype for a twentieth-century revolution in retailing.

*   *   *

The tremendous interest that accompanied the announcement of Polk Bros.' closing was surprising to the family but perhaps should not have been so unexpected. After all, for more than half a century Polk Bros. had made news — and it had made history.

From the beginning, Polk Bros. broke and then rewrote the rules of retailing. Dealing in volume buying, rapid turnover, and rock-bottom prices, Sol Polk challenged the appliance industry's most sacred shibboleth in the 1950s by daring to sell nationally advertised products below manufacturers' list prices.

Polk Bros. was the first retailer in the industry to open its stores on Sundays. It was the first dealer to bring color television and microwave ovens into the market and was among the first to open up the U.S. market to Japanese electronics. Polk sponsored Chicago's first color television broadcasts, hosted the nation's first telethon, and created the first infomercial. The concept for one of the longest running advertising campaigns in history — the lonely Maytag repairman — originated on the Polk Bros. sales floor.

Hailed by *Fortune* magazine in 1955 as "Chicago's Red-Hot Merchandiser," and by the *Saturday Evening Post* in 1963 as "The King of the Discounters," Sol Polk pioneered merchandising strategies that foreshadowed by decades today's Kmart and Wal-Mart stores. Polk templates such as neighborhood merchandising, patriotic marketing, and on-time buying have been reinvented as the retailing buzz words of the 1990s. When Polk Bros. closed its last store, the company was recognized as the business that invented the retailling phenomenon of the 1980s — the electronics superstore.

When people remember Polk Bros., they remember above all else that shopping at Polk's was fun for the family. Polk sales floors were perpetual carnivals of promotions and entertainments. Although the hoopla generated around a Polk Bros. promotion will never be equalled, the combination of merchandising with show business is a strategy that has now been taken up by every major retailer in the country.

*   *   *

When she learned that Polk Bros. would close Judith Semon, a widow and great-grandmother, sat down, at the kitchen table in her home in suburban Elgin, Illinois, to compose a letter:

> I was your customer since 1941 when we bought our wedding furniture. Maybe you don't remember this, but you kept it for us and didn't charge us anything, until we could find an apartment, which was very hard to do then. . . . I miss your store very much.

Over the next several months hundreds of letters like this flooded Polk Bros. offices: "It's like a death in the family. . . ." "I don't know what we are going to do without you. . . ." "My father made going to Polk Bros. a family outing. . . ." "Just about everything we have was purchased at Polk Bros. . . ." "Goodbye Old Friend. I will miss you."

*   *   *

The closing of the Polk Bros. stores after fifty-seven years was indeed the end of an era. It was also a beginning. Polk Bros.' star as a retailer had dimmed, but Polk Bros. Inc. was neither broke nor bankrupt. Far from it.

Polk Bros. had always been an unusual business, known for its tightly held and intensely private financial structure as much as for its hellza-poppin' public promotions. But nothing in the long circus that was Polk Bros. was so unexpected by the Chicago business community as the retail chain's parting gesture. The entire wealth of the company, which came to total some $220 million, had been devolved upon the charitable Polk Bros. Foundation. The goal was clearly defined by the family and outside directors: Giving Back to Chicago.

Polk Bros. has been imitated, many times over, but the extraordinary confluence of events, technologies, personalities, and place that created the Polk Bros. phenomenon is unlikely to occur ever again. Here is what Polk Bros. was, how it did what it did, and the story of the people who made it happen.

1

The World's Largest Birthday Party

"Polk Brothers, those fabulous neighborhood merchandisers . . ."
> — **The Leader**
> September 30, 1953

"They built a 'city' from a small appliance store."
> — **Chicago American**
> April 28, 1955

In 1935 Sol Polk, a young man just out of high school, opened up a small appliance store in a Northwest Chicago neighborhood and brought his four older brothers and his sister in to help him run it. Twenty years later that little family business dominated the Chicago appliance market and was well on its way to revolutionizing the way that America's retailers did business.

In the beginning, the Polk family ran scared and they worked hard. During the war years, the threat of failure was never far from their minds. By 1950, however, these fears were no more than a fading memory. Polk Bros. was a success. It was a huge success.

In the rapid-growth years that began with the return of the veterans in 1945, Sol Polk persistently challenged both the bastions of fair trade pricing and the traditional patterns of distribution in the appliance and housewares industries. From the beginning, old-line retailers had dismissed Polk as an upstart and something of a nuisance. It didn't take Sol long to prove them wrong. Within the decade of the opening of the first store, the company was recognized in the national press as "a Chicago institution" and "the country's fastest mover of home appliances."

Polk Bros. was as famous for its sensational promotions and the carnival atmosphere of the "Polk City" complex of stores on North Central Avenue as it was for its rock-bottom prices and unsurpassed selection of brand-name merchandise. In the early 1950s, something like eight thousand shoppers a day visited Polk City and the company's two South Side stores. By 1955 more than a million Chicago families had shopped at Polk's, furnishing their kitchens and their homes with the best and the newest products that American industry had to offer — at the lowest prices.

As the twentieth anniversary of the opening of the first Polk Bros. store approached, the family decided that it was time to celebrate. The event would be master-merchandiser Sol Polk's grandest promotional effort to date: He bought out the entire Chicago Stadium on the night of March 13, 1955, to treat Polk customers, suppliers, and friends to "The World's Largest Birthday Party."

Tickets were distributed free through the stores and were given out at the box office to anyone who could produce a Polk Bros. receipt, new or old. The show would be an entertainment blockbuster: Ed Sullivan's "Toast of the Town," the most successful variety show on television, was to be broadcast live from the Chicago Stadium that night. The Sullivan show would be followed by an opening-weekend performance of the Ice Capades of 1955.

On the Wednesday before the event, Congressman Richard W. Hoffman declared on the floor of the U.S. House of Representatives that

> A birthday celebration of this magnitude is typical of the way Sol Polk does business. In the past twenty years he has made merchandising history in Chicago as a retail dealer in home appliances.

Twenty thousand people — all guests of Polk Bros. — jammed the Chicago Stadium on the night of the big party. The event was pivotal, not just because it was so memorable, but because, in the eyes of the Polk family, it marked the transition of the company from an aggressive adolescence to a mature, though no less boisterous, status as a powerful presence in the city and in the industry.

*   *   *

The choice of an ice revue as the big birthday present to Polk Bros.' customers was not at all accidental. In hitching Polk Bros.' party to the Ice Capades show, Sol was recreating a memory of one of Polk's most popular promotions to date — the midsummer installation of an actual ice-skating rink in the parking lot of the Polk City complex on North Central Avenue.

The ice-rink idea had popped into Sol Polk's mind in the spring of 1953. At that time Chicago Blackhawks hockey, and a goalie named Glenn "Iron Man" Hall, were almost as big in Chicago as Chicago Bulls basketball and a player named Michael "Air" Jordan would be thirty-five years later. The Blackhawks, Sol could not help but notice, drew standing-room-only crowds.

Lester Bachmann, who for nearly fifty years was Sol Polk's right-hand man, remembers that Arthur Wirtz, who owned the Chicago Stadium and who had bought the Blackhawks team in 1952, agreed that if Sol set up a refrigerated rink, he would send the Hawks out to run some practice sessions in front of the Polk Bros. stores.

Getting the Blackhawks was not much of a problem for Sol Polk. The problem of keeping the sun from turning the ice to slush was harder to solve. Sol's answer was to cover the rink with a full-size circus tent. The Blackhawk practices drew so many spectators into the stores that the Polks decided to keep the festivities going through the summer.

Sol, a man with mile-a-minute imagination, came up with another plan. He would invite the Ice Capades to use Polk Bros.' rink for a Sunday dress rehearsal before the revue's 1953 Chicago opening. On the Sunday that the Ice Cadets and Ice Capettes came out to Polk Bros.' parking lot, some twenty-one thousand people passed through the Polk City stores. For the rest of the summer the Polks kept the event alive by offering evening ice-skating free to everyone.

*   *   *

Sol Polk always thought big. When the idea of having a twentieth birthday celebration came to mind, Sol levelled his gaze on the Chicago Stadium. The stadium was known as the world's biggest and noisiest barn. When it was built in 1929, it was the largest auditorium of its kind anywhere, seating thousands more spectators than even New York's Madison Square Garden.

Everything about the Chicago Stadium was larger than life. The stadium was a sports palace without compare — a building built for spectacle. It was designed to accommodate world champion boxing matches and six-day bicycle races. It had been the home of the Blackhawks since 1929. The Chicago Bulls would make it their own in the 1960s. The World Champion Chicago Bears, frozen out of Wrigley Field, played the first National Football League playoff game under the dome of the Chicago Stadium.

The stadium was the scene of the quadrennial Democratic National Convention from 1932 through 1944. It was here that Franklin D. Roosevelt first made his promise of a New Deal for the American People. Mayor Richard J. Daley's torchlight parade and nationally televised, all-star Democratic rally staged at the Chicago Stadium on November 4, 1960, was said to have won the presidency for John F. Kennedy.

The amphitheater had been host to circuses, rodeos, and wrestling matches. It was home to the big-band dance parties of the 1940s and would become home to the big-time rock concerts of the 1970s and 1980s. The Chicago Stadium was the birthplace of the opulent ice revues that reached dazzling heights in the Sonja Henie ice shows of the 1940s and the Ice Capades and Follies of later decades.

From the beginning, the Chicago Stadium was a blue-collar hall, beloved by the people of the city. It was the scene of the hottest tickets in town. And the biggest events. It was the place to go to have a grand old time. The venerable Chicago Stadium was also part of the old neighborhood for the Polk family. Located at 1800 West Madison, the stadium was just blocks from the walk-up flat on West Taylor Street where Sol and three of his brothers had been born.

Where else would Polk Bros., billed as the world's largest dealer in brand-name appliances, go to stage the world's largest birthday party, for one of the largest crowds ever to gather for an indoor event in Chicago?

*   *   *

The Ice Capades, a glittering entertainment guaranteed to be fun for the whole family, fit Polk Bros.' criteria like a hand in a glove. Polk Bros. already had a relationship with the Ice Capades organization, and Polk's entree to the Chicago Stadium was assured by a long-standing association with stadium owner Arthur Wirtz.

Lester Bachmann recalls the negotiations over the deal. The date chosen was March 13, the second night of an eleven-day run of the "Fabulous Fifteenth Ice Capades of '55," then billed as "The Greatest Show on Ice." The Stadium seated between sixteen and twenty thousand people, depending on the event. Polk Bros. bought out the house. Sunday morning reviews of the opening night performance described the spectacle as "a stunning package" but advised Chicago readers not to rush to the box office: "Tonight's show is completely sold out, all seats bought by a local firm, which is celebrating its 20th anniversary."

*   *   *

Ed Sullivan's "Toast of the Town" program was riding the top of the charts in 1955. The show was aired live from the CBS-TV studios in New York City at eight o'clock on Sunday nights, peak family viewing time. From there it was transmitted into millions of homes across America.

In early 1955, Sullivan and network executives at CBS-TV were looking for an opportunity to take "The Toast of the Town" out of New York for a remote broadcast from another major American city. Chicago with its sophisticated broadcasting facilities seemed like the right place, and a tie-in with the Ice Capades was the right format for the family-oriented Sullivan show.

Lester Bachmann believes that when the Sullivan people scheduled their Chicago telecast for the night of March 13, they did not realize that while Sunday nights across the country were presumed to belong to Ed Sullivan, the Chicago Stadium that night belonged to Polk Bros.

Historian David Halberstam has described Sullivan as "on the screen and in real life, a stiff — a staid, humorless, rather puritanical man." In 1955, Ed Sullivan was at the height of his power. He was also, Halberstam suggests, "most assuredly not a man to cross."

Sullivan was then sponsored by Lincoln-Mercury. When he requested the usual block of tickets for his sponsor's Chicagoland dealers, he was dismayed to discover that a local appliance store had pre-empted the night. "We had twenty thousand seats, and Sullivan had none," Lester Bachmann recalls. "Sullivan was so mad about this that he made things very difficult."

In a conciliatory gesture, Polk Bros. offered Sullivan five hundred tickets to distribute among his Chicago dealers. Sullivan accepted the tickets but became even more "stiff," "staid," and "humorless" than usual in the presence of anyone from the animated Polk Bros. camp. "On the night of the show, he was still mad," Lester says. "He even refused at first to have his picture taken with Mr. Polk."

*　*　*

There is some history behind his behavior. This was not Ed Sullivan's first encounter with Sol Polk and the Polk family appliance business. Some months before the Chicago Stadium ticket debacle, Sullivan had announced to the nation that "Next week on our r-e-a-l-l-y big show we will bring you, live from New York, none other than Sergeant Bilko: The always marvelous Phil Silvers!"

Phil Silvers did not appear live on the next week's "Toast of the Town" show, as Sullivan had promised, for this reason: Silvers, who played master sergeant and master schemer Ernie Bilko, was busy in Chicago that weekend. He was doing a promotion for Polk Bros., from a makeshift stage set up in the parking lot of Polk's new store on Cottage Grove Avenue.

"Sergeant Bilko's" appearance at the Polk Bros.' opening was arranged personally by George Foerstner, founder and chief executive officer of the Amana Refrigeration company. Amana at that time was sole sponsor of the "Phil Silvers Show."

Foerstner, a brilliant engineer who had been Charles Goren's bridge partner, nonetheless had down-home ways about him. When he was in Chicago, he liked to drop by Polk Bros.' makeshift offices upstairs over the store at 2850 North Central Avenue and shoot the breeze for an hour or so.

Lester Bachmann recalls that on one of these informal

occasions, Foerstner asked, "Could you do anything if we brought Phil Silvers out to your stores?" Lester remembers:

> I said yes, because Sergeant Bilko was one of the most popular half hours on television. Mr. Foerstner said, "Give me the telephone." I handed him the phone and he called Las Vegas and got hold of Phil Silvers.
>
> He said, "Phil, when are you coming east?" Phil gave him the dates that he was due in New York. Mr. Foerstner said, "I want you to do me a favor. I want you to bring your whole crew out here to Chicago on that Saturday and Sunday and put on a couple of shows for some friends of mine." And he hung up, just like that.

Sol Polk and Lester Bachmann started making plans for the Phil Silvers' Amana promotion. They advertised the forthcoming visit, placed displays in Polk Bros. stores, and had a stage built in the parking lot at the Cottage Grove store. Sol contacted the Fifth Army Headquarters and borrowed a recruiting tent — and an army tank — as props for the occasion.

Lester, understandably, was alarmed on the Sunday before the scheduled appearance when he heard Ed Sullivan tell the nation that Phil Silvers was going to be in New York, not Chicago, the next Sunday.

> First thing in the morning I got on the phone and called George Foerstner in Iowa. I said, "George, did you see the Sullivan show last night?"
>
> He said, "Yes."
>
> I said, "What are you going to do about it?"
>
> He said, "Nothing."
>
> I said, "Well, we have this whole thing planned. What are we going to do?"
>
> He said, "I told you that Phil is going to be there Saturday and Sunday. And he is going to be there Saturday and Sunday. Don't worry about it."

On the Friday evening before the event, Sol and Lester met Phil Silvers, his wife-to-be, and the show's producer at the Chicago airport. The party went together to a Chicago hotel for an affable dinner. Nothing was said about the Sullivan show. Other "Phil Silvers Show" cast members arrived that night and the following morning.

Silvers and his crew spent Saturday and all day Sunday at Polk Bros.' big, new store at 85th and Cottage Grove Avenue. They chatted with shoppers, handed out Silvers-style black eyeglass frames to the kids, and did stand-up performances from the stage in the parking lot. After the last performance, they went over to the CBS studio in Chicago and did a remote telecast to the Sullivan show in New York.

*   *   *

The story is significant for what it says about the economic relationship between brand-name national manufacturers such as Amana and a trend-setting, high-volume dealer such as Chicago's Polk Bros.

Foerstner and Amana Refrigeration, at the time of Phil Silvers' visit to Chicago, were struggling to make a place in the American family life-style for Amana's principal product, the home freezer. They were also preparing to launch a new specialty item, the combination refrigerator-freezer. Polk Bros., with its saturation of the Chicago consumer market, could make or break a new product. When it came to a showdown over Silvers' schedule — Sullivan or Chicago — there was no contest. Polk owned the Chicago appliance market, and Amana owned Silvers.

*   *   *

The afternoon of the World's Largest Birthday Party was clear, sunny, and cold, even for Chicago. People began gathering early along West Madison Street, hoping to get a glimpse of arriving celebrities. Scalpers circulated among the crowd, holding two fingers, or four, over their heads as they bargained for tickets to the sold-out event.

The World's Largest Birthday Party, the scalpers said, was the hottest show in town. Competition was stiff: "South Pacific" was at the Opera House; Deborah Kerr in "Tea and Sympathy" was playing the Blackstone; Ralph Bellamy in "Oh Men! Oh Women!" was at the Harris Theatre; Yul Brynner was at the Shubert, starring in the first run of "The King and I"; and Tallulah Bankhead was playing in "Dear Charles" at the Erlanger. If that weren't enough, the Shrine Circus was at the Medinah Temple that weekend.

Ed Sullivan and the "Toast of the Town" cast arrived around five o'clock to rehearse the show that would be telecast nationwide at seven, Chicago time. Pianist-comedian Victor Borge ran through his act, supported on both arms by Ice Capades skaters as he made his way to the piano. He dubbed his appearance, his first on skates, as his way of "breaking the ice."

Seating for the VIP spectators and guests had been a touchy matter for Polk Bros., the host of the evening's events. Chicago elections — always a matter of great interest in the city — would be held three weeks later, on April 5. The governor of the state was in Springfield that night, but he sent the lieutenant governor to represent him. Richard J. Daley, who was making his first run for the office of mayor, had a front-row seat. So did his hapless opponent, Alderman Robert Merriam. The mayoral race, at this point, was thought to be close. Chicago precinct captains and ward bosses roamed the mezzanine hustling votes for Daley, the choice of the powerful Democratic machine.

The Chicago-area Lincoln-Mercury dealers and their families filed into the reserved section designated for them. Coca-Cola dealers and their families, special guests of Polk Bros., settled noisily into another reserved section.

Sam, Harry, Morrie, and David Polk and their families also arrived early. Sol Polk, a bachelor, was then just thirty-seven years old. Chicagoans, aware that they were celebrating

Polk Bros.' twentieth year in business that night, were surprised to see how young the company's founder appeared. A writer for *Fortune* magazine commented at the time that Sol Polk "doesn't look like a titan of the marketplace." In fact, the writer said, "He looks more like Bob Hope." Many who knew Sol then agree.

The name "Polk Bros." was always something of a misnomer. The five Polk brothers had an older sister, Goldie Polk Bachmann Luftig. Goldie, who had been left a widow with two young children in the early 1940s, was the brains behind the successful home furnishings branch of the business. She was accompanied to the event by her second husband, Morris Luftig, and her grown son and daughter, Bruce Bachmann and Roberta Bachmann Lewis, along with Roberta's husband Irv Lewis.

*   *   *

Moments before 7 p.m., the house lights went down, the hot television lighting went up, and Ed Sullivan made his entrance. The show went off without a hitch. But the effect was curiously flat. Maybe it was the cavernous space of the Chicago Stadium. Maybe it was the all-Chicago audience. And maybe it was the collective sense that Sullivan's show was merely a prelude to the main event.

A review that appeared the following day was terse in its summary comment:

> That friendly intimacy that Sullivan establishes regularly in the New York Theater where he usually telecasts his show was largely lacking last night. Come again, Ed, and try a smaller place.

A well-known Chicago celebrity watcher and newspaper columnist noted Sullivan's pique and remarked that "Ed Sullivan is getting a Polk complex. It seems every time he wants to do something in Chicago, he has to get permission first from Sol Polk."

At 8 p.m. the Ice Capades ensemble launched their own show and the party began in earnest. The crowd seemed to come alive as music swelled to fill the huge Stadium and long spotlights swept back and forth across the silvery ice, tracking dazzling virtuoso performances by Donna Atwood and her partner Bobby Specht.

For sheer spectacle, the show, it was said, was the greatest Ice Capades ever, featuring ten lavishly costumed production numbers. These included George Gershwin's "An American in Paris" and a condensed version of the musical comedy "Wish You Were Here." For the children, there was a comedic Mother Goose fantasy entitled "Humpty Dumpty on Ice" and a dramatization of "How Much Is That Doggie in the Window?"

At intermission, master of ceremonies Howard Miller, a popular radio personality, signalled the spectators to remain in their seats for a birthday surprise. Two dozen Ice Capades skaters swept onto the ice and circled the arena. Each was carrying a large, mock birthday cake with a sparkling candle. Each cake was marked with a single giant letter. The skaters fell into formation, and the crowd cheered when they saw that the letters spelled out "HAPPY BIRTHDAY POLK BROS!"

As the skaters circled the Stadium, an army of Coca-Cola employees flowed into the aisles. Their job was part of a choreographed and well-rehearsed drill that was carried off with the precision of a massive military maneuver. Within a matter of ten minutes, they had served twenty thousand Cokes and as many birthday cupcakes to Polk Bros.' guests.

The five Polk brothers and their sister Goldie came briefly to center stage to wave and acknowledge the crowd. Though they would have no way of knowing, it would be one of the last times that the six of them would be together. Within a matter of weeks, David, who was the youngest next to Sol, would fall ill suddenly and die of complications of a heart ailment.

Many years later, Goldie's daughter Roberta Bachmann Lewis recalled the night of the World's Largest Birthday Party:

> Although they had all worked so hard in the business for so many years, I don't think my mother or any of my uncles realized until that night just how big the business had grown, how many people they had touched, and how far they had come together.

2

American Dream

"To our father and mother who brought us to this country."

— Polk family toast

"No one was ever more enthusiastic about the opportunities our free enterprise system affords."

— Earl Lifshey
Weekly Home Furnishings News

The excitement of the sprawling Polk City complex on North Central Avenue has been compared to the great bazaars of Eastern Europe. The comparison is a fair one, but the spirit of the Polk Bros. stores can be traced even more directly to the hustle and energy of Chicago's Maxwell Street Market.

The Polks' flamboyant style and their talent for drawing huge Sunday crowds into their stores may have seemed extraordinary in the American midwest in the middle of the 1950s. But the phenomenon was not at all without precedent. It came straight out of the Pokovitz family's earliest experiences in America.

At the turn of the century a writer for the *Chicago Tribune* spoke of the same phenomenon when he noted that "La Salle Street and Dearborn Street may busy themselves with a business which involves millions [of dollars] every week. But both of them combined will not expend more nerve tissue, action and volubility than does commercial Maxwell Street in the very center of hard times."

Maxwell Street — and the culturally rich ethnic neighborhood surrounding it — is the milieu in which the six children of Yetta and Henry Pokovitz were raised. The spirit of the bazaar was in their blood. Their experience as first-generation Americans growing up within a resolutely cohesive old world family is the canvas upon which much of the later history of the Polk brothers' enterprises would be written.

* * *

Henry Pokovitz, like his brother Leon and sister Caroline, was born in the independent state of Romania and was living in Bucharest at the time of his marriage to Yetta Reyen. Yetta came from a family of eight brothers and sisters, living in close proximity to a score of Reyen aunts, uncles, and cousins. The family home was the village of Yakubovka (Jakovowka), midway between the cities of Lvov and Chernovtsy in what was then Eastern Galicia. This politically turbulent region was within the boundaries of the Austria-Hungarian Empire in the late nineteenth century. It is now part of Ukraine.

Henry, a tinsmith, was a blond, strongly built young man with a large, open face that matched his broad body. Yetta, in striking contrast, was a tiny woman with clouds of dark hair and the intense, focused gaze that emerged as a distinctive familial feature among her children.

The first of the couple's six children — and their only daughter — Ghisella, always known as Goldie, was born in December 1904. Henry was then twenty-six years old; Yetta was in her late teens. Their first son, Samuel, arrived just a little more than a year later, in January 1906.

The precise circumstances of the family's emigration have not been recorded and are not now remembered. But the likely events can be readily reconstructed. The social and political pressures that would have compelled a young Jewish family to scrape together every meager penny and sell their belongings to raise passage to America in 1906 were enormous.

The primary force behind Henry and Yetta Pokovitz's decision to flee Bucharest undoubtedly was economic. The urban economy was then stressed to the limit by a massive influx of landless peasants seeking work as laborers. Despite some constitutional reforms, political persecution of Jews remained widespread, and resentments ran deep. Henry, as a Jew, would not have been able to find work in the city of Bucharest, even if there were work to be had.

But there was also real danger. Strikes and famine were widespread in Romania after 1900. The lawless mood of the Russian pogroms of 1905 had spilled over the borders and would culminate in 1907 in a widespread peasant uprising in Romania, with incendiary mob action directed first against Jews in the cities and then against the large landowners.

The Pokovitz family was by no means alone in its flight. In a single generation — the span of the twenty-some years since the first Russian pogroms in 1881 — more than a third of the Jews of Eastern Europe were driven from their homes by political oppression and economic hardship. By 1906 and 1907 the steady tide of Jewish emigration from Russia, Poland, Austria-Hungary, Romania and the rest of Eastern Europe had reached flood stage.

Mass emigration from Romania had been dramatized in 1899 by the marches of the wayfarers, bands of young men who set out to cross Europe on foot. But these were a minority. The emigres of 1906 were neither the pioneers of the 1880s nor the adventurers of 1899. By the time Henry and Yetta left Bucharest the road was well traveled. The preferred

route was the long overland trip by train through Vienna and
Frankfurt to Amsterdam or Hamburg. There a family would
board one of the several steamships, such as the U.S.S.
Amerika, that catered to the Eastern European immigrant
trade.

The Atlantic crossing by then had become regular and
fast. Fares in steerage had dropped to as little as twelve dollars, and the length of the trip had been reduced to ten days
or less. But with some three thousand persons crowding each
ship leaving for America, the passage could not have been either comfortable or easy. Most of these Eastern European
emigres, as many as ninety thousand a year by 1906, flowed
through Ellis Island into the Battery and the Lower East Side
of New York City. But others proceeded directly to ports in
New Jersey, and from there headed to industrial centers such
as Pittsburgh and Chicago — cities where relatives and neighbors were already settled and where a man with a trade could
expect to find work.

Such was the case with Henry and Yetta. Two of Yetta's
seven brothers and sisters had made the journey to America
before her. An older sister, Minnie, with whom Yetta would be
reunited many years later, was the first to emigrate. Minnie's
passage to Canada was paid by an uncle, for whom she worked
as a housekeeper until her marriage to Canadian-born Adolph
Feuerstadt.

An unmarried younger brother, Benjamin, was the next
of the Reyen family to come over. Ben settled in Chicago,
where he found work as a tailor's apprentice, married, started
a family, and eventually was able to save enough money to
open Ben's Grocery and Meat Market, a small family-run
shop located on the city's South Side.

Henry Pokovitz also had family in Chicago. Max, Leon,
and Herman Greenberg, the sons of Henry's sister Caroline,
had immigrated in the years before 1910. Max, who was ten
years younger than his uncle, Henry, married a Chicago girl,
raised five children, and for a brief time in the mid-1930s was
a silent partner in the Polk brothers' first appliance store.

These family members, and other families whose friendship dated from the coming-to-America years, together with
a host of American-born nieces, nephews, and cousins, would
over the next decades become interwoven into the life of the
Pokovitz family. In many cases they also became involved in
the Polk family business.

*   *   *

At the turn of the century somewhat more than half of
Chicago's eighty thousand Jews were recent arrivals from
Eastern Europe. The great majority of these newcomers gravitated to the congested, Yiddish-speaking ghetto centered at
Halsted and Maxwell streets, south and west of the Loop, near
the railroads. Henry and Yetta Pokovitz, like so many others,
sought lodging within the community of fellow immigrants
upon their arrival in Chicago.

The densely populated "Old West Side," as the district
came to be known, was considered in 1910 to be Chicago's
worst slum. But the judgment was relative. Life for the Eastern European immigrant families who poured into the Old
West Side was abrasive, clamorous, and burdened with the
hardships of making a bare livelihood. But it was also rich in
communal tradition. To newcomers like the Pokovitzes, the
neighborhood was both sociable and sheltered. Here familiar
ways were perpetuated, and here they readily found acceptance among relatives, friends, and countrymen.

Goldie's daughter, Roberta Bachmann Lewis, says:

> My mother's first memories were of that neighbor-
> hood, where there were cousins — first cousins and
> second cousins. It was a community, which is not
> uncommon among immigrants. You cling to your
> own.

Yetta found companionship and links to the homeland
within the structure of the Romanian synagogue, where she

maintained a strong connection throughout her life. Henry's pastimes were more secular. Like other men of his age and background, his day-to-day social life was centered around the Romanian coffee house where menfolk congregated to play cards and trade stories, fortified by glasses of strong, sweet tea or tumblers of homemade wine.

Daily life in the congested streets of the Old West Side faithfully reflected much of the old world experience of the first-generation immigrant families. In fact, many of this generation, once they arrived, never left the neighborhood. The final leg of the long journey to America, assimilation into the mainstream of American life, was left to the children — the next generation.

During the week peddlers with their ubiquitous pushcarts followed circuitous routes through the narrow back streets and alleys, selling fruits and vegetables, housewares, and notions. The familiar chicken stores, fishmongers, and kosher markets were clustered along Jefferson, Halsted, and Taylor streets. Most of these small shops were run by families, who lived over the stores or in the back rooms.

On Sundays, when stores everywhere else in the city were shuttered, the Maxwell Street bazaar burst into life. For eight blocks or more, pushcarts, open-air stalls, wooden stands, and second-hand dealers jostled for space among teeming crowds seeking bargains in hats, socks, suits of clothes; oilcloth, shawls, spectacles; bananas, apples, garlic. Unlike the downtown stores where prices were fixed, on Maxwell Street haggling over prices was the rule.

While few newcomers could write or read English, families kept up with news from home through ethnic newspapers such as the Yiddish-language *Jewish Courier*, published in the Maxwell Street area. The popular and influential *Jewish Daily Forward*, which was delivered from New York, with Chicago pages added, regularly reported on the anti-semitic rancor in Romania.

There is no known record of Henry Pokovitz's addresses in his first years in Chicago, a fact that suggests the family moved frequently. Journalist Ira Berkow recalls the experience of his grandfather, who, like Henry, was a Romanian-Jewish sheetmetal worker: "Like most of the breadwinners in this area, my grandfather, Israel Hersh Berkovitz, moved his family from flat to flat, seeking little by little to better their lot."

The question of housing would have been an important one. The Pokovitz family was growing. A second son, Harry, was born in 1907. Goldie was then three years old; Sam was just fourteen months. Morris arrived in 1911, followed in 1913 by the fourth boy, David. All, it appears, were home births, as was usual for the time and the neighborhood.

For Henry Pokovitz, the streets of Chicago were not paved with gold. Work, at best, was intermittent, and the housing situation must at times have been precarious. Whatever promise a new life in America had held out was tarnished by hard facts brought on by hard times. The Chicago construction industry on which Henry depended for his livelihood was crippled in the years between 1903 and 1912 by waves of work stoppages and sympathy strikes inspired by an active and often militant labor union movement.

Around 1910 Henry was hired to work on the roof of the People's Gas Building, on South Michigan Avenue. It was a major construction project and might have led to more work with subcontractors to the architect, D. H. Burnham and Company, but Henry's luck was short lived. The now-landmark building, famed for the quality of its brass and metalwork, was barely completed when a general strike brought Chicago construction to a virtual standstill.

Things were probably looking up again by 1914. This is the year that Henry Pokovitz's name appears for the first time in the Chicago city directory. His occupation was given as "tinner." The Pokovitz address, 1413 Taylor Street, was one of the three-story, brick tenement buildings (called "double deckers") that sprang up on the Old West Side after the turn of the century, built to house an ever greater press of immigrant families.

These buildings looked substantial enough on the outside but the accommodations were desperately meager. A three-room flat consisted of a kitchen and a parlor with a windowless bedroom between them. A dozen or more people might be housed in these three rooms. Typically a single cold water tap and one water closet were shared by all the families along a hallway. Often the only source of heat was a coal or wood-burning stove, making the kitchen the most desirable place to sleep.

While the conditions under which the Pokovitz family lived in these years were impoverished by any standard, their circumstances were no worse than those of their neighbors. Arthur Goldberg, who became a United States Supreme Court Justice, was a contemporary of the Pokovitz boys and lived near them at Halsted and O'Brien streets. Goldberg recalls that after his father's death in 1914, his mother and eight children were crowded into two rooms. "We were a damn poor family, yet without resentment," Goldberg has said. "We lived in this enclave because we were so poor, but we moved at various points."

In many respects it appears that the Pokovitz family fared somewhat better than other families in the neighborhood. Sometime between 1917 and 1923 the Pokovitzes moved again, to a three-story brick apartment building at 1422 Taylor. Although the move was only across the street, the new flat undoubtedly represented another small step up for the family.

* * *

On May 14, 1917, Sol Pokovitz, the sixth and last of Henry and Yetta's children, was born at home at 1413 Taylor Street. Henry was then nearly forty. Yetta was in her early thirties. Goldie was a young teenager and had taken her place as a second mother to the younger brothers. Although relatives described Sol as his mother's "little prince," it seems that he never assumed the traditional role of baby of the family. Quite the contrary. Even as a child, Sol was taken very seriously. All the Pokovitz siblings were known within the extended family by nicknames and diminutives: "Goldie," "Sammy," "Harry," "Morrie," "Davy," and "Sollie." Sol, although the youngest, was the first to shed his childhood nickname.

*　*　*

Abraham Lincoln Marovitz, a much-honored Chicago legislator and federal court judge, grew up at 1100 Laflin Street, just around the corner from the Pokovitz flat on Taylor Street. Abe Marovitz and Sam Pokovitz were within a year of one another in age; they moved to the Taylor Street neighborhood at about the same time; and they became fast friends. It was a friendship that lasted a lifetime.

Judge Marovitz's recollections help fill out the picture of what daily life was like for boys growing up in a close-knit family such as his own and the Pokovitzes. "There's not a day passes by that I don't think of Sammy and Sol, and the other brothers, and my little friend Goldie," Marovitz said in 1992.

> I take pride in the fact that they were my friends more than seventy-five years ago. We shared the good times and the bad times. I don't think you would say we were poor. We weren't deprived of anything. We had three meals a day. My mother would give me two cents and I'd go next door to the grocery store and they would fill up my bag with soup greens a foot high, and mother would throw a few beans in there and once in a while a little meat. We never went hungry and never had any fancy meals, except on Friday night which was something very special. The Sabbath meal was often shared among several families so that everyone would have enough. Each one did what they could.

Marovitz's father, Joseph, like so many Russian immigrants in the Maxwell Street area, was a tailor. His mother,

Rachel, owned the neighborhood penny-candy store where, Judge Marovitz recalls, the pickle-on-a-stick, a somewhat whimsical Chicago specialty, was invented. In its original form, at least as it was served in Mrs. Marovitz's candy store, this was half a dill pickle speared with a lemon or peppermint stick. "The Polk boys were in our candy store all the time," Marovitz recalls.

Photos from the period show neighborhood boys in caps and knickers and high-top boots playing street hockey and stickball in the alleys behind Taylor Street and the Hull House Settlement a few blocks away, while girls in muslin dresses and smocks look on from the sidelines. But life on the Old West Side was not necessarily that benign.

Because living quarters were invariably cramped, children were likely to spend their days in the street. It could be a rough and hostile environment. Indeed, the Maxwell Street area, a few blocks east of the corner of Taylor and Laflin where the Pokovitz and Marovitz families lived, was identified by the *Chicago Tribune* in 1906 as "the crime center of the country." Every corner had its own group of hoodlums. Street fights and territorial incursions of warring Irish, Jewish, and Italian gangs were part of daily life.

There were good kids and bad kids. The lines were cleanly drawn in Judge Marovitz's mind. But to be merely good was not good enough. To survive on the streets a boy had to be as tough and as shrewd as he was honorable. He had to be a scrapper. Abe Marovitz himself became an amateur boxer. He expresses sincere admiration for the Pokovitz brothers when he describes them as "honest boys: good and tough."

Child labor in the sweatshops of the garment industry or the cigar factories on Halsted Street was common, even after the turn of the century. Families that arrived in the later waves of immigration, however, placed greater value on keeping their children in school, at least until the age of fourteen — the legal age for a work permit. Even so, it was expected that children of any age would contribute to the family income by working odd jobs after school, at night, and on weekends.

If children did not work in a family store, they found other ways to earn pennies. Girls did piecework with their mothers in home workshops. Boys sold fruit and vegetables, they hauled wood and coal, and of course they worked as newsboys. Abe Marovitz worked in the candy store from the time he was seven years old. When Abe was nine, he and Sam figured out that they could beat other newsboys to the street by selling papers to men coming off night work shifts and then dashing over to Holy Family church to catch people arriving for early mass.

At that time Abe and Sam were fifth-graders at Thomas Jefferson Grammar School, a looming red brick fortress built so solidly in 1884 that it still stands at the corner of Laflin and Fillmore, diagonally across the street from the now-vacant lot where the Marovitz candy store once stood. Goldie was a year ahead of Sam. Harry, Morris, and David were enrolled at Jefferson in due course.

"Sam and the other boys were just like me: not too smart and not too dumb," Marovitz asserts. "But I never missed a day of school, and neither did the Polk boys." The statement, while true in spirit, may suffer from less than perfect hindsight, at least as it relates to the middle Pokovitz boys. Sam, then as in later life, felt his responsibilities as the eldest brother keenly. He was steady and responsible. Harry and Morrie had more latitude. They were street-smart.

School offered another kind of experience for Goldie. School was the place where the process of turning immigrant children into Americans began. As a child Goldie was shy and bookish. She was eager to carry what she learned at school home to her parents. She was the assimilator — and the only grammarian that the family would produce. David, for other reasons, might have welcomed the haven from street life that the school offered. Frail from birth, and gentle by nature, David did not share his brothers' zest for the fray.

The brothers' education was definitely ecumenical. At

home they learned the cultural values of their parents. At Jefferson Grammar School they learned to read and write English. After school they attended classes at the Chicago Hebrew Institute on Taylor Street. But this did not preclude them, Marovitz recalls, from participating in social and community activities at St. Ignatius, the Catholic high school. They may also have had some contact with Jane Addam's Hull House, as did other boys from the neighborhood, including Arthur Goldberg and Benny Goodman. Judge Marovitz remembers:

> We were all different religions, but not too many different colors. Our friends were primarily Irish-Catholic, Italian, and Jewish. We had a great many Italian friends and Irish friends. That was mainly what the neighborhood consisted of. We were exposed to a lot of nice people. We learned the art of living together.

All the boys, and Goldie, not only stayed in school but went on to graduate from high school. Goldie, Sam, and Harry went to the Joseph Medill High School on 14th Street. Morris, David, and Sol graduated from Marshall and Manley high schools in the Lawndale district. This was a considerable achievement and one that could not have come easily in a family that depended on the income that the boys brought in from full-time and night jobs.

*   *   *

Much has been written about the remarkable accomplishments of the graduates of a single Harvard Business School class: The Class of 1949. Less likely to be noted is an equally remarkable constellation of talent that emerged, at about the same time, among the first-generation Jewish-American boys of Chicago's Old West Side.

The alumni of Taylor Street may not have thought of themselves as Harvard material, but the fact remains that the neighborhood was a crucible of ambition and energy. The names of boys who grew up in the same era as the Pokovitz brothers, on the same streets, and in the same circumstances, are well known. They include Supreme Court Justice Arthur Goldberg, who served also as U.S. ambassador to the United Nations; musician Benny Goodman, whose childhood home was on Washburne, just two blocks from the Pokovitz family; Columbia Broadcasting System founder William Paley, who was born in the back room of the family cigar store on Maxwell Street; and Barney Balaban, who became president of Paramount Pictures, and his seven brothers.

They include also such Chicago movers and shakers as Democratic party kingmaker Colonel Jacob Arvey; trucking tycoon John L. Keeshin; sporting goods magnate Morrie Mages; and, of course, Judge Abraham Lincoln Marovitz and the Polk brothers. It should be said that the neighborhood produced more than its share of famous hoodlums as well, including Jacob Rubenstein, better known in later life as Jack Ruby.

There are many ways to account for this phenomenon, not the least of which is the immigrant experience itself and the collateral drive to succeed that was instilled in the immigrant family's American-born children.

Judge Marovitz attributes the extraordinary number of success stories that emerged from this one small area, at a particular point in time, to the quality of family life and a standard of rectitude transmitted to children by parents who lived by a centuries-old code of honorable behavior.

> We are what we saw in our homes. The Polk parents, like mine, I'm sure weren't able to read or write, but the values all those boys learned, they learned from their parents. Our parents taught us the simple decencies of life: what we call **menshlichkeit**.
>
> A good name, a wholesome name, is very important. What matters is the family, holding the family together. That is why there was such a bond

among those brothers. Whatever little differences the Polk family may have had, they kept on the inside and it worked out. There isn't any mystery. Those of us who were privileged to know them understand what made them tick.

Independent entrepreneurship such as that evidenced in the Pokovitz family was a common response among the sons and daughters of Eastern European immigrant families. But the opportunity that America offered, and the background from which they came, was not forgotten by the children of Henry and Yetta Pokovitz. The family toast over the years was: "To our mother and father who brought us to this country."

3

Growing Up

*...obility. Services came
...ne ice cream vendor,
...who sold lamps and
...ere were the knife
...e whetstone and the*

*...trice Michaels Shapiro
...mories of Lawndale"*

By the early 1920s America was changing. The austerity of the war years had given way to an exuberant postwar economy and the open life-style that characterized the new decade. Chicago was booming. The fortunes of the Pokovitz family were also on the upswing. These were the growing-up years.

By 1924, Goldie, Sam, and Harry had completed high school, and all were bringing home paychecks. Goldie, who had taken business courses, worked as a typist at Stein and Company, a small manufacturing concern that made candy. Sam had turned a night-messenger job at the Postal Telegraph Cable Company into a full-time position as a clerk. Harry was working for a company that went by the name "Flashtric Sign Works."

Even before World War I, the Old West Side district around Maxwell Street was in transition. Expansion of the railroads and a proliferation of small factories fragmented familiar neighborhoods. A new wave of immigrants, black laborers from the American South, began to take over the tenement housing that at the turn of the century had been the enclave of Eastern European families.

As the economic status of these families improved, the locus of the Jewish community itself shifted: First to Polk Street; then west to Ashland Boulevard; and then on to the Lawndale district, which by the early 1920s had become the up-and-coming Jewish neighborhood.

In 1923 the Pokovitz family, too, left Taylor Street behind and moved to Lawndale. The new apartment, at 1523 South Ridgeway, was on the second floor of a sturdy red brick building in the middle of a block of brick and graystone six-flat dwellings, each with three front and three rear apartments. At each address, a flight of steps led from a small yard to a common front entrance. The Pokovitz family had five rooms and a sheltered brick porch overlooking the street.

The move to a residential district with broad tree-shaded boulevards and quiet side streets was a breath of fresh air for the family. The change was especially opportune for Goldie who, as a young working woman, welcomed the respectability that came with the new address. But it was also comfortable for the Pokovitz parents. The neighborhood, populated principally by families of Russian and Polish immigrants, was flushed with tradition. Chicago writer Beatrice Michaels Shapiro in her essay, "Memories of Lawndale," captures much of the character of neighborhood life as it was in the 1930s, and much as it must have been for the Pokovitz family.

> The immigrant mothers, their chores finished, sat on benches outside their dwellings. They wore housedresses and spoke in their common language,

Yiddish, their words punctuated by dramatic gestures. Relatives and countrymen lived close to one another, sometimes in the same buildings. Visiting was a favorite pastime. The fruit and vegetable peddlers, as in the old neighborhood, plied their trade in the streets and alleys. The great variety of small, family-run shops so commonplace in the Maxwell Street district emerged again in Lawndale.

Shapiro writes: "Every street had a corner Ma and Pa grocery. Butter was scooped out of a container and sold by the pound; dill pickles were marinated in a wooden barrel, and lox was sliced from a whole fish."

Along Roosevelt Road, the Pokovitzes found the customary Romanian restaurants and coffee houses, the bakeries, butter and egg stores, hat shops, and second-hand furniture outlets. Nearly every block had a newsstand carrying magazines, national and Yiddish language publications, and as many as eight local newspaper editions a day. There was no need for "Ma" and "Pop" Pokovitz to travel very far from home.

*   *   *

In the Lawndale years, the family had no car and no telephone. But the Ridgeway apartment was in a choice location, just a block south of Independence Square, between Garfield and Douglas parks. The imposing Theodore Herzl Public School, at Ridgeway and Douglas Boulevard, stood just a few doors to the north of the Pokovitz apartment. The Chicago Hebrew Institute, renamed the Jewish People's Institute, had moved, with its constituency, from the Old West Side to a new location at the intersection of Douglas and St. Louis Avenue. The Romanian Synagogue on Douglas Boulevard at Millard Avenue was convenient for Yetta. The family undoubtedly would have been among the crowd of thousands who gathered at the synagogue in 1928 to catch a glimpse of the visiting Queen Marie of Romania.

The streetcar line on Roosevelt Road tied the Lawndale community directly to the Old West Side neighborhood and gave Sam ready access to the Postal Telegraph office in the Board of Trade Building. In the 1920s, all the boys — with the exception of Sol, who did not enter high school until 1930 — would grow up and move into full-time occupations.

Sam's career path followed a straight line from his schoolboy years into adulthood. Back on Taylor Street, while still in their early teens, Sam and his friend Abe Marovitz had evening jobs with the Postal Telegraph company (merged with Western Union in 1943). Marovitz went on to other jobs, to the study of law, and eventually to a seat in the state legislature and a federal judgeship. Sam stayed with Postal Telegraph after his graduation from high school. By 1930 he had become night manager for the Chicago office, in charge of the midnight to 8 a.m. shift.

For a time after high school Harry joined Sam at Postal Telegraph. From that staging point, he moved on to a job as a driver with the U.S. Post Office. When Morrie graduated from high school in 1928 he went to work for his cousin, Max Greenberg, a plumber, who, with his grown sons, had launched an appliance sales and service business that specialized in refrigeration and cooling.

David was still in grammar school when the family moved to Lawndale. Born with a lame foot, he was the most protected of the brothers. While the older boys chose more robust lines of work, David found a job as a delivery boy in a neighborhood drug store. He became an apothecary's assistant and learned to mix prescription medicines. This was a job, his family remembers, that David truly loved. However, when he graduated from John Marshall High School in 1930, David chose another career path. He went to work at the stock exchange as a runner for Hornblower & Weeks, with plans to become a stockbroker.

Most close families can identify stories that are passed along through the generations. While the particulars may change, the essential truth invariably is a communication of family values. In the case of the Pokovitz family in this period, the story of the shirts communicates this truth:

> They were very poor in these days. There were five boys, but they didn't have five white shirts. Whoever got up got a clean shirt. You got up late, you got no shirt.

The variation on the shirt story is that among them the boys had one good suit. Whoever had to go to a job first got to wear the suit.

Clearly, Yetta was the emotional center of the family — the stable force that bound them together. It was a bond that would not be broken or breached. The heart of the household was the kitchen. The immigrant Jewish mother had a mission in life: She had mouths to feed, and Yetta saw to it that her family was fed. Even in the 1940s, when her sons were building a multi-million dollar business and the family lived over the store at 2850 North Central Avenue, Yetta expected the boys to come upstairs for dinner.

*   *   *

While the boys were tall, loud, boisterous, outgoing, Goldie was small — barely five feet tall — and delicate by nature. She walked a fine line between the European ways of her parents and the ambitions of a young, largely self-educated, first-generation American woman. Work in the clothing factories as an operator or a finisher, the fate of so many immigrant girls, was not for her. Nor, apparently, did Goldie seek the comfort of early marriage. A position as a typist or as a saleslady represented status, respectability, and some measure of independence.

Goldie would be a typist. When she landed her first full-time job, as a secretary with Stein and Company, the family was justifiably proud of her achievement. But the transition from home and school to the business world was not easy for her. Goldie herself would later say that life in the outside world, where "she had to speak," was difficult for one so painfully shy. That admission would come as a surprise to friends, vendors, and employees who found her in later life to be a commanding presence as a manager and buyer — as hard-driving as any of her tough-minded brothers.

In the summer of 1928, Goldie married Louis Astrov Bachmann and entered into a life that would be very different from that she had known in the sheltered environs of her parents' home. Goldie was then twenty-four years old. Louis Bachmann was a professional musician, who as a teenager had played with Benny Goodman at Hull House. When Goldie and Louis married, Lou was the featured pianist with a Chicago jazz band. He later became a staff musician for Don McNeill's popular "Breakfast Club" radio show, which was broadcast nationally through the NBC network.

Like Goldie, Louis came from a family of five brothers and an older sister. The two had met "in the neighborhood," introduced by a friend who was then dating one of Lou Bachmann's brothers. There was a closer, but coincidental, link: Lou's brother Max was general manager of the Chicago Postal Telegraph office, where Goldie's brother Sam was also rising through the ranks. It is not at all coincidental that, except for Sol, each of the Pokovitz boys, and Max's son, Lester, would work for Postal Telegraph at one time or another during their growing years.

Newly wed Goldie and Louis Bachmann found a first-floor, two-bedroom apartment in a courtyard complex at 211 North Central Avenue, in the heart of the comfortably middle class Austin neighborhood. Louis's mother, Rebecca, lived with them until her death two years after their marriage. When Goldie and Lou's daughter, Roberta, was born, the bachelor uncles were elated. When son Bruce arrived four years later, Goldie and Lou's family was complete.

* * *

In this period, Yetta and her brother Benjamin Reyen were reunited with their sister Minnie, from whom they had been separated since childhood. Minnie, her husband Adolph Feuerstadt, and their two sons, Irving and Saul, had moved from Canada to Coney Island, New York, where they opened a small grocery store. At the urging of a sister-in-law, Minnie placed an ad in a Chicago ethnic newspaper: Searching for Yetta Reyen. This was a common practice among separated immigrant families. Yetta was found. Years later, Irving and Saul would both make careers with Polk Bros. After World War II Minnie and Adolph joined their sons in Chicago.

In 1935 the Pokovitzes moved again, following a northward movement of Jewish families from the West Side to Chicago's Logan Square and Albany Park neighborhoods. The Pokovitz apartment in Albany Park, at 4612 North Drake, was no larger than the Lawndale apartment, but it was the scene of perpetual activity. Roberta remembers, from her perspective as a very small child, that when the brothers were there "the walls just shook." She says,

> The boys were a handful. Morrie and Harry and David and Sol were a rambunctious crew, surrounded by friends, phone calls, teasing, laughter.
>
> Sam, on the other hand, had a quiet, dignified demeanor — conscious of his place as the eldest brother.

Speaking of "The Uncles," as the five brothers were known to the next generation, Roberta observes:

> I don't think they had the kind of childhood that allowed them to do very much. But in the 1930s they had jobs and the world was starting to open up for them. They were having a lot of fun.

Bruce Bachmann recalls:

Morrie and Sol were the rough and tumble, fun-loving, lady chasers of the group. They had lots of girlfriends. Morrie was really the dandy. Girls telephoned him all the time. We knew the call was for Morrie when they asked for "George." Morrie and Sol were very close, they hung out together, and they kidded around, and pushed and wrestled.

Henry Pokovitz is described as "a charming man who loved life and good times." But as a father it seems that he did not exert a strong presence in the household. He was, family friends would recall, "just there." In the eyes of his first granddaughter, however, Henry cut a colorful figure. Roberta notes:

Grandpa had a Balkan background, and in my mind, he was kind of exotic. On Sundays he wore an embroidered red cap, and a vest, and red sash. He and friends played a loud card game at the dining room table — one where they slammed down the cards — while Grandma worked in the kitchen.

In the tradition of the Balkans, meats in the Pokovitz household were broiled until blackened on a charcoal grill set up outside on the porch. The image of Grandpa presiding over the grilling of the meat is common among the grandchildren, who have similar memories of Henry's devotion to Turkish coffee, Greek wine, and cigars. David's son Mitchel, like Roberta, was impressed by "that noisy Russian card game he played with seven decks of cards." No one of this generation remembers Henry working outside the home.

An obituary notice published at the time of his death in 1951 described Henry as a "retired sheet metal contractor." The absence of a family memory of his wage earning years, however, is probably accurate. As the Pokovitz boys grew older and provided primary support for the family, Henry worked less. The onset of the Great Depression, and a hiatus in the construction industry that would not end until after World War II, sealed the deal. By 1930, Henry Pokovitz, for all practical purposes, was retired.

The same would never be said of his sons. Especially Sol.

4

The First Store

"In the utility business you have to have volume to make money. You have to get people to use electric power. So in the depression era we sold appliances door to door. Mostly irons, because irons use a lot of power.

"Sol got his training selling house to house. He got to understand the customer better than most people because he saw them in their homes. He was a crack salesman. The best Edison had."

— Thomas Ayers
Commonwealth Edison

Sol "Mr. Wow" Polk is described, without exception, as a merchandising genius, a mastermind of competitive marketing. A man of volcanic energy, endowed with a twenty-two track mind that spun off ideas at the speed of sound. He was born to sell.

While many men of extraordinary ability may not show what they are made of until later in life, such was not the case with Sol. Roberta Bachmann Lewis recalls that even as a child she knew that:

> With Sol, there was something different. When he walked into a room, it was special. The other uncles were wild and wonderful. Sol was electric.

The stories of Sol Pokovitz's talents as a schoolboy entrepreneur are legion. There may be some hyperbole in the tales, but there is no revisionist history. Accounts of his early exploits are remarkably consistent.

In keeping with the newsboy tradition popularized by Horatio Alger stories such as "Tattered Tom" and "Ragged Dick," Sol had established a reputation as an aggressive magazine salesman by the time he entered elementary school. An anecdote related in the old *Chicago American* in 1953 goes like this:

> When Sol Polk was only six his mother took him to the dentist for a painful session. The boy made no protest. In the office he behaved well, sat in the chair without howling and even cast frequent smiles at the doctor. When the session was over the dentist congratulated him and told his mother: "My, but you have a charming boy." Whereupon the tyke whipped an order book out of a back pocket, grinned hugely, and asked: "Wanna buy a subscription to a magazine?" The dentist signed.

By the age of eight, it is said, Sol had five other boys working for him, peddling the *Saturday Evening Post* and other popular magazines door to door. It was not a trivial occupation. Before the days of radio and television, magazines were primary transmitters of popular culture. In 1929, one issue of the *Saturday Evening Post* ran to two hundred seventy-two pages, weighed five pounds, and was supported by two hundred fourteen national advertisers. It cost five cents.

When he was twelve Sol became neighborhood branch manager for a magazine publisher, operating out of an office he established in the basement of the family apartment building at 1523 South Ridgeway. At that time, as the story goes, he had two dozen junior salesmen working for him. When cash flow slowed, Sol went out door to door selling cosmetic items individually from kits that he purchased. He was said to be bringing home twenty-five dollars a week in these days, a nice sum in the early years of the depression.

Some thirty years later Sol Polk would revisit his legendary accomplishments as a newsboy. When Polk Bros. agreed to run a series of full-page ads in the regional edition of the *Saturday Evening Post*, the magazine photographed Sol, the adult appliance mogul, carrying a canvas *SEP* delivery boy's satchel over his shoulder. Sol later had the photograph made into a life-size cutout that was displayed at Polk Bros. sales motivation meetings.

While still in grade school Sol hit upon another idea that he would turn to advantage in his later business life: As a student at William Penn Elementary he raised a record amount of money for the school Red Cross drive by auctioning old magazines and unsold stock. In just the same way, he would later donate used appliances, taken as trade-ins on the sale of new merchandise, to schools and other institutions for use in vocational training programs.

By the time Sol entered high school in 1930, the population of Greater Lawndale had reached nearly one hundred thousand, making the district the city's largest predominantly ethnic community. Children no longer were put to work at the age of fourteen, and the schools were overflowing.

In the summer before his senior year, Sol transferred from overcrowded John Marshall High School to the newly opened Hugh Manley Vocational High School at the corner of Sacramento and Polk streets. There Sol found a group of pals who would become friends for life. The foursome was made up of Sol Pokovitz, Henry "Hank" Schneider, Saul Cohn, and Eddie Rabinovitz.

As a senior in a new school, Eddie Rabinovitz shortened his name to Robbins. Sol made a similar move. When the first yearbook came out, Sol Pokovitz's senior photo identified him as Sol Polk. "Polk" rather than "Poke" was an easy translation for a young man who had lived all his life in the vicinity of Polk Street, named for the American president.

Within five years, the brothers would make the name

change official. Cook County Circuit Court records from December, 1940, show that petitions for official name changes, from Pokavitz [sic] to Polk, were granted to Samuel H., Harry H., Morris G., David D., and Sol Pokovitz.

Harry's son Edward Polk later was told that the middle names (Samuel **Henry**, Morris **George**, and David **Dan**) were assumed, perhaps to lend stature to the Polk brothers' signatures. Since the name "Henry" had been claimed by Sam, the first-born son, Harry settled for the initial "H." alone. Sol didn't chose even an initial.

Sol's many sales enterprises were more important to him in his high school years than any academic program. (He once told an associate, no doubt facetiously, that the only reason he stayed in school was to keep warm in the winter. School, he said, was where he learned to sleep with his eyes open.) The organizational side of extra-curricular activities was another matter. Hank Schneider recalls that as a member of Manley's first graduating class Sol took charge of ad sales and promotions for the school's fledgling newspaper, the *Manley-Gram*, and was a powerhouse behind the organization of school dances and events.

"Sol was always business minded," Schneider recalls.

> He more or less kept other things locked in himself.
> He was not outspoken. But if he could advise some-
> one on what they were doing, he was always willing
> to do so. If anyone had problems, he would come up
> with solutions.

They were solutions that worked. A decade later both Sol Polk and Hank Schneider had caught the tide of the times: While Sol and his brothers were building a $100-million-a-year appliance empire, the Schneider family was building On-Cor Frozen Foods, a food processing giant that emerged with the development of the home freezer. On-Cor grew out of Hank's father's frozen egg business, a family enterprise that, in the Lawndale days, shelled and sold eggs in bulk to bakers.

*   *   *

In 1933, the darkest year of the Great Depression and the summer before Sol Polk's senior year of high school, Chicago mounted a great world's fair. The "A Century of Progress" exposition celebrated the forces of science and the ingenuity of industry. It held out the promise of a better life and brighter future for depression-weary American families.

If Sol Polk can be said to have experienced a prophetic revelation of what his own future would be, it surely occurred here, at the Century of Progress, where he had a job selling oriental rugs. That summer he certainly would have visited and grasped the impact of the technological marvels displayed at the exposition's modernistic "House of Tomorrow." He probably also lingered at the General Electric "House of Magic" pavilion where the most imaginative offerings of the home appliance industry were displayed and sold.

Sol Polk glimpsed opportunity. While Sol could not have foreseen how far the idea would take him, historian William Manchester addresses the magnitude of that opportunity in hindsight. He writes that in 1932:

> Appliances, gadgets, and creature comforts of the 1970s were rare. There were no power mowers, home air-conditioning units, automatic dishwashers, clothes driers [sic], electric blankets, clock-radios, . . . automatic coffee makers, cordless shavers, . . . hi-fi stereo sets, . . . home freezers, cassette recorders, . . . garbage disposal units, tape recorders, snow blowers, electric knives, home hair driers [sic], electric can openers, . . . no television, not even plain black and white.

The revelation that fifteen-year-old Sol took away from the 1933 exposition was no less than a prescient vision of the mechanized modern household. The Pokovitz boys had grown up in a home where their mother was captive to the dawn-to-dark drudgery of cooking and cleaning and washing.

Sol saw this as a wrong that could be righted. The capacity of electric appliances to free the housewife for time with her family would become a Polk Bros. litany in years to come.

In a 1955 interview with *Fortune* magazine, Sol confirms his new-found preoccupation with home appliances: "I was very interested in growth. When I went to Manley High School we had the project of laying out a store, and the store I picked was in the appliance field." If home appliances were Sol's idea of the future, the spectacle of the fair itself was the setting for the store of his dreams. Riotous with color and a carnival atmosphere, the exposition was an advertising man's dream, as it was intended to be.

Within months of the opening of the world's fair, Sol returned with enthusiasm to door-to-door sales. But magazines and cosmetics were a thing of the past. Sol became a dynamic house-to-house salesman of light bulbs and the small appliances offered by the Commonwealth Edison Company as an inducement to customers to use more electric power in their homes.

His specialty was Sunbeam electric irons. The electric irons available to homemakers at that time weighed five to six pounds. Sunbeam came out with a three-and-a-half pound model, billed as the first light-weight, fast-heating electric iron. As an added benefit, it was housed in a "fireproof box." It sold for $7.95.

While a heavy electric iron had been on the market for some time, many families still depended on the old gas iron or the even older flatiron. The Sunbeam lightweight electric iron was innovative; it was an exciting new product. Max Greenberg's daughter Rose remembers "Auntie Yetta showing us these irons piled in back of the sofa. She was so proud of Sol."

Sol's sales manager at Sunbeam was Robert P. Gwinn, who started his career with Sunbeam in 1928. Gwinn subsequently became chairman and CEO of Encyclopedia Britannica, Inc. Sol remembered that it was Bob Gwinn who taught him how to balance an ironing board on one shoulder while carrying his stock door to door. Gwinn recalls that "Sol was amazing, there just was no one like him. He sold a tremendous amount."

If Sol happened to catch the housewife on ironing day, he suggested that he take over the task. With the new Sunbeam iron in hand, and in record time, he would finish a few pieces out of the ironing basket himself. While in the home, he made a pitch for Commonwealth Edison, which was then promoting the use of higher wattage bulbs. Sol asked to see the kitchen, saying, "We have a special today on a kitchen light; it's a one-hundred-watt bulb." To demonstrate Edison's slogan "Better Light, Better Sight," he replaced the old forty-watt bulb, and another sale was made.

Sol Polk's first principle of merchandising was to keep his capital working for him. As a door-to-door salesman, his hard-driving strategy was to sell two irons to raise the money to buy three and sell the three so he could buy five. Later, when Polk Bros. was buying in great volume, Sol and Sam showed a keen sense for the velocity of money. A primary goal was to turn their inventory before it was paid for. For instance, they might negotiate thirty-day terms with their supplier, sell the merchandise in ten days, and re-invest the supplier's money for another twenty days.

*   *   *

Within a year and a half of the time he began selling for Commonwealth Edison, Sol was clearing one hundred to one hundred fifty dollars a week in commissions. By 1935 he had assembled enough capital to open his own small appliance outlet in a sliver of rented space in a blue-collar neighborhood on Chicago's Northwest Side.

While it may seem improbable, or at best improvident, for a seventeen-year-old boy to launch such an enterprise, the fact is that Sol Polk's timing, as it so often would be, was excellent. The appliance business was an economic niche that in the mid-1930s spelled opportunity to ambitious entrepreneurs from immigrant families. The same had been true of the

movie business a decade earlier, as witnessed by the careers of
Samuel Goldwyn, Harry Warner, Sam Katz at Paramount,
and Katz's Chicago partners, the Balaban brothers.

Sol risked his entire savings, one thousand dollars, in the
fledgling business. Uncle Max Greenberg put up another
thousand. Max's son Arthur worked part time with Sol for a
short period of time. The Greenbergs' primary commitment,
however, was to their own store, Northwest Appliance. When
Sol was able to buy Max out, the Greenbergs were entirely
agreeable. The arrangement was satisfactory to both parties.

That first store, ambitiously named Central Appliance
and Furniture Company, was located at 3334 North Central
Avenue, a few blocks north of the intersection of Central and
Belmont. The twenty-five by thirty-five-foot space, smaller
than many mobile homes today, was at the corner of a large
gray brick apartment block on the west side of Central. Over
time, this apartment building would become home to a host
of Polk family members and relatives, including Yetta
Pokovitz's sister, Aunt Minnie, and her family from New York.

*   *   *

Sam formally joined Sol in the business as a partner and
store manager in 1937 although his role behind the scenes had
begun much earlier. Sam, who had a night job, minded the
store days, freeing Sol to go out selling door to door to raise
the capital needed to keep the business afloat. Harry came in
at night, after his day job at the post office. David did the
same, coming in after the stock exchange closed. None were
on salary in the first years, except Sol, who allowed himself fifteen dollars a week.

The brothers were salesmen during the day. At night
they painted and cleaned, swept the floors, made deliveries,
and hauled hard-won inventory as it became available. Typing, filing, and other office work fell to Goldie who, even with
a young family of her own, began taking the Central Avenue

bus from her home at 211 North Central to help out at the store at 3334 North Central.

The brothers continued to make house-to-house calls throughout the early years, selling small appliances, introducing themselves to the neighborhood, and inviting housewives to bring their laundry into the store to try out the new automatic washing machine. In this way they created a creed of word-of-mouth advertising that would become a cornerstone of Polk Bros.' later business. The theory was, "If we don't sell a customer, at least we'll make a friend."

And their friends were innumerable. In their business and social relations, each of Sol's four brothers projected an individual, barely concealed, personal charm that is often remarked upon by those who knew them. Their personalities were very different. What they had in common was a hard-won reputation for being rough-and-ready guys. With hearts as soft as marshmallows.

That "tough guys" image was enhanced by the brothers' ability to wreak havoc on the language. They were "'dese, 'dose, and 'dem" speakers. Family members have commented: "None of them could pass an English exam, but they got the message across," and "What was on their minds was on their tongues."

The accent, such as it was, was characteristic of families of European, particularly Russian, origin whose native language has no equivalent for the English **th** or **w** sounds. But the Polks gave colorful speech a distinctly local twist. The vernacular of the Polk brothers was **Chicago-ese**: English, Chicago style — a manner of speaking made famous by "Da Mare," Richard J. Daley, and his cohort on the "Fif' Floor" at City Hall.

This tendency to massacre English syntax, however, was probably quite volitional, and particularly so for Sol and Morrie. Harry often revealed a fine command of English grammar. Goldie, with her polished, second-generation sense of style, spoke the language elegantly. Sol, on the other hand, never stopped referring to the brothers as "my brudders." He no doubt could have refined his speech, had he had a reason to do so. But he was not the kind of self-made man to be embarrassed by his background. On the contrary; he was proud of it.

From the beginning, the brothers established a pattern of family involvement in a business where "everybody did everything" and where most of the real business was done, in effect, over the kitchen table in after-hours meetings. For fifty-seven years, Polk Bros. would remain an intensely private, family-held and managed financial empire where, even with seventeen stores and sales over $150 million a year, one or more of the brothers reviewed every invoice and signed every check.

Similarly, the eighteen-hour work days that the Polks required of themselves throughout their lives began at the original Central Appliance and Furniture store when working the equivalent of three jobs was not a choice but a necessity. It is not merely an eccentricity that in later years this traditional Jewish family celebrated family togetherness on Christmas Day — one of the three days of the year that the stores were closed.

*   *   *

It often is said that the luck of the Polks was in being in the right place at the right time with the right idea. Chicago in the prewar years, with its broad manufacturing base, was definitely the right place.

From the beginning Sol pursued Chicago-area manufacturers, and in the process forged valuable friendships with men who would later become industry leaders. These included Ross Siragusa at Admiral, Paul Galvin at Motorola, and Bob Wallace at Zenith Radio. The lesson, and the loyalties, were not forgotten during times of wartime scarcity, nor later as Polk Bros. rose to become the world's largest independent center for brand-name appliances.

Paramount among these was R. Cooper, Jr., Inc., General Electric's Chicago distributor. R. "Dick" Cooper had come

into the business when the first automatic refrigerators became popular in the 1920s. As General Electric grew, so did
the R. Cooper, Jr. distributorship.

When Sol and Sam launched Central Appliance and Furniture, Dick Cooper and his son Doug gave them their first
credit line and provided many of the small appliances that Sol
sold door to door. Their trust was well placed. Doug Cooper
would often say "There's one thing about dealing with the
Polks: They always pay their bills." The Coopers over time
helped pave the way for Sol's contact with other key suppliers.
Sol spoke with great affection of "The Old Man," and Cooper
in turn "treated Sol like a son."

Cooper was an early mentor, but Sol also worked his own
personal magic on the men, and the women, who could help
him get the product he needed. Secretaries to suppliers were
beguiled by his courtesies and small gifts. Another valued
early ally, in fact, was a woman: Lockie Luehrman, who at that
time was a representative at the Merchandise Mart for the
Eagle Foundry Company, a manufacturer of kitchen ranges.

When Eagle refused to extend a five-hundred-dollar
credit line for the purchase of eight gas ranges to this boy, just
out of high school, Lockie, known professionally by her
maiden name, "Miss Edwards," put up her own commissions
as a guarantee. She knew that Sol was going to make it in the
business. When other distributors saw that Eagle Foundry
was servicing Central Appliance, they too began to sell to the
Polks. "She made it look like Sol had more than he had," Miss
Edwards' son, William Platt, explains. Sol did not forget the
favor. Miss Edwards serviced the Polk Bros.' account for many
years, and, like the Coopers, became a close family friend.

To the extent that their capital and an expanding reserve
of good will among suppliers allowed, the brothers began to
build a more diversified line of home and electric appliances:
ranges, refrigerators, vacuum cleaners, toasters, phonographs,
radios, even children's wagons.

In the beginning Sol bought what he could, wherever he
could get it, and even as the business grew he continued to

court a variety of suppliers. In this way, the Polks broke with the common practice among retailers of handling only one brand of major appliances. As late as 1951, the majority of re-tailers still carried a single line; fewer than five percent carried more than three brands of major appliances. Polk Bros. even-tually would carry the products of nearly two hundred brand-name manufacturers.

By 1937 business in America was looking up. New Deal wage and price regulations had restored a measure of mass buying power, followed by a surge of prosperity generated by the late-1930s arms buildup. New housing starts in Chicago, combined with the Depression generation's hunger for durable goods, delivered the demand.

The Bendix Corporation introduced the world's first au-tomatic washing machine to the market in 1937. In that same year *Life* magazine advertised the first air conditioners for the home. Electric refrigerators were coming on line to replace superannuated gas models and even older iceboxes. The Polks' little Central Appliance and Furniture Company car-ried them all.

5

The War Years

"During the war, more jobs were held by more Chicagoans in more new factories that paid more money than at any other time in the twentieth century. Moreover, the abundance of money was in the hands of the many, not the few.

"Amidst this abundance, however, there seemed to be shortages of almost everything, including housing, consumer goods, factory workers, and raw materials."

— Perry Duis and Scott LaFrance
We've Got a Job to Do:
Chicagoans and World War II

For the Polk family, the 1940s began as the best of times and became the worst of times. The decade opened with a rush of prosperity and optimism that fortified the growing business. But by 1943 the very survival of the Polk's Central Appliance and Furniture Company was balanced precariously on the vicissitudes of wartime allocations.

For one sweet moment in the late 1930s, however, fate smiled on the beleaguered American economy. The middle class had survived the Depression, and had emerged stronger and in greater numbers than ever before. Distinctions between the rich and the poor — between those who had things and those who did not — had all but disappeared in the reshuffling of wealth that occurred in 1930s. Middle-class families were in a buying mode. And they were paying cash.

Central Appliance and Furniture was beginning to show a profit. The only downside of growth for the Polks was that they had no space to grow into. The cramped sales floor at 3334 North Central Avenue served them well, but the room was packed to the rafters. The piecemeal solution was to rent garages in the alley behind the store to house inventory as they acquired it.

In 1940, buoyed by rising sales revenues, the brothers purchased a vacant building and the adjoining lots in the middle of the 2800 block of North Central Avenue. The two-story building was on the west side of the street, just four blocks south of the store at 3334 North Central.

By 1950 this property — which took the number 2850 North Central Avenue — would be the nucleus of the massive Polk City complex. But when the Polks bought it the building was a boarded-up tavern that had fallen on hard times after the murder of a child on the premises. Or so the story goes. Whatever the actual circumstances, Sam Polk and Sol got a deal on the property. The street-level floor provided warehouse space; the bonus was that there were two, two-bedroom apartments on the second floor that could be converted into a new home for the family.

The building was just north of the intersection of Central and Diversey avenues. Henry and Yetta Pokovitz took the south apartment; Morrie and David shared the second bedroom in the parents' apartment. The north apartment, which had a large, open porch, was a bachelor pad, shared by Sam, Harry, and Sol. Irving Feuerstadt, Yetta's nephew, had come to Chicago from New York in 1940 to work in the store, and for a time Irv, too, lived with the family. Yetta's new kitchen was furnished with the best that Central Appliance and Furniture could provide, including a Bendix automatic washing machine.

*   *   *

The year 1940 turned out to be memorable in other respects. In the fall of this year the family hired a sixteen-year-old neighbor to come in and help out after school. Lester Bachmann would stay on with Polk Bros. for more than fifty years. He became Sol Polk's right-hand man, the company's purchasing czar, and ultimately he would serve in Sol's absence as president of the company.

Lester was the Polks' first non-family assistant. But the brothers did not go far outside the family to find him. As mentioned earlier, the Bachmanns and Polks were connected in various ways. Lester was Louis Bachmann's nephew, and thus Goldie's nephew by marriage. His father, Max Bachmann, had been Sam Polk's supervisor at Postal Telegraph for some fifteen years.

Since 1938 the Bachmann brothers, Louis and Max, and their families had been next-door neighbors in the apartment building at 211 North Central Avenue. Lester at the time was a student at Austin High School and was working a variety of after-school jobs, including a Saturday job in a factory.

Hearing that Lester was looking for another weekend job, Goldie suggested that her brothers could use some part-time help at the store. Lester Bachmann began work as a stockboy at the 3334 North Central store in September 1940. When he graduated from high school in January 1942, he enrolled at Wright Junior College, just three blocks west of the store. The proximity to Central Appliance and Furniture was seductive. Lester began to take on more, and more diverse, duties at the store.

Central Appliance and Furniture made its first cautious forays into print advertising in this period. The medium was the classified pages of small neighborhood papers. "Classified was inexpensive, and it didn't take a lot of talent to write six or seven lines," Lester Bachmann claims.

For a company that in the 1960s would routinely run more than 40,000 lines of print advertising in any given week, a few lines in the classified pages may seem a puny beginning. The effort may even seem casual. But the strategy was right on the mark. The Polks were into neighborhood merchandising. Their customers were the Northwest Side families that for years they had sold door to door. In 1940, with jobs and money coming back into the economy, and housing at a premium, the classified pages were hot. The Polks were practicing the first principle of modern advertising: targeted marketing. Bang for the buck.

These early ads revealed another practice that was carried over into Polk Bros.' future promotional activity: Do the common, uncommonly. In the early 1940s electric trains were a popular Christmas season item, and Central Appliance and Furniture did a brisk business in Lionel train sets and accessories. Lester Bachmann recalls that "The whole trick was not to have any carryover, but in 1941 we did have some carryover in the trains. We probably had ten to fifteen sets. It was not a lot. But for us it was." The Polk solution was characteristically uncommon: In mid-summer a classified ad was placed in the *Chicago Tribune*, promoting train sets as a "Fourth of July Special." Lionel trains literally flew off the shelves.

*   *   *

In the late summer of 1941 Sam Polk married Miss Thelma Amelia Bank. He was thirty-seven years old, and the first of the brothers to marry. The wedding was a momentous event for the family.

Thelma was born at the family home in Chicago's Wicker Park neighborhood, but spent her early childhood —

the years spanned by the First World War — in Europe with
her widowed mother. After their return to Chicago, Thelma
completed high school and began work at Goldblatt's department store. She soon found a better position, in the credit department at the Philco corporation, which happened to be
one of the Polk brothers' major suppliers.

Thelma and Sam's middle daughter, Barbara Polk Milstein, remembers being told that Thelma's first meeting with
Sam was engineered by amateur matchmakers at Philco:

> The men at the managerial level were always trying
> to find a nice Jewish boy for her to marry. They re-
> ally wanted to look after her. So one of the fellows
> came to her and said, "There are these five Jewish
> boys who just started a business. Their books are in
> a mess. Why don't you go over there and help them,
> and see if you can do yourself some good."

Barbara continues: "So Mommy had a new fur wrap, and
she dressed herself all up, and marched in there, and cleaned
up their books." Sam noticed. He asked Thelma out. The
courtship, however, was somewhat non-traditional. No dancing at clubs until the wee hours. Sam was then working the
equivalent of three jobs: There was the store during the day;
law school in the early evening; and Postal Telegraph from
midnight until eight in the morning.

"He was tired," Barbara says. "Their dates consisted of
him coming to Grandmother's home and falling asleep on the
couch. He'd sit down — then have a nice nap." Thelma, apparently, became a little weary herself. After two or three
years of courting, on the night of the Hadassah Ball, a big dinner dance, she said, "Sam, I'm leaving." He proposed.

On August 10, 1941, Sam and Thelma were married in
the Skyline Grand Ballroom at the Morrison Hotel at 181
West Randolph Street in Chicago. The Polk family's invitation list included all of Central Appliance and Furniture Com-

pany's carefully cultivated suppliers. More than six hundred guests were present for the ceremony. Roberta Bachmann was the flower girl; seven-year-old Bruce Bachmann was the ring bearer. The marriage certificate was signed by Sam's lifelong friend, Abraham Lincoln Marovitz, who was then an Illinois state senator.

*   *   *

These were the good times, but the political climate was turbulent. By 1940 America had assumed an attitude of preparedness with regard to the war in Europe. In September of that year the Selective Service Act was passed. For the first time, American boys were being drafted during peacetime.

On December 7, 1941, the Japanese attack on Pearl Harbor brought America into the war on the side of the Allies. War on Japan was declared on December 8. On December 11, the United States declared war on Germany and Italy. The declaration of war opened the floodgates for a tremendous infusion of cash into the economy.

New factories, geared to defense efforts, were springing up throughout the Chicago area. Men were working longer hours and bringing home larger paychecks. In the winter of 1941 department store sales in Chicago hit record levels. Wholesale orders for furniture at Chicago's Merchandise Mart rose twenty-four percent over sales for the same period in 1940. Goods were still plentiful, but shoppers, and dealers, anticipated wartime restrictions. They were buying everything they could.

In an effort to curb competition from Johnny-come-lately dealers, Chicago's old-line department stores drafted an industry code designed to curtail "no-down-payment" advertising claims made for major appliances. Electric refrigerators especially were targeted, but so were the other fast-moving items such as radios, stoves, washers and ironers, and vacuum cleaners.

That sword cut both ways. In mid-1942, a wholesale and retail inventory policy committee within the War Production Board's Division of Civilian Supply was set up to study the necessity of inventory control. In this case, the larger and financially more powerful stores — those capable of stocking disproportionate shares of what merchandise remained on the market — were the target.

Disposable income was rising, but the nation's inventory of durable goods was shrinking. Refrigerators, ranges, and radios had been snatched up in the flush of the 1940 to 1941 prosperity. In mid-1942 the War Production Board issued a draconian list of controlled materials that would drastically curtail any further manufacture of goods for stateside consumption.

The home appliance and home furnishings industries were hit hard by a reallocation of rubber, iron and steel, silk and wool to the defense industries. Rationing of raw materials was followed by even more stringent orders shutting down assembly lines that had turned out hundreds of categories of consumer goods.

In early 1942 the War Production Board halted the manufacture of cars and light trucks. In May, production of some fifty types of electrical appliances — including toasters, percolators, griddles, waffle irons, and heaters — was curtailed. Metal household furniture, which had become popular during the 1930s, and wool carpeting were history.

*   *   *

There would be no more Fourth of July specials on electric train sets at Central Appliance and Furniture. And very little activity in major appliances. A bellwether for the industry, the Sears, Roebuck 1942 fall and winter catalogues, were almost bare of any hard lines.

When factories quit manufacturing automatic refrigerators, the Polks bought and sold ice boxes. When factories had exhausted their reserves of steel, leaving unfinished goods on the assembly line, Central Appliance and Furniture bought the skeletal innards of gas stoves.

By late 1943 consumer durable goods of any description had all but disappeared from the market. War production was in full gear. The new American industry was armaments. Thirteen million men between the ages of eighteen and fifty had enlisted or had been called into the armed services. Three of the five Polk brothers would be among them.

So would Lester Bachmann. Lester, just one year out of high school, enlisted in December 1942 in the Army Signal Corps. He attended Signal Corps' training classes in Chicago in 1942 (as did Robert Galvin, who would later succeed his father Paul Galvin as president of the Motorola corporation) before being posted to the China-Burma-India Theater as a radar specialist.

Harry, who was then thirty-one and unmarried, was drafted in late 1942 and assigned to the U.S. Military Post Office in San Francisco. At the time Harry was engaged to marry Miss Pearl Luftig, a strong-minded and artistic young woman whose widowed father, Morris Luftig, owned the Superior Belt Company, a successful leather-goods manufacturing business.

The declaration of war and the specter of men shipping out for overseas duty had changed the ground rules that governed courtship and marriage. Traditional large ceremonies, such as Sam and Thelma's 1941 wedding, gave way after Pearl Harbor to quick marriage services in the office of the county clerk.

When Harry was drafted, Pearl Luftig let it be known that she did not intend to wait out the duration under her father's roof. Pearl followed Harry to San Francisco. The two were married there in early 1943. The festivities were limited to a brief honeymoon at San Francisco's famous old St. Francis Hotel. Harry served his entire tour of duty with the military post office in San Francisco. Pearl kept herself busy working as a saleswoman in a millinery shop.

Sol was drafted in late 1942. He was inducted into the U.S. Army in February 1943 and spent six months stateside before being posted to the European Theater. Sol, a supply sergeant, served two-and-a-half years in England. He may have talked himself into Special Forces; family members say that Sol Polk had the enviable job of driving World Heavyweight Boxing Champion Joe Louis around when Louis visited the troops. Others say that Sol, as a photographer, had the less enviable job of accompanying the American forces into the death camps of Central Europe in 1945.

Sam's civilian status for a time seemed more secure. He was nearly forty years old. He was married. And by the late summer of 1943, Sam and Thelma were expecting a child. With two brothers already in the service and with the draft deferment for fathers still in force, Sam probably could have stayed home.

His eldest daughter, Sandra Polk Guthman, believes that Sam "sort of forced his way in." He was inducted into the army in November 1943 and became active in January 1944. Sam was able to stay in the United States for another six months — until after Sandra's birth in March of 1944 and long enough to attend his brother David's wedding in June. In August Sam was posted to Belgium where he served fourteen months in the 798th Port Company as a marine engineer, ferrying barges between Europe and Britain.

Sam's departure left only Morrie and David at home. David, whose hypertension was first discovered during his Selective Service physical, had a IV-F draft classification from the beginning. Morrie also remained at home, in the status of head of the household.

From the early 1940s Goldie's husband, Louis Bachmann, had been working side by side with the brothers in the store. His help became even more critical in 1943 with Harry, Sol, and Lester Bachmann in the service, and Sam preparing to go. But this was not to be. Louis was not well. The diagnosis was leukemia, and the disease progressed quickly. Louis died at home on December 21, 1943, with Goldie at his side. He was then just forty-two years old.

Bruce Bachmann, who was a grade-schooler at the Robert Emmet Elementary School, remembers the day.

> I had come home for lunch. My father was in the bedroom. I knew he was sick. I remember my mother saying goodbye to me when I went back to school, and as I left the house I remember hearing her calling my father's name. When I came back in the afternoon, my Uncle Morrie was there on the steps waiting for me. I could tell the news was not good. Then I realized what had happened.

When Sol and Harry went into the service, Sam and Thelma took over the north apartment at 2850 North Central. David and Morrie continued to share the parents' apartment next door.

When Louis died, Goldie had to give up the apartment at 211 North Central Avenue. She moved, with her children, to the family residence at 2850 North Central, to share Sam and Thelma's apartment with Thelma and her baby. Thelma and the infant, Sandra, had one bedroom; Goldie and her daughter, Roberta, had the other. Nine-year-old Bruce slept in the kitchen.

*   *   *

Although 1943 ended in personal tragedy for the Bachmann and Polk families, the mood of America in that year was not all grim. This was the era when families gathered around the radio every evening, not only to get news from the front but also for relief from the war news. Radio was a lifeline, and the comedy-variety programs — Jack Benny, Fibber McGee and Mollie, and Edgar Bergen and Charlie McCarthy — became a part of family life.

Outside the home, nightclubs were thriving and ball-room dancing was never more popular. Young people thronged Chicago ballrooms to sway to the recorded music of Glenn Miller, Tommy Dorsey, Benny Goodman, and the Andrews Sisters. David Polk, in spite of his lame foot, was a superb dancer. And so was blond, vivacious Marian Cole.

In the summer of 1943, Morrie Polk was dating a young woman who, like David, was an accomplished dancer. When David asked if there were "any more like her at home," she gave David the names of two friends. "I was his second choice," Marian claims.

> He called a few times, and he was a little bold. I later found out that was not at all like him. He was such a sweet and gentle man.

Marian, who had attended Central YMCA College (now Roosevelt University) was then taking night courses at Northwestern University and was working for the United States Treasury, Bureau of Public Debt. It took several calls from David, but Marian finally agreed to meet him. "It clicked," she remembers.

David and Marian were married on the 25th of June 1944 in the presence of some forty guests at the famed Edgewater Beach Hotel, the Chicago home to the big bands of the thirties. Harry was in San Francisco and Sol was in Europe, but Sam, in uniform, made it to the wedding. Morrie was his brother's best man.

* * *

With Harry, Sol, and Sam gone, Central Appliance and Furniture had become Morrie's eighteen-hour-a-day job, as it was for David and Goldie. The family was locked in a perilous fight for the very life of the business. "It was a battle to get equipment, anything. It was a time when you tried to get whatever you could. The goal was to keep the store open," Lester Bachmann says.

The winter of 1944 to 1945 was a time of agonizing austerity. And it was an especially bitter winter, even for Chicago, accustomed as it was to the arctic blasts that typically swept the city in the dark days of January and February. Coal and oil for heating were scarce. Neon signs were forbidden, and stores had to close at dusk to save precious fuel. Food rationing was in full force. It was a time of meatless meals. Real butter was only a memory. In the spring, the family planted a Victory Garden in the vacant lot adjacent to the apartments at 2850 North Central.

"They were just holding on to the company, just getting the bills paid. That was my mother's job," Roberta Bachmann Lewis recalls. "She would come home from the store after dark and put on her apron to prepare the meals, and then settle down at the kitchen table to work on the books until after midnight." Roberta's own job, besides working in the store after school and on weekends, was to write a letter every week to the brothers in the service.

For a time, after hard goods disappeared from the market, Goldie and David struggled to supplement the family income with furniture and carpeting sales. As early as 1940 Goldie had recognized a secondary market among Central Appliance customers. If a family were shopping for appliances and kitchenware, they might also be furnishing homes, she reasoned. Roberta recalls: "When people came in to buy a roaster, she would ask, 'What else are you buying?'"

David at the time had begun ordering carpeting for Central Appliance customers through the Strauss-Rose carpet distributorship at the Merchandise Mart. Even before the brothers went into the service, David and Goldie were taking customers to the Mart to select furnishings. In this way, Goldie began to forge relationships at the Merchandise Mart that, in the postwar years, she built into the highly successful furniture division of the Polk Bros.' operations.

But by early 1943 furniture, too, was in short supply.

Competition for scarce merchandise was keen. *The New York Times* reported in early 1943 that attendance at the annual January furniture market in Chicago was unprecedented in its numbers. Most of the registrants were small merchants. The *Times* took this as "strong evidence that the average small dealer in home furnishings fears an end to his business and is determined to fight to the last to survive." There were few, if any, as determined to endure as the Polk family.

* * *

The secret of Central Appliance and Furniture's survival through the war years and remarkable growth of the company in the immediate postwar period lay in the family's ability to stock merchandise even in times of factory backlogs and profound shortages. There has long been speculation around the question of how they did this. The answer is deceptively simple: They were scavengers.

For a time, War Production Board policies actually worked to the advantage of small and energetic retailers, especially family-owned businesses such as Central Appliance and Furniture which were unencumbered by formal management and purchasing structures.

Inventory control measures introduced in 1942 targeted the largest retailers, because these outlets were the easiest to control. The process in effect gave priority to smaller retailers, who stood to benefit most in the redistribution of inventories that had been stockpiled by manufacturers in 1941. Until shortages of raw materials shut down the pipeline, wholesalers were happy to reroute available product, in smaller lots, to retailers such as the Polks.

Right up to the day he went overseas, Sol haunted local distributors with whom he had established friendships. He bought whatever he could, in whatever numbers he could get it — even item by item. Many less competitive operators, including the pre-war boomers, had been forced out of business by 1942. When they unloaded what remained of their inventory, the Polks were waiting on the doorstep to buy it. Sol bought out of storefronts, out of warehouses, out of store-rooms, and even out of garages.

And the Polks had friends. Their friends included Lockie Edwards, who had personally guaranteed Sol Polk's credit with the Eagle Foundry Company in the late 1930s. Up through 1943 Eagle Foundry was one of the few manufactur-ers in the country that was permitted to make stoves, along with the production of magnesium bomb casings.

Miss Edwards, as the Eagle Foundry representative, prospered in the early years of the war. She sold to the largest outlets: Marshall Field and Company, Goldblatt's department stores, the Fair Store. But she did not favor her large accounts over Central Appliance. Lockie Edwards was a working mother, with a son close in age to Goldie's son Bruce, and a close friendship developed between the two women. Orders for gas stoves were written up over dinner in Yetta's kitchen, recalls Lockie's son, William Platt. "It was a very informal deal; my mother was very successful in these years, but she al-ways looked to Goldie for advice."

Bill recalls that when Goldblatt's refused delivery of a carload of gas ranges because the car was damaged, Lockie called Sol.

> She said, "Sol, come on down. I want to see if you want anything on this car." One of the things she liked about Sol was that he could make up his mind. Sol took the whole car. It was real big for him. And she got the commission.

As shortages worsened, so did black market trade in scarce goods. It wasn't the crime of the century; although some activities clearly were more flagrantly illegal than oth-ers. In the early 1940s, for example, cattle rustling reappeared in the Old West. Most black marketeers, however, were oth-erwise legitimate businessmen who devised various ways to circumvent price ceilings and rationing programs.

This kind of activity was not within the Polks' venue, for the obvious reason. They had other objectives. Black marketeering implies scarce goods at high prices. The Polk strategy was just the opposite: more transactions at lower prices. The Polk business secret, from the days of the Sunbeam irons on, was never tied to inflated price; it was pegged to low overhead, high volume, and fast turnover.

But as 1944 dragged on into 1945, even the Polks ran out of merchandise.

6

The Boys Come Home

"The veterans were coming home, the building trades were booming, it was the beginning of the housing developments — and everybody needed something."
— Roberta Bachmann Lewis

The war in Europe ended in May 1945. By August 14, the day of the Japanese surrender, it was all over. The boys were coming home.

Sam Polk boarded a troop ship out of Belgium in October 1945 and arrived at Great Lakes Naval Air Station north of Chicago in early November. Harry Polk and his wife Pearl returned from San Francisco at about the same time. Sol was discharged in early 1946, leaving the U.S. Army with the rank of master sergeant.

"The uncles were back and suddenly the place just pepped up," Roberta Lewis recalls. "There was energy everywhere. When the factories started to tool up, I think Sol was probably first in line for the merchandise. They just had this tremendous sense of optimism."

And so they should have. The postwar mood in America, in Chicago, and on Central Avenue was exuberant. The term "The Home Front" took on an altogether new meaning. Women were being pressured out of the work force to make room for returning GIs. ("Do You Want Your Wife to Work After the War?") Exit Rosie the Riveter; enter Betty Crocker. The years between 1945 and 1951 were heady times indeed.

Dreams of owning a home and raising a long-postponed family seemed now to be within the reach of middle-class Americans. The rush to acquire was on. Enforced saving during the war years had put cash in people's hands. Wartime technologies were bringing altogether new products into the market. Young families had homes to furnish, and consumer demand was at a fever pitch. A hit tune of the day, "I'll Buy That Dream," was music to the ears of the Polk brothers.

Sol Polk at the age of twenty-nine was no longer a boy wonder. He was as focused and ambitious as ever, but by 1946 he was also a seasoned entrepreneur — and a war veteran. He was of that generation of able, supremely confident, goal-directed men who stormed back onto the national scene after the war, determined to revolutionize American business. From the day of his return, Sol was consumed with rebuilding Central Appliance and Furniture. He was a dynamo of restless energy. He needed more merchandise, more space, more people.

The goal was nothing less than to supply Chicago's working- and middle-class families with the stuff of the American Dream: automatic washing machines, refrigerator-freezers, dishwashers, radio-phonographs, contemporary furniture, and eventually television.

*　　*　　*

When Lester Bachmann returned to Chicago in the spring of 1946, his plan was to continue his studies in electrical engineering at the Armour Institute (later renamed the Illinois Institute of Technology). This was not going to happen. He says,

> I went over to the store to say hello to the boys, and they asked me what I was doing. Sam called that night and said, "Why don't you come back just until school opens. We could use somebody to help out."

That casual invitation marked the end of Bachmann's plans to become an electrical engineer and the beginning of a lifetime career at the very heart of the Polk Bros. operation. Lester remembers that the character of the business had not changed much while he was gone:

> I was working with Sam when I came back, but I did everything. I did bookkeeping. I did selling on the floor. I handled the cash register. Everybody did everything, from opening the mail to sweeping the floor to waiting on customers. It was a real family operation.

And so it was. All of the brothers, and Goldie, were now working seventy and eighty hours a week in the business. By mid-1946, Sol had hired two young women to help out in the office. The Polks' cousin Irv Feuerstadt returned from the service and went back to work on the sales floor. One by one a broader circle of family members were called in to work in the store, and Sol began hiring salesmen from outside the family.

John Szilagyi, an experienced salesman, and Ernest J. LaSalle, who was trained in appliance servicing, were among the first of these outside hires. Szilagyi and LaSalle, together with Irv Feuerstadt, office manager Vera Smith, and delivery driver Willie Hawkins formed the core of a group of committed employees who started with Central Appliance and Furniture in the 1940s.

Another key figure entered the management circle in June of 1946 when Sol persuaded twenty-five-year-old Georgia Rice to leave a more glamorous job at Helene Curtis to become his secretary. Like the brothers, Georgia would devote her life to the business; and like Sol, she never married. Georgia, together with Lester Bachmann, was one of two non-family executives who operated at the exact center of the organization. Others close to the inner circle included the brothers' attorney, Ben Crane, who had been a friend and compatriot from childhood, and Polk Bros.' outside accountant Ben Beckerman.

*   *   *

The demand for consumer goods in the immediate postwar period was matched only by the relentless problem of shortages. Although factories had gone into overdrive converting to the manufacture of peacetime consumer goods, an overloaded distribution system still struggled with a backlog of orders. The wait for a family's first postwar Ford or Chevy was likely to be as much as six months. The same was true of electronics and appliances.

The Polks' scavenging instinct returned with a fervor. Again, as in the war years, they bought whatever they could get, often in war surplus sales and warehouse clearances. From time to time, the shelves of the store were stocked with such diverse items as steel wool, aluminum pans, and flashlight batteries. Lester Bachmann remembers the times:

> After the war there was war surplus. Batteries weigh a ton, but it was something to sell when we didn't have washers or ranges to sell. We would scrounge around to see who had anything, whether it was a retailer, a vendor, distributor, a manufac-

turer. We would get anything we could to satisfy a customer.

But steel wool was not the Polks' stock in trade. What Sol needed was the big stuff. This he acquired in deals that as often as not reflected unusual ingenuity.

Ernie LaSalle recalls, for example, that right after the war Sol Polk was able to buy several hundred wringer washers from the Thor company. He got them cheap; they had no motors. These were outdated models that had ossified on the assembly line when the War Production Board cut off supplies of copper wire. Thor was glad to part with them because the company was then rushing their new automatic washer into production. Sol then went to another supplier and bought several hundred washing machine motors. LaSalle vividly remembers the circumstances because he installed every one of those motors himself. The machines were sold as reconditioned merchandise.

Space heaters, both oil and gas, were another item in great demand after the war. Sol Polk at one point was able to buy a boxcar load of oil heaters. He was notified on a Friday evening that the shipment was standing on a siding at the railroad terminus in Galesburg, Illinois, and would not be moved out until Monday. On Saturday morning, Sol and Lester took a truck down to Galesburg. Bachmann recalls:

> There was no one around there. Finally we found an agent and talked him into opening up the car so we could unload the merchandise ourselves. We pleaded that there were children in Chicago who were cold and were waiting for the heaters. Something like that. We got the goods and filled our customers' orders on Sunday.

The Galesburg trip was not at all unusual in the postwar period, according to Bachmann:

Sol and I almost lived at warehouses. We got to know every receiving clerk and every shipping clerk by their first name. When they got a shipment of goods, we'd be there to get our share. We wouldn't take no for an answer.

Sol Polk himself once told an interviewer that when he needed refrigerators after the war, and there were few to be had, he would go directly to the suppliers' offices.

I'd ask to see the guy in charge of sales. They'd say he was busy. I'd say, OK, and I'd sit down. I'd sit there all day long. Then I'd go back the next day and I'd sit there. Finally they got so tired of seeing me, they would give me some merchandise.

The statement is probably unnecessarily humble. While Sol may indeed have sat in vendors' waiting rooms in the first years of the business, after the war Sol Polk went back to his friends. He revived the cornerstone relationships that he had forged in the pre-war years. He called on suppliers and they called on him. Irv Lewis, who became a key member of the operation in the late 1950s, says that the significance of these friendships, nurtured as they were in the immediate postwar period, cannot be underestimated.

The Coopers [R. Cooper, Jr., Inc.] were the first to give Sol Polk a franchise. He never forgot that; he never forgot General Electric. It was the same situation at Zenith. And at Admiral, where he dealt with Ross Siragusa, who was the founder and chairman of the Admiral Radio Corporation.

The senior Mr. Galvin at Motorola, which is now the cellular giant of the world, and his son Bob Galvin would come in because they were interested in selling radios to us. All these people grew up in

the business in the years right after the war. Sol had
a relationship with them.

Again, time and place were important. The radio and
electronics industries that were born in Chicago in the 1920s
and 1930s became critical in the war effort. In the postwar period they converted quickly to the production of radios,
record players, and telephone equipment for civilian consumption. The Polks' old friends at Zenith, Admiral, and Motorola soon dominated the national market for these products;
by 1950 they would make Chicago the nation's leading center
for production of television sets.

David Polk's son Jeffrey notes that the success of Central
Appliance and Furniture in the immediate postwar period
rested on Sol Polk's remarkable ability to keep the merchandise rolling in.

> The business didn't thrive because of normal chan-
> nels. It thrived because Sol had a strong relationship
> with R. Cooper, Jr., and other suppliers. After the war,
> when everybody had money and there was nothing to
> buy, you're going to do pretty well if you have an
> abundance of toasters — especially if you discount
> them as well. Sol had an abundance of toasters.

Jeffrey Polk adds a further insight — one that cuts to the
heart of the Polk brothers' business strategy:

> They didn't make their money on the wealthy ten
> percent of consumers. They made it on the other
> ninety percent. The middle class uses a lot more
> toasters.

*   *   *

The return of the brothers and the burst of new activity
in the business set in motion a round robin of Polk family

moves that began with the family apartments at 2850 North
Central and ended with a virtual colonization of the large
apartment complex at 3334-3370 North Central, where the
first store was located.

It started with Goldie. In 1946, in her early forties,
Goldie married Morris Luftig, the aforementioned owner of
the Superior Belt Company and the widowed father of Harry's
wife, the former Pearl Luftig. He was a warm-hearted man in
love with life.

The new Mrs. Luftig, with Bruce and Roberta, moved to
Morris's apartment at 5522 West Jackson Boulevard, in the
Austin neighborhood where she and the children had lived in
the 1930s. Sam moved back to the family apartment that
Thelma and Goldie had shared during the war years. Morrie
had moved to a bachelor apartment on West 63rd Street, and
Sol, on his return from Europe, took over Morrie's old room
in the Polk parents' apartment at 2850 North Central.

Harry and Pearl Polk lived up the street, in the 3334-
3370 complex, as did Irv Feuerstadt and his wife, the former
Ruth Freed. Apartments were hard to come by in 1946. But,
then, so were appliances. Ruth recalls that Sol traded the land-
lord a refrigerator for the lease on the Feuerstadt's two-and-
a-half room apartment. Irv's parents, "Aunt Minnie and Uncle
Adolph," also lived in the building. Lester and Gail Bachmann, who married in 1944, had an apartment at 3366, in the
same complex.

The men all worked in the store at 3334 North Central.
So did Irv's brother, Saul, and Abner Rand, a Polk cousin
whom Sam and Sol had located in a concentration camp after
the war and had arranged to bring to America. Others, including Ruth Feuerstadt's brother-in-law Mel Arbeit, would
soon be drawn into the circle. Such was the sheer centripetal
force of Sol's personality.

The families living at both 2850 and 3334 were close; the
living conditions were almost communal. Ruth Feuerstadt remembers that Irv and Lester shared a company car with David
Polk:

Irv would have it one weekend; Lester would have it the next. When Lester and Gail's son David was born, Irv drove Gail and Lester to the hospital. When I went into labor with our daughter Karen, it was Lester's week to have the car. So Lester drove me to the hospital.

Living over the store did have its advantages. More often than not the men were able to come upstairs for supper and to change to a clean white shirt before returning to the evening shift on the sales floor. The proximity to scarce appliances was convenient. The Feuerstadts and the Bachmanns did their family laundry after hours in the demonstration washer at the 3334 store. Later, when Sam and Thelma bought their first home and Harry and Pearl moved to the apartment at 2850, Pearl kept groceries in a store refrigerator.

But living over the store had disadvantages too. Lester Bachmann recalls that when Central Appliance put one of the first black-and-white television sets on display in the store, it became a tremendous draw to building residents, who had the habit of dropping in after supper to watch the televised wrestling matches.

The store was open until ten o'clock at night, but that didn't matter. When I got ready to close, the neighbors would say, "One more match, we'll just watch one more match." So I had to wait until the wrestling was over before I could close up and go home.

In early 1946, the brothers bought a building at 3110 West 63rd Street, on Chicago's Southwest Side. The building had housed a National Tea Company store and had apartments over the street level store front. Morrie Polk took over the management of the property and opened a second Central Appliance and Furniture outlet at this address.

At this time Morrie hired Harold Millard, who was married to Lester Bachmann's sister Shirley, to help out part-time with orders in the 63rd Street store. Like the rest of the family, Millard soon became full time. In 1950 he was seconded to the headquarters store at 2850 North Central, where he became lead buyer for two of Polk's highest volume products — television sets and air conditioners — and developed the inventory control system that came to be known as right-on-time buying.

*   *   *

Sol Polk's primary move, after re-establishing his contacts with his suppliers, was to add additional floor space to the North Central Avenue building where the family apartments were located. Before the war, the brothers had bought the vacant lots north of the 2850 apartments. This property would became the site of the Polks' first expansion. *Fortune* magazine reported some ten years later that Sol was so eager to get started on the addition that he acted as his own contractor on the building job:

> The result had its ludicrous side: The building that went up in the center of Polk City didn't have any downspouts. These were later installed **inside** the store, where they are still visible, a perpetual monument to Sol's passion to get on with life's main business.

"There was never 'tomorrow' for Sol Polk," Ernie LaSalle remembers. "To him, everything had to be done today." Sol was in such a hurry to use the expanded space that he began storing merchandise there even before the roof went on. "If it rained, we just covered everything up," LaSalle says. "Sol would tell us, 'I've got merchandise rolling in; I've got to put it someplace.'"

Lester Bachmann agrees that "putting up that building was quite a story." He says,

We didn't have an architect, and we didn't have any plans when we built it. When we laid the foundation we had floors that were just dull, gray concrete. We couldn't afford tile or carpet or anything like that. But Sol found a kind of red powder that could be mixed with the concrete to color it, so he hauled a load of that stuff over. It worked pretty well on the floors, but the powder seeped out of the bags and dyed the trunk of his car an even brighter red.

The coloring agent worked so well that a few years later when the sidewalks around the front of the store were replaced, the same red-dyed concrete was used.

*   *   *

When the 2850 addition was finished in 1947 it was used primarily as a showroom for refrigerators and large appliances. David Polk was put in charge of that outlet, which he staffed with the assistance of one salesman, Charlie Restano.

At the time, Lester Bachmann recalls, the company had only one cash register. That was located at the original store at 3334 North Central. Every evening David Polk collected the day's receipts from the 2850 store in a cigar box and walked four blocks north to 3334 so that Lester could ring up the sales. The joke between them was that if the new store ever did enough business, they would buy a second cash register. They needn't have worried. Within a decade that second store would become the heart of the sprawling Polk City complex.

The headquarters of the Polks' operation gradually shifted from 3334 to the 2850 North Central location as the area under roof there expanded. When the first addition was completed, the garages behind the buildings were connected to the main building; soon a further expansion was made to the south. Eventually the family apartments would be torn off, except for one bedroom which Sol used as his office and, occasionally, his sleeping quarters.

Sam was the first to move his office to 2850. Sol and Georgia Rice followed, bringing some sales people with them. Lester was left at the original store for several months longer. Then he, too, went over to the main store, as it had come to be called. The little store at 3334 North Central was closed in 1948. Yetta Polk, for one, was happy with the new arrangement. She was accustomed to calling her boys at the store to remind them to come upstairs for dinner; when they couldn't make it, she would send a pot of spaghetti down to the sales floor.

*   *   *

The move to 2850 was followed by the Polk brothers' decision to open the store on Sundays. Sunday retail sales (other than alcohol or motor vehicles) did not violate any Illinois statutes of the time. But the Polks' decision to open their doors on Sunday did defy a long-standing and time-honored practice within the Chicago retail community. Most merchants slavishly followed the lead of the old-guard department store bloc, which since the days of the first Marshall Field had decreed there would be no sales activity in Chicago on Sundays.

The decision to open the stores on Sundays coincided with the Polks' first venture into radio advertising. This was a Sunday morning spot on a small one-thousand-watt station out of the village of La Grange, south of Chicago. An aluminum roasting pan — there were about one hundred in Polk's surplus inventory — was offered as a free gift to anyone who came into the store that day and mentioned the name of the station that broadcast the ad.

Lester Bachmann recalls that the spot ran at nine-thirty

in the morning. When the store opened at ten o'clock, there were no customers.

But by eleven-thirty, quarter to twelve, the place was a hornets' nest. People were driving up at all angles in the parking lot and rushing into the store wanting their free roasting pan. When we ran out of roasting pans, we started giving away other things to keep people happy.

I'll never forget Mr. Polk saying to me, "Set up a card table in the middle of the store. Get the names and addresses when they get the roasting pans. I want to know where these people came from." I couldn't write that fast. We had to call all our friends to come in and help us manage the crowds. . . .

We were on the map after that Sunday.

In 1949, acting on the suggestion of Hal Newbold, general manager of the General Electric Supply Corporation, distributors of Hotpoint products, the brothers agreed to change the name of the company to Polk Bros., Inc. Sol liked the brevity; it meant less copy in print ads, larger headline type, fewer costly seconds wasted in radio commercials.

The change was made gradually. Print ads were not too problematic. In the transitional logo, the name "Polk Bros." flew like a flag over the word "Central," followed in smaller type by "Appliance and Furniture." Telephones were more difficult. Until 1950 at least, operators struggled through a lengthy salutation: "Good morning. Polk Bros.' Central Appliance and Furniture Company. Can we help you?" In time, the name was compressed to the ultimate in brevity, dropping even the period in print ads. The elimination of the period — making the name just "Polk Bros" — created a nice graphic balance, but the unconventional usage forever after created havoc for newspaper and magazine proofreaders.

*   *   *

By the time of the opening of the store at 2850, the Polk brothers were casting their eyes on other real estate in the area. In these early years, the Polks, as real estate entrepreneurs, hopscotched their way up and down both sides of the two blocks north of the headquarters store. They acquired vacant lots and small buildings with the zeal of men circling a giant Monopoly board.

In these two blocks of North Central Avenue, Sol Polk was becoming king of the hill. With one exception. Sol was never able to buy one property he coveted. This was the southwest corner lot at 2900 North Central, which directly faced Polk's main entrance. That lot and the building on it belonged to Sol's old friend — who became his nemesis — restauranteur Joe Bruno. It would forever stick in Sol's craw that Bruno would not only refuse to sell the building but would thumb his nose at the Polks by opening his own store there in 1950 — defiantly naming it Bruno's Appliance and Furniture Co.

*   *   *

Morrie and Sol were the bachelor uncles. In the spring of 1947 that, too, would change. Morrie met Marion Bauer, a graceful, soft-spoken honey-blond. It was a blind date, arranged by family friend Ben Crane. Morrie was then thirty-six. Marion was just twenty-two.

As had been the case with Sam and Thelma, the course of the courtship was governed by Morrie's hours at the store. Throughout the fall Marion took a bus in the evening to meet Morrie at the 63rd Street store, where she waited for him to close up at 10 p.m. They just had time for a late supper before Morrie drove Marion back to her parents' home in his big, green Packard car.

In January, at the wedding dinner celebrating the marriage of Ben and Elaine Crane, Morrie proposed to Marion, in an unusual way. He stood to offer a toast to Ben and Elaine, and seized the occasion to announce his own engagement to Marion. It was news to everyone present, including Marion. "I was a little surprised," she says. "But then he always was kind of a take-over guy."

A large, formal wedding, to be held at the Palmer House Hotel, was planned for May of 1948. But an event that proved to be devastating to the family intervened. On April 2, a Friday, Harry's wife, Pearl, had taken her mother-in-law, Yetta, for a fitting for the hat Yetta planned to wear to Marion's first bridal luncheon. Pearl left Yetta at her door and went to her own apartment across the hall to leave her packages. In the few moments after her return home, Yetta suffered a massive stroke. She died instantly.

The rabbi advised that Morrie and Marion's marriage should take place as planned. But because the family was in mourning, all of the pre-nuptial affairs were canceled. Marion was able to return her wedding dress. The service, and a modest dinner, were held on the scheduled date — May 9, 1948 — in a small hall, without music, and with only family and close friends present. It was Mother's Day.

At that time, the stores were open on Monday and Thursday nights. When Morrie and Marion returned from a brief wedding trip, Morrie was told that the family had decided to keep the Central Avenue store open every evening, Monday through Saturday. "It didn't take long before they decided to open up on Sundays, too," Marion recalls.

"From the day we got home from our honeymoon he worked every single night," Marion Polk remembers. Her three sisters-in-law could have warned her of what it meant to be a Polk wife — and probably did. The brothers were devoted husbands, and loving parents to their children. But they just never were home. "The store was number one in Morrie's life," Marion says. "I'm sure it was number one in all their lives."

The families themselves were not exempt from Sol's relentless drive to keep the sales floor stocked and the merchandise moving. Marion Polk recalls in acute detail the day that Morrie sold her new GE electric refrigerator right out of the kitchen of their apartment on 63rd Street.

Bruce Bachmann recalls an experience that was common among the Polk children:

> As you would expect, we were one of the first families in the neighborhood that had a television set. But we knew that sooner or later the television would disappear. Wrestling was the only thing on, but every ten days or so a truck would come and carry the set away because that was the model that Sol needed to sell.

In at least one case, proximity to the family business worked in reverse. When a customer that David had taken to the Merchandise Mart changed her mind about the three custom tables David had ordered on her behalf, David was forced to keep the merchandise himself. His wife, Marian, says she lived with those tables — blond veneer with black surfaces — for twenty-five years: "The darn things never fit in and they never wore out."

Another of the family parables concerns the timing of the arrival of Polk babies. In the beginning, the stores were open only two nights a week: Monday and Thursday. David's wife, Marian, jokes that she was lucky. Two of her sons were born on a Tuesday and the third was born on a Friday. Morrie's wife, Marion, didn't have that option. When the time came for their daughter, Linda, to be born, Marion took her watch and waited out the early stages of labor in the Marquette Theater across the street from the 63rd Street store.

> When it got close to ten o'clock, which was closing time for the store, the pains were five minutes apart. I walked out of the movies and went across the street to the store. I said to Morrie, "Now, you don't have to rush, but it's time to go to the hospital."

When Marion's second child was due, in December of 1951, the timing was a little closer. Morrie's joke was: "Don't bother me until after the Christmas rush." Marion didn't. She went into labor on December 26th; their son Howard arrived the next morning.

*   *   *

The period from 1946 to 1951 — roughly the years between the end of World War II and the beginning of the Korean conflict — could be considered the adolescence of the company. This was the time in which Polk Bros. made a dramatic transition from a small family business to the seasoned operation that it became in the decades of the 1950s and 1960s.

The family's sheer drive to succeed, their ability to put in almost superhuman hours, and their daring as a young, renegade company competing in a market dominated by old-guard retailers made the difference. But when it came to generating consumer demand, Polk Bros. had a great deal of pro bono help from a revitalized advertising industry.

In the immediate postwar period, pent-up demand guaranteed a ready market for durable goods. Even before the war ended, manufacturers were racing to convert their assembly lines from the production of thirty-seven-millimeter cartridge cases to the production not only of washers, ranges, and refrigerators but also to the production of altogether new products, such as chrome dinette sets and aluminum pressure cookers.

The buzz words right after the war were "New" and "Newest." Advertisers fanned the flame of consumer demand for the very latest models of everything. They saturated the market with broadsides such as one prepared in late 1945 for the "Postwar Electric Appliance and Radio Show." This ad featured cartoon figures exclaiming over the wonders of appliances. A serviceman in uniform and his wife, for example, rejoiced over a refrigerator decorated like a gift package and proclaimed, "We'll want these new appliances in our dream home." Dialogue captions for other characters in the ad advised readers: "This certainly is the place to get new ideas for that new home"; "It's so exciting! The new appliances we've been hearing about for so long"; and "I declare . . . Those new ranges just think for themselves." A child dragging his mother by the hand says, "C'mon Mom. Let's see the new radios now."

Even the venerable *Saturday Evening Post* got into the act. A 1945 institutional ad promised consumers: "You'll See Your New Washing Machine First on the Advertising Pages of *The Post*. Millions will turn to *Post* advertising pages for their first news of the many exciting products for better living."

The other calls to action were the words "Electric" (or better, "All-Electric") and "Automatic." The first GE electric ranges came off the line in September 1945. Although historically Chicago had been a "gas market," within weeks of the introduction of the electric range, an advertisement placed by R. Cooper, Jr., the General Electric supplier, proclaimed that now "electrical equipment stands near the top in postwar wants." By 1947 the "all-electric kitchen" was being promoted as the heart's desire of the American homemaker. The gas stoves of the 1930s were out. Electric ranges were in.

A product that was "New," "Electric," and "Automatic" as well, was irresistible. Commonwealth Edison invited customers to see "the new automatic electric ranges." The automatic electric water heater was touted, as were automatic electric clothes dryers, automatic ironers, and automatic console-combination radios. Advertisers' reach for the limits of new, electric, **and** automatic products was surpassed when the Thor company came out in 1947 with its "Auto-Magic" combination clothes washer and dishwasher.

The Polks did not get into display advertising themselves until 1950. They didn't have to; it was being done for them. What they did have to do was differentiate themselves from competitors who were as likely as Polk Bros. to catch the fallout of the postwar advertising blitz.

Thus, while other retailers slept, Sol Polk set in motion practices that had the potential to destroy his valuable supplier relationships but that ultimately would see him recognized by the national business press as the man who virtually invented modern discount retailing.

7

Fair Trade Isn't Fair

"The Polks' unique talent was an ability to stock merchandise even in times of profound shortages.

"Their genius — the cornerstone of Polk Bros.' spectacular success — was offering these goods at prices that defied the 'fair-trade' codes observed by other retailers of the day and that foreshadowed, by decades, the modern phenomenon of discount retailing."

— Crain's Chicago Business
April 1992

Reflecting in the early 1960s on the extraordinary success of the Polk Bros. stores, the *Saturday Evening Post* dubbed Sol Polk "King of the Discounters." No title could be less acceptable to Sol himself. In fact, the writer of that article acknowledged that "the word makes him wince."

The Polk brothers did not consider themselves discounters. That type of merchandising was something they associated with lower Manhattan and a type of sideline operation that, in Lester Bachmann's words, offered "a bunch of catalogues, maybe a few pieces of merchandise, and no service, no delivery, no sales people."

Sol Polk had another idea. He knew that to beat the competition in the wide-open postwar economy, he had to do something different, something better. From their first days as neighborhood retailers, the Polk brothers had cultivated their reputation as the place to go to get a deal. In the postwar period, Sol Polk became the first retailer in America to openly discount the price of brand-name, nationally advertised appliances. In doing this, he willfully, purposefully challenged the appliance trade's most protected privilege: resale price control.

*   *   *

The notion that the price of an item, particularly an item such as a major appliance, was "fixed" at a certain dollar figure had become rooted in the public mind by the end of World War II. The concept began with the New Deal wage- and price-control policies first embodied in the National Industrial Recovery Act of 1933. More relevant to the evolution of what came to be called fair-trade codes were the provisions of the 1936 Robinson-Patman Act. Robinson-Patman was designed to protect small businesses from "price discrimination" by making it illegal for suppliers to offer more favorable prices to volume buyers, such as Sears, Roebuck and Co. and Montgomery Ward.

Sears and Ward reacted to price control, and more specifically the Robinson-Patman regulations, by establishing their own private brands, which they advertised as "below the fixed price" for comparable merchandise. The stratagem kept the big stores within the letter of the law. But it did not immunize the gigantic Sears organization from Sol Polk's one-man battle against "off brands" — or "ghost brands" as Sol called them. The Polk brothers were perhaps both amused and flattered by a petulant letter on the subject dispatched in 1953 by Sears general counsel Arthur M. Wood. Wood, who would later become chairman of the mammoth Sears conglomerate, complained that the Polk brothers' "derogatory remarks with reference to 'off-brands'" constituted, in his opinion, "unfair competition."

In practice, by the end of World War II, New Deal fair-trade policies had the effect of protecting not the small dealers but the manufacturers, who, under the umbrella of the fair-trade codes, were allowed to name, or "fix," the retail price for goods bearing the manufacturer's trademark. Given the history of price-control regulations, the implication was that any challenge to "fair trade" was nothing less than un-American. The dealer who defied industry practices was condemned by his fellows as a "price-cutter."

Sol disagreed. As he so amply demonstrated in later life, Sol Polk was the consummate patriot. He fervently believed that the health of the American economy depended on mass selling to keep production lines rolling. He believed with equal fervor that the average American family was entitled to enjoy the fruits of American industry and should have these products for better living at a price that reflected their actual value. "Waste in distribution and extravagant overhead," by Sol Polk's reckoning, were the enemies of the people. "Fair trade," Sol declared, was decidedly **unfair** to the consumer.

Concurrently, Sol Polk was also the consummate businessman. He knew that big-ticket purchases such as major appliances were highly price sensitive. He recognized that if he could be the first Chicago retailer to offer top-quality merchandise at ten to twenty percent below the manufacturers' suggested list prices, the public would beat a path to his door. Major appliance buyer Jerome Ungerleider (known in the business as Jerry Unger) described the scope of Sol Polk's vision:

> When they started, there was a list price for everything. Mr. Polk felt that if he could take a refrigerator that was list-priced at, say two hundred dollars, and sell it for one hundred fifty dollars, the customer would have fifty dollars to spend on something else. In this way you build traffic. And you have more

people buying, with more money to spend, on more merchandise. With more merchandise being sold, you keep the factories running and the punch presses going.

It was a grand idea, but for nearly a decade Polk Bros. walked a precarious path, balancing industry pressures and carefully cultivated supplier relationships against Sol Polk's own fiercely independent free-market philosophy.

Manufacturers enforced the fair-trade codes by refusing to sell their trademarked product to a retailer who was not willing to honor the manufacturer's suggested list price. In a time when merchandise was hard to come by, and demand was voracious, the sanction was a powerful one. In the early days, such major manufacturers as Magnavox, DuMont, Frigidaire (which sold to Marshall Field), and even Chicago-based Sunbeam, were among those that held a hard line on the price-maintenance issue. They had a strong voice in the industry.

The hard-liners had allies among the traditional retailers such as Chicago's Marshall Field & Co. and Carson, Pirie Scott & Co. department stores. As the market stabilized and competition for market share grew hotter, the old guard department and appliance stores began to view the activities of the upstart Polk Bros. company with alarm.

These traditional retailers needed fixed pricing. The manufacturer's suggested list price was scaled to cover the dealer's cost plus the normal mark-up. Retail appliance dealers' overhead was estimated at about twenty-eight percent at this time. Markup might be as much as thirty-eight percent over cost. Sol Polk claimed that he could cut overhead to nine percent, sell the product below list price, and still make a profit. (It was commonly believed by the early 1950s that Polk was getting near distributor margins on the merchandise it sold. Sol did not deny the rumor.)

The trade magazine *Electrical Merchandising* reflected on the super-heated emotional climate of these times in a 1953 article titled "Sol Polk: Price Cutter or Pioneer?"

Every generation has something that local taboos consider most holy. Today, one of the things considered sacred is the list price of an appliance. So much kowtowing has been done before the idea that the man who would tamper with it is considered a cur. If he cuts it, he is barred from heaven and despised in hell. Or so society would have you believe.

Polk Bros.' response to the invective of the industry, however, was simple and direct. They turned the other cheek to suppliers who would not deal on Polk's terms. And they bought, in large volume, from suppliers who were more than happy to work with them. In this respect, Sol Polk relied heavily on his friends and on a history of honorable relationships forged in the pre-war years. These included long-standing friendships within Chicago's growing electronics and home-entertainment industry.

They included also such old friends as Dick and Doug Cooper, the GE suppliers that had given Sol his first franchise in the mid-1930s. Bill Platt, a representative for the Hardwick Stove company, relates a story told to him by Doug Cooper. The occasion was a meeting with suppliers called shortly after the war by all of Chicago's State Street dealers:

> Sol Polk had come in with his concept of pricing. Up to that time no one had even heard of discounting. Right there in that meeting the State Street dealers told Dick Cooper, "If you sell to Sol Polk, you're not going to sell to us."
>
> The reply from GE, through Cooper, was: "That's your choice, gentlemen."

While the industry seethed at Polk Bros.' refusal to sanctify the canons of resale price maintenance, the Polks nonetheless were able to sustain speaking relationships with even the most obdurate of these manufacturers. Polk played by the rules of the game. "We didn't try to get around fair trade," Lester Bachmann says. "We honored it." He continues:

> We knew what the manufacturers were attempting to do. We went along with that, although not whole-heartedly. Fixed price was not our philosophy. But we recognized that the manufacturer had a right to state the terms by which he wanted his product sold, or displayed, or advertised. If we told the manufac-turer we would do certain things, we did them. Our word was our bond. If we said we couldn't meet a certain requirement, and the manufacturer objected, that was all right. We would remain friends. We just didn't do business with them.

*   *   *

Ultimately Polk Bros. beat fair trade to the ground by virtue of their sheer buying power. But in the early years, the path to lower prices was sometimes more circuitous. The com-pany perfected the practice of offering a high trade-in allowance on a customer's old appliance. *Fortune* magazine, in a 1955 arti-cle, took pains to point out that "this technique was not devised to circumvent fair trade." In practice, it did just that.

Fortune gave the example of a refrigerator listed at four hundred twenty dollars. Polk's price for that model might be three hundred ten dollars: "If the customer has an old, near-worthless box that he wants to get rid of, the salesman will quote an allowance of one hundred ten dollars, which brings the price to three hundred ten dollars." If the old appliance had some resale value, the trade-in allowed might be even higher.

The Polk brothers themselves were entirely open about the trade-in option. In fact, they advertised that "Polk Bros.' tremendous King-Size Trade-In allowances provide the great-est savings anywhere on nationally advertised appliances, TV, furniture, and carpeting."

If Polk Bros. had ever been called upon to justify King-Size Trade-In allowances — and it was not — it would not have had any difficulty. When Sol Polk found himself with a mountain of old appliances, he gave Ernie LaSalle, Polk Bros.' one-man maintenance department, what amounted, in LaSalle's words, to a "field commission." LaSalle's job was to develop a Polk Bros. reconditioning center.

Eventually, Polk Bros. opened a rebuilt-appliance outlet store on Grand Avenue. It became a major profit center. The company, as will be seen, also garnered both a public relations bonanza and a useful tax break by donating large quantities of this merchandise to trade schools and prisons for use in vocational training programs.

*   *   *

By the mid-1950s, the fair trade issue had become a battle of loyalties among those suppliers who remained faithful to fair trade and the apostates who were willing to sell to Polk Bros. When the Polks announced the opening of their 60,000-square-foot store on Cottage Grove Avenue, they sent out press releases accompanied by a glossy photograph of the exterior of the new building. As at Central Avenue, the facade was emblazoned with the larger-than-life brand-name signs and logos of Polk Bros.' suppliers.

Lester Bachmann recalls that the president of Magnavox responded by sending a letter to his dealers, with a copy of the photograph, asking them to note which logo was missing from Polk Bros.' parade of brand names. "He used our store as an example of the restricted distribution they had at the time," Bachmann says. "But Mr. Polk never spent a minute on anything negative. There was always something positive around the corner."

Another encounter with Magnavox exemplifies the Polks' attitude. In the period when Magnavox continued to hold out against Polk Bros., the Polks bought out a retailer who operated a small dealership in a Chicago suburb. Bachmann recalls that the transaction was done in one of Sol Polk's typical post-midnight business meetings.

> We got our accountant and our lawyer out of bed, and we signed the deal that night. The owner happened to be a Magnavox dealer, and he had just received a relatively large shipment of Magnavox product. It was brand new, still in the cartons. The next morning I called the local Magnavox representative and told him that we had just bought this store and we had this inventory of Magnavox merchandise. We said that if he'd send a truck over, we'd make out a bill and sell it all back to them.
>
> That's what we did. We sold them every piece. We walked away from the opportunity to abuse the product, because that wasn't necessary. We wouldn't have gained anything by doing that. They did not forget that, and a couple of years later we were carrying Magnavox.

The Polks were faithful to their word to customers as well. Lester Bachmann recalls that in 1946 when demand for radios was at its peak and the wait was as much as six months, the little store at 3334 North Central set up a display and took orders for Zenith Radio Corporation console and table model radios that Zenith representative Bob Wallace had made available to the Polks. In the months between the time the demonstration display was set up and the product became available, Zenith's price for the top-of-the-line console model increased from three hundred ninety-five dollars to four hundred ninety-five dollars. In filling customer orders, the Polks honored the three hundred ninety-five dollar price.

* * *

Polk Bros., however, did not depend entirely on the normal distribution channels. They had a sharp eye for distressed dealerships and closeouts. In the 1930s and 1940s the public utilities in Chicago operated retail stores, selling appliances to promote the use of electricity and gas in the home. When People's Gas Company closed down their retail sales operation after the war, the Polks negotiated to buy the entire inventory at cost. And they did not cut the retail price further in resale. Polk's primary purpose in this deal, Jerry Unger recalls, was to keep the merchandise out of the hands of other retailers.

Thomas Ayers, who became chairman and CEO of the Commonwealth Edison Company, has another memory of Sol Polk's dealings with the electric company's retail appliance stores. Ayers recalls that Edison operated forty to fifty retail stores in Northern Illinois after the war.

> I became convinced in the late 1940s that it was ridiculous for us to be in the appliance business. We could have sold appliances for less, but a big utility couldn't sell at cut rates because the smaller retail stores thought that wasn't fair.
>
> I had gotten to know Sol and his brothers because they were the leading lights in serving people who wanted so badly to get these new appliances. I thought the Polk brothers had the best operation that we had seen. Their goal was to serve the customer. I persuaded my bosses that Edison ought to get out of the appliance business.

One would think that Sol, who had once worked as a door-to-door salesman for Commonwealth Edison, would have been pleased by Edison's withdrawal from the market. But he wasn't. Ayers says,

> Sol didn't like that one bit. He wanted us to stay in business because he liked to tell customers that if they wanted to see what a good deal they were getting at Polk's, they could go down to the Edison

store and see what these appliances are really selling for.

Ayers adds, "I used to kid him about it. I'd say, you want me to keep these outrageously expensive stores open so you can sell for less? He did, but we closed them all anyway."

*   *   *

One by one, suppliers began opening their lines to Polk Bros. They crossed over when the price — gauged in terms of the size of an order — was right. In 1946 Polk Bros. Central Appliance and Furniture had been just another small independent dealership in a crowded market. Sales in 1946 were estimated at one million dollars. But as Polk Bros.' annual revenues multiplied — reaching, by conservative estimates, $14 million in 1952 — distributors began seeing the dollar signs on the wall.

Tom F. Blackburn, who was Chicago editor for *Electrical Merchandising* magazine in this period, relates a story that goes to the heart of suppliers' divided loyalties. "The question arises," Blackburn writes,

> as to why the industry continues to sell to Polk Bros. when price-cutting is demoralizing to the appliance business.
>
> The answer may be found in the story of a group of distributors who had lunch and agreed to cut him off. The elder statesman of the group was delegated [to go to Polk Bros. offices] and perform the excision. "I had just told Sol and was pulling away from the curb," he said, "when who should drive up but one of the other men who had attended the meeting."

Blackburn tells a similar story illustrating the dilemma faced by suppliers. When one supplier made a deal to sell a few units of his product to Polk Bros., a Chicago dealer who considered himself to have a "more or less exclusive" relationship with that supplier objected. In the fallout, Polk was canceled out. But not entirely. Polk Bros. "was thereafter sold through the back door," Blackburn says. The story was not disputed by Polk Bros. executives who read Blackburn's article before it was published.

If the anecdote is true, it is not surprising that the supplier would risk his old account by continuing to deal with Polk Bros. Blackburn notes that in the first month Polk sold five hundred seventy-two units of that supplier's product. S. R. Bernstein, editor of the influential trade magazine *Advertising Age*, observed in 1955:

> Every time Marshall Field & Co. sells an appliance, Polk Bros. sells ten appliances. Every time Carson Pirie Scott & Co. sells a single appliance, Polk Bros. sells sixteen. So, in cold, hard terms of moving merchandise, this discount house is worth ten accounts like Marshall Field and sixteen like Carson's.

As the saying went at the time, there were those suppliers who would not sell to Polk Bros., and there were those who were afraid not to. There were also those who tried to keep a foot in both camps. Some agreed to sell to Polk, but refused to offer price concessions or advertising allowances.

*   *   *

By the time Polk Bros.' third store, on Cottage Grove Avenue, opened in 1954, the Polks were able to run a full-page advertisement in the *Chicago American* listing ninety-one nationally advertised brands of appliances, electronics, furniture and housewares that could be found in Polk Bros. stores. The copy did not mention the industry phrase "manufacturer's suggested price." Nor did it use the tainted word "discount." Polk Bros. merely assured customers that these brand-name goods were available at "our common, sensible prices."

The company was presenting itself by this time as the largest outlet for brand-name merchandise in the city. This kind of advertising brought heavy leverage to bear on manufacturers who wanted to hold their place in the Chicago market.

Inexorably, in the case of each supplier, a point would be reached when the size of an order from Polk Bros. had the effect of softening the heart of even the most reluctant distributor. The Polk brothers were not only good for a supplier's business. They were good people to do business with. The Polks pushed high volume and rapid turnover. They kept their word. They paid on time and in cash. They were straight shooters.

In a vignette newspaper advertisement that ran in 1958 the company made this statement:

> We believe in advertising a manufacturer's list price, and we've never lost the trust of a manufacturer because we've made a price leader or a football out of a product that he has spent millions of dollars perfecting.

These were not empty words. Unlike many of the discounters and so-called bargain-barn retailers that rushed onto the scene in the 1950s, Polk Bros. never spent a day in court over a fair-trade issue. They were never sued by a manufacturer or a supplier. And, so far as anyone can remember, they were never served with a summons or an injunction charging violation of a contract or agreement.

By the mid-1950s the partisans of fair trade were beginning to lose ground in the arena of public opinion. S. R. Bernstein took a fresh look at the resale price maintenance issue in a 1955 address to the Association of National Advertising. Using Polk Bros.' operation in Chicago as his example, Bernstein speculated on what supporters of list-pricing policies would say to the Polks: "You would probably explain that they have caused you a great deal of trouble, because they have 'disturbed the retail price structure,' and because they have upset your 'normal distribution channels.' "

Bernstein then presented his response to the manufacturers' argument:

> In my opinion, your job is to move the goods you make, as quickly and as effectively as possible. It is not your job to maintain "normal distribution channels." It is not your job to protect lazy or inefficient retailers. And it is certainly not your job to see to it that the consumer pays a higher price for your goods, if he can get them at a lower price, and still have everybody in the distribution chain make a reasonable profit.

Bernstein identified the battle over resale price maintenance as "that little drama entitled 'Turmoil in the Marketplace' — or 'Who's on Which Side, and What the Hell Kind of Game Are They Playing Anyhow?' " The speech and the ensuing reprint in *Advertising Age* was not a "little drama" for Polk Bros. It was a triumph. Polk Bros.' operation, heretofore not widely known outside of Chicago, was being discussed and evaluated by the entire retail trade. Lest anyone miss the import of the story, Sol's good friend Congressman Richard W. Hoffman had Bernstein's speech, introduced by his own remarks, read into the *Congressional Record*.

The impact had a ripple effect in the industry. Later that year the trade magazine *Electrical Merchandising* held:

> Mr. Polk's philosophy and business methods are an important guidepost to the phenomenon of discount selling.
>
> By deliberately violating the principle of list price, he has built Polk Brothers into a better than $12-million-a-year Chicago dealership, and his

methods, although both admired and condemned, are imitated — which makes them important.

*　　*　　*

By 1960, discounting and the phenomenon known as "off-price" stores was on the rise nationally. The fair trade codes were becoming more and more difficult to enforce from within the industry. But the concept died hard. In 1983 — even after the U.S. Supreme Court had repeatedly found manufacturers' fixed pricing to be an automatic violation of the Sherman Antitrust Act — the Reagan administration, under pressure from powerful lobbying groups, petitioned the court to legalize resale price maintenance. Even into the 1990s the Federal Trade Commission continued to investigate appearances of illegal price-fixing by major appliance manufacturers.

The word "discount" was never spoken in Polk Bros. stores, nor was it used in their advertisements. Yet, ironically, Polk Bros. quickly became known as a "discount house" whose founder was widely described as the father of modern discount retailing.

The apparent contradiction is easily explained: By combining high sales volume of **top quality merchandise** with deep reductions in operating costs, Polk Bros. was able to cut its own margin of profit on each transaction. What Polk Bros. did was give the word "discount" an entirely new meaning. In this respect, Polk executive Irv Lewis says, "Sol Polk educated a generation." He goes on:

> I don't know what the word "discount" means anymore. All I know is we took the goods to market as quickly and as inexpensively as possible. It was a basic, honest, hard-driving philosophy.

Jules Steinberg, a former executive of the National Appliance and Radio-TV Dealers Association (NARDA), recalls the drama and the politics surrounding the issue in the 1950s and early 1960s. "Sol Polk," Steinberg says,

> was an inspiration to independent retailers every-
> where. However, he was not viewed as a friend by
> the trade: Even as they unloaded carloads of mer-
> chandise at his central warehouse, manufacturers
> despised him for defying the "fair trade" laws of the
> land by consistently selling below supplier-estab-
> lished minimum retail selling prices. And as might
> be imagined, that tactic did not endear him to his
> fellow merchants.

In 1961 Steinberg sponsored Sol's application for mem-
bership in NARDA. The application was blackballed. Three
years later, with fair trade finally overturned by the U.S.
Supreme Court, Sol Polk was not only welcomed into the association; he was proclaimed NARDA's "Man of the Year" in
recognition of his "outstanding service to the industry." Victory was sweet.

8

The Great American Shopping Spree

"Modernism came to America through the kitchen door."

— Richard Guy Wilson
The Machine Age

"Isn't it better to be talking about the relative merits of our washing machines than the relative strength of our rockets?"

— Richard M. Nixon
Moscow "Kitchen Debate," 1959

Long before the fair trade issue was finally fought to the ground, Polk Bros.' flamboyant merchandising style and capacity for moving massive amounts of merchandise had made national news. *Fortune* headlined a 1955 feature story with these words:

> Sol Polk has set a whole market on its ear. A combination of carnival man and evangelist, he has become the country's fastest mover of home appliances, grossing $40 million a year in his colorful stores.

103

It was quite a story. In less than a decade Polk Bros. had grown from a small family business to acknowledged status as a mega-player in the American home appliance industry.

As shown earlier, the company's spectacular growth in the postwar period was the result of many factors: dogged hard work, audacious marketing, and incredible foresight. But the greatest of these was providence. Polk Bros. in the decade of the 1950s mirrored the image and the aspirations of the American public. The products that Polk Bros. brought to the marketplace were the very symbols of a new, more affluent, more leisured way of life.

Nostalgia for the "Fabulous 'Fifties" may evoke memories of Chevrolet convertibles and Cadillac tail fins, but the true memorabilia of the age — the objects that forever changed American life-styles — were the lush new products of the home appliance industry, paired with the arrival of commercial television. It is no fluke that America's sweetheart in the summer of 1952 was not a blond starlet with a Hollywood wardrobe, but Betty Furness, the Lady from Westinghouse. She sold refrigerators, and they made her famous.

Refrigerators, and all that went with them, were what people wanted. While many families were buying their first appliances, even more were buying the latest appliances, the newest and the best. America in the 1950s was riding a soaring economy. Life was good and it was going to get better. Real income was on the rise, and a confident people were spending as never before. The phrase "never before," in fact, became something of a slogan for the era. Never before, said design critic Thomas Hine, had so many people been able to acquire so many things, and never before had there been such a choice.

The technological revolution that was to radically transform American life-styles in the mid-twentieth century did not burst on the scene riding the nose cone of an Atlas rocket. It crept in more quietly — by way of the kitchen door. The middle-class family of the prosperous postwar period was infatuated with appliances, electronics, and housewares. Young marrieds acquired the furnishings of the modern kitchen with astonishing speed: electric ranges, automatic washing machines, double-door refrigerators. That done, they hungered for more and even newer products: electric clothes dryers, dishwashers, home freezers, garbage disposals.

Small appliances such as electric frying pans, blenders, hair dryers, and electric shavers were snatched up almost as soon as they were invented. Transistor radios, forty-five-RPM record players, and wire recorders appeared in the stores in the 1950s, the vanguard of an immense home entertainment industry to come. By 1957 appliances had become a five-billion-dollar industry in America.

Polk Bros., which carried more of these products for the home, in greater variety, than any other Chicago outlet, was at the heart of the action. It could be said that Polk Bros. grew up with the new American family of the 'fifties. The converse is also true: In Chicago tens of thousands of postwar families grew up with Polk Bros.

*   *   *

For the Polks, the decade of the 1950s was a time of electrifying energy, perpetual motion, and spectacular growth, as the brothers and Goldie expanded the Polk City complex of stores and pushed the company's volume up into figures that quickly ran into the tens of millions of dollars.

The "main store" that was built around the family apartments at 2850 North Central Avenue in the late 1940s was not enough to keep up with the growth. By the mid-1950s, that store had exploded into a dynamic mosaic of permanent and temporary buildings that came to be known, quite aptly, as "Polk City."

The Polk City complex — which ranged up and down Central Avenue in the two blocks between Diversey and Wellington — was a patchwork of supermarket-sized sales floors; specialty stores featuring contemporary, colonial, and nursery furniture; a lawn and garden center; a boating store;

parking lots, canvas pavilions, massive outdoor boards, and flashing neon displays.

A block north of the 2850 headquarters building was the futuristic Today store, Goldie Bachmann's province, which sold the best in contemporary furniture. North of that, under a huge outdoor canopy, the Four Seasons store sold summer furniture, lawn equipment, and backyard swimming pools. Across the street were campers and boats. The first furniture store was at 2901 North Central, across from the Today store. Farther south, past the main parking lot and across from the 2850 store, was the carpeting outlet.

Eventually, Polk City encompassed nearly a dozen permanent Polk Bros. buildings, and any number of temporary structures, including quonset huts, circus tents, and, in 1953, the world's largest portable ice skating rink. The headquarters store at 2850 itself was a veritable midway, emblazoned with the neon and lighted logos of Polk's suppliers: GE, Admiral, Philco, Motorola, Zenith; Westinghouse, Maytag, Kelvinator, Whirlpool; Norge, Roper, Hotpoint; RCA Victor, Necchi.

Polk Bros.' inimitable merchandising style emerged full-blown in the 1950s, distinguishing Polk Bros. from other dealers of the day and earning the company its place in retailing history. This was the period when Polk became as well known for its spectacular promotions, its colorful sales force, and imaginative advertising campaigns as it was for its famous rock-bottom prices.

The early 1950s were also the years that America became wired for television. Sol Polk was among the new medium's most fervent messengers. Polk Bros.' aggressive approach to marketing black-and-white, and then color, television sets and the company's pioneering forays into live television advertising catapulted Polk Bros. into the national retailing arena.

Sol Polk embraced the spirit of the times with an almost messianic fervor. In Sol's mind, unrestrained consumption was the engine that drove the great American economy. The materialism of the decade was, in his terms, not an expression of idle hedonism but an act of patriotism. A 1954 Polk Bros. advertisement was unabashed in its statement of this philosophy:

> The story of Polk Brothers is essentially the story of America, where you get more and have more than you can get or can have anywhere else. You are America, and your standard of living represents the bountiful American way of life. People that HAVE are HAPPY people.

Lester Bachmann, as the principal buyer for the company, saw the phenomenal growth of the home appliance industry in the 1950s and early 1960s in more institutional terms:

> The industry was growing and we were growing up with it. We happened to be in a very dramatic business. We saw the first electric ranges, the first home freezers, the first dishwashers, the first color television sets. We were part of this revolution in the industry.

Polk Bros. from the beginning had been one of the few outlets in the country to stock both appliances and electronics. By the early 1950s the combined force of Polk Bros.' reputation for negotiated prices, a virtually untapped demand for television sets, and the extravaganza of Polk's zany promotions had driven store traffic up into near stratospheric numbers.

By the mid-1950s the stores were open seven days and six nights — a total of eighty-five hours a week. At least nineteen carloads of merchandise rolled into the Polk warehouse each day. The company was turning its inventory as often as fifteen times a year, a writer for *Fortune* magazine estimated. On an average weekday some 7,750 people passed through the Polk City complex. On Sundays that number rose to 9,500 shoppers and their families.

These figures are particularly amazing when we see that even as Polk Bros. became a Goliath, it continued to be run, not by a cadre of highly trained executives and marketing MBAs, but as a family business whose principals, in effect, were still "living over the store." While none of the brothers ever carried an official title, the five Polk brothers settled into individual roles that suited each and that defined each man's place in the business.

*   *   *

Sol, possessed of a native brilliance and single-minded ambition, was the idea man. The company was created in his image and dominated by the sheer, driving power of his personality. Sol was the master merchandiser, the master pitchman, the master of the deal. No one would deny that he was charismatic; few would say that he was beloved.

Sam Polk, the oldest of the brothers, was the steadying presence and the financial arm of the business. He was the company's "inside man," solid and sure, close to the administrative staff and savvy about the company's growing investment portfolio. He personally signed every check and managed the company's cash flow, even when volume grew into multi-million dollar figures. It was Sam, people remember, who knew every employee by name and never failed to ask about their families.

Harry built a career as a floor manager and operations man at the main store at 2850 North Central Avenue. His territory was major appliances. Salesmen used to joke that if you wanted to find Harry, head for washers and dryers, and if that failed follow the trail of ashes from his ever-present cigar. Harry was the salesmen's salesman — one of the guys — and the man they counted on to close a deal when negotiations reached a stalemate.

Morrie ran the South Side stores in the 1950s and acted as a roving trouble-shooter for all the operations. Noted for his quick temper — a rough exterior hiding a tender heart — he was known throughout the stores as "Morrie Thunder." Energetic and voluble, Morrie was a master of Don Ricklesstyle one-liners. "You want the latest model?" he might ask a customer hesitating over a purchase. "Wait until the day before you die. You'll get the latest model."

David, more gentle by nature than the hard-driving brothers, worked with Goldie Bachmann to establish the highly profitable furniture and carpeting branch of the business. Like Goldie and the other brothers he drove himself mercilessly in the high-growth years of the 1950s. His untimely death from heart failure in 1955 left a gaping hole in the family.

The scene of the action in the 1950s was a chaotic warren of small offices and partitioned work spaces carved out of the former family apartments at 2850 North Central Avenue. The work areas overflowed onto a balcony built out over the major appliance department and connected to the lower level by a wooden stairway.

Irv Lewis has a lasting memory of that balcony and his first encounter with the five Polk brothers. It was a fall evening in 1952. Irv was meeting Roberta after work at the 2910 North Central furniture outlet. He had chosen that night to give her an engagement ring. Roberta suggested, given the occasion, that Irv should go down the street with her to the headquarters store at 2850 "to meet the uncles." Irv remembers:

> I walked over to 2850. This was the first time I had ever been there. And there was a wooden staircase with a landing that went up to the office on the second floor. I looked up, and there were these faces looking down at me. Three or four of them were cigar smokers. There were these tough-looking guys with cigars, standing there looking at me, waiting for me to come up the stairs.
>
> I thought, "Holy cow, what is this?" I've been around, but here was this bunch of tough-looking guys, not saying anything, just looking me over. This was their oldest niece, their princess; they want

to know who this guy is. I went up those stairs with my heart in my throat. It was a tense moment, believe me.

But then they were very, very cordial. I'm sure they had already made all kinds of inquiries about me. I found out right away that they were tough, but like most tough guys, they were also marshmallows. Like Goldie, they were just wonderful people. Bobbie [Roberta] introduced me, and soon everybody was laughing and congratulating me.

*   *   *

The stairway and balcony was also the place where vendors lined up after the store closed at 10 p.m. to wheel and deal with Sol Polk and Lester Bachmann. These meetings, which sometimes went on until three in the morning, may have seemed as intimidating to a sales representative approaching the Polks for the first time as it had been to Irv Lewis. A long-time manager remembering these midnight meetings says, "Before the Polks agreed on anything they could cut your heart out, but once you came to an agreement, you could go to the bank on it."

Daniel Seligman, writing for *Fortune*, has recorded his impressions of the normal daytime activity in Sol's offices in the mid-1950s:

> Visitors may be confounded by the informal, not to say chaotic, atmosphere of Sol's office. Distributors, salesmen, bookkeepers, kibitzers, pile into it steadily. They come to see Sol, but often remain to talk to each other while he merchandises over the telephone, pouring milk from a container, doodling on a large artist's drafting pad. Virtually no daylight penetrates to this room, which is cluttered with Sol's huge conference desk, a record player, a projection machine, and half a dozen bright red Fiberglas

chairs, which frequently are not enough to seat all of Sol's visitors; as many as ten people may be standing around.

Sol Katz, who did some printing work for Polk Bros. in the 1950s, recalls that the offices over the stairs were "a madhouse."

Everybody was coming up to see them. They were friends with everybody. No matter who you were, they treated you the same. Everybody was equal and the same to them. That's why they stayed in business for so long.

In 1954 the brothers expanded Polk Bros.' sales operations — but not the balcony offices — into a more modern setting when they built the first of the very few stores they would design and construct from the ground up. This was the 60,000-square-foot outlet at 85th and Cottage Grove Avenue, famed in the mid-1950s as the site of Chicago's televised All-Star Bowling competitions.

The investment at the time seemed enormous, and the decision to build was undertaken with considerable apprehension. But the Cottage Grove Store incorporated Sol's ideas of what a retail outlet should be. The parking lot was designed to hold four thousand cars; the main floor was the size of a football field; the sales floor was plumbed and wired to display and demonstrate as many as five hundred major appliances and three hundred brands and models of television sets.

*   *   *

The rapid growth years between 1945 and 1955 were a tumultuous time in the business. These were dynamic years for the Polk families as well, as the brothers and their wives established their own homes and began raising families.

When Yetta Pokovitz died in the spring of 1948, the

heart went out of the household. As the main store was built out around the 2850 North Central family apartments, the family's widowed father, Henry, was moved to a residential facility on West Jackson, near Goldie and Morris Luftig's home, and the parents' apartment gradually was taken over as the upstairs office for the new headquarters store. After Henry Polk died in May of 1951, Harry and Pearl gave up the remaining family apartment over the store at 2850.

Although they lived comfortably, the brothers and Goldie all lived frugally throughout their lives. Even as the business became hugely successful, they lived, in the words of a close friend, "well below their means." The Polk brothers made money, but they didn't make money either to spend it or display it. The first principle of child-rearing was "Never, never spoil the children." As they reached their early teens, each of the twelve Polk sons and daughters went to work in the stores on weekends and during school vacations, not because of economic necessity but because it was the right thing to do.

The pace of the Polk business in the 1950s and the brothers' own relentless work ethic took a toll on family life. The Polk brothers were never the type to bounce their kids on their knee or take the boys to a ball game. There was no time for that. Howard Polk jokes that he never saw his father until he was ten years old, but tells a greater truth in his recollection of Morrie coming into the children's rooms after midnight and sitting with them for some time in the dark before going downstairs to start the paperwork.

Time with the fathers was precious. Sandra Guthman and her sister Barbara Milstein both recall the Sunday mornings when Sam would take them with him to the darkened store and let them play house in the model kitchens while he worked in his office upstairs over the sales floor. "Who wants a doll house when you can have that?" Barbara recalls. "If we got tired of one kitchen, we would move on to the next."

Edward Polk remembers that Harry spent sixteen hours

a day at the store, six and sometimes seven days a week. "He'd come home for dinner at 5 p.m., and go back at 5:30." Edward recalls that as a child he would go into the Polk City store after school just to spend time with his father. "I would do little things and they would pay me a quarter an hour." In high school he got a regular job as a stockboy.

* * *

It was 1955 when Polk Bros. had their famous twentieth-year birthday party for Polk Bros. at Chicago Stadium. A little over a month later the families' buoyant spirits were shattered by the illness and sudden death of David Polk. He was just forty-one years old. His three sons were all under the age of ten. His wife, Marian, remembers that on Sunday, April 24, David had tried several times to go into the store but became increasingly weaker. On Monday he was admitted to Michael Reese Hospital; he died in the early hours of Wednesday morning. David had long suffered from a chronic hypertension, but his sudden death dealt a staggering blow to the family. The *Chicago American* reported that "Sol Polk, thirty-seven, youngest of the brothers and president of the firm, collapsed when he learned of the death and was placed under the care of a physician."

On Thursday, the day following David's death, the Illinois House of Representatives adopted a joint resolution acknowledging that "David Polk and his brothers have contributed greatly to the happiness and welfare of countless people through the merchandising and charitable policies of their stores" and extending sympathy to the family. As a "further mark of respect," it was moved that the house stand adjourned until the following Tuesday. A newspaper headline on the day following the April 29 services for David read: "Hundreds in Last Homage to Polk." Another headline placed the number of mourners in the thousands. The accompanying article reported:

Hundreds of persons from all walks of life paid their respects last night at the bier of David Polk, one of five brothers who built a "city" from a small appliance store. Civic leaders and prominent personages in the business and entertainment field were among the many who visited [the] chapel.

* * *

At the time of David's death, the Polk Bros. chain included the 2850, 2901, and 2910 North Central Avenue stores in the Polk City complex; the southwest Chicago stores at 3110 63rd Street and 8530 Cottage Grove Avenue; and a Near North store at 1754 Belmont Avenue. By 1960 another four stores would be added to the chain. These were the 5711 North Milwaukee outlet in Chicago's predominantly Polish Northwest Side, and suburban stores in Joliet, Arlington Heights, and River Grove.

Polk Bros. never released sales figures, but there are benchmarks that give a picture of the breadth of the operation and the rapidity of its growth curve in the 1950s and 1960s. Business analyst Daniel Seligman, writing for *Fortune* magazine in 1955, estimated that Polk Bros.' gross revenues had risen from one million dollars in 1946 to $30 million in 1952, and projected gross revenues of $45 million in 1955. In 1958, *Sports Illustrated* described Polk Bros. as a $60-million housewares chain, which sold television sets at the rate of one thousand a day. By the mid-1960s Polk Bros.' sales volume had topped the $100-million mark.

As early as 1952 Polk Bros. had been recognized in the national press as both "a Chicago institution" and "the country's fastest mover of home appliances." It was also fast becoming close to the hearts — in fact, part of the lives — of three generations of Chicago families, with customers eventually numbering in the millions.

The story of Polk Bros. in the 1950s is broader than the numbers reveal. The larger story is that of the emotional significance of the merchandise they sold and the role these appliances came to play in the lives of growing families. Acquisition of an automatic washer, or a home freezer, or, later, a dishwasher, was invested with significant symbolism for 'fifties families. But few events are as memorable as the day that father brought home the family's first television set. Ask any Chicagoan what he remembers about that first black-and-white TV, and he is very likely to say, "We bought it at Polk Bros."

9

Queen of the Home Furnishings Floor

"There will be a hell of a lot of houses built after the war. . . . just plain, good American twentieth-century houses, and they will need good American twentieth-century furniture to put inside them. . . . good, down-to-earth, inexpensive contemporary furniture."
— T. H. Robsjohn-Gibbings
***Architectural Forum**, 1942*

"Furniture was never more straight-forwardly a practical manufactured good than it was during the immediate postwar period."
— Thomas Hine
Populuxe

When Sol Polk and his brother Sam opened the Central Appliance and Furniture store in 1935, it is probable that furniture was among the furthest things from their minds. The force behind Polk Bros.' home furnishings and carpeting business was their sister, Goldie Bachmann Luftig.

In the mid-1940s, when the World War II veterans returned to buy new VA-financed houses and start their own young families, Goldie saw an opportunity. She began to develop furniture and carpeting sales into an important ancillary business for Polk Bros., complementing the tremendous demand in this period for home appliances such as refrigerators and washing machines.

While the brothers may not have taken furniture seriously in the early years, the growth of the furniture division speaks for itself. Furniture and carpeting sales soared in the 1950s and 1960s, with three stores in the Polk City complex devoted entirely to these products: the carpeting outlet at 2836 North Central Avenue, a major furniture store at 2901 North Central, and the trendy Today store at 2910 North Central. In the 1970s Polk Bros. claimed to be "the largest independent retailer of furniture in the country," with furniture showrooms in ten Chicago and suburban Polk Bros. stores. When the company announced major expansion plans in the late 1980s, furniture was said to account for well over one-third of the company's revenues.

*   *   *

Goldie, like Sol, built the furniture business around personal relationships cultivated over many years with furniture manufacturers and representatives. As had been the case with the brothers and the appliance industry, the growth of the Polk Bros. furniture division was largely a matter of the right person being in the right place at the right time.

Even before Chicago became a center for the electronics industry, the city had been a major supplier of furniture to the nation. In the mid-1920s, some three hundred Chicago area factories — many of them very small — produced as much as one-fifth of the furniture made in the United States. Similarly, Chicago was a magnet to furniture buyers who came from all over the country to shop the manufacturers' showrooms at the massive American Furniture Mart, built in the 1920s at 666 North Lake Shore Drive, and at the even more massive Chicago Merchandise Mart, which opened in 1930.

The Great Depression put many of Chicago's smaller manufacturers out of business, while in the same period, advancing age and immigration restrictions reduced the number of European-trained craftsmen working in Chicago factories. But in 1941, the year that Goldie began visiting the Merchandise Mart, Chicago still ranked as the foremost producer of furniture in the country, turning out an estimated three million pieces in that year alone.

Early in the 1940s Goldie began asking people who came in to the first small store on Central Avenue to look at refrigerators or radios or roasting pans if there were something else they might need for their homes, and offered her assistance in finding furniture or other items. In this period, with David's help in the carpeting field, Goldie began to generate new business for the company and, simultaneously, to build the relationships at Chicago's Merchandise Mart that in the postwar years would form the base for expanding the furniture and carpeting divisions of Polk Bros. operations.

There was never enough floor space at the first Polk Bros. store at 3334 North Central Avenue to show carpeting or furniture. David and Goldie operated in these early years in much the same way that a decorator or an interior designer would today — taking customers to the Mart, or making selections for them. Goldie made friends in this period who were happy to help her get a footing in the business, including Maurice Mandle (Mandle and Co.) and the R-Way furniture representatives at the Merchandise Mart.

Between 1943 and 1945, with Sam, Harry, and Sol serving in the U.S. Army, and the manufacture of appliances halted by wartime restrictions on rubber and steel, the furniture and carpeting orders that Goldie and David brought in went a long way toward sustaining the struggling family business through the last two years of the war.

Even so, it was an uphill battle. By 1943, wartime shortages of raw materials had halted the manufacture of furniture for civilian consumption almost as completely as they had frozen production of major appliances. Metal hardware, steel springs, feathers, down, cotton webbing, and even upholstery tacks, were among the materials subject to stringent restrictions. In the years before the war, some five hundred new items were introduced each year at the American Furniture Mart. During the war, the number of new offerings fell to as few as five per year.

*   *   *

Morrie, David, and Goldie were running the business alone, barely keeping the family afloat through the lean last years of the war. Roberta Bachmann Lewis, who was then enrolled at Austin High School, remembers this period more vividly than other members of the family. These were the difficult years, perhaps more difficult for Goldie than anyone. "I think she did what had to be done day by day, in the best way she could, and then prayed to get through another day," Roberta says. "She would never have said so, but I know they were all fighting exhaustion all the time."

Driven by wartime exigencies and the challenge of raising two children alone, the shy girl that Goldie had been showed a backbone of steel. A powerful personality began to emerge. "When the boys came home, she was not the same lady," Roberta recalls. "She began to move from the background to the foreground."

But there were always two Goldies. She was a woman of great dignity, able to silence the raucous profanity of the sales floor with a single withering glance. But when the store closed at ten, Roberta recalls, she would come upstairs and slip into an apron to stir up a pot of soup. In business Goldie could cut men dead. At home she was one-hundred-percent mother and grandmother.

*   *   *

Goldie's side of the business — which always was uniquely her own — grew apace with the predicted demand in the postwar period for carpeting, furniture, lamps, and accessories. But those who knew the family in this period acknowledge that Goldie had to fight her way into the business.

In 1946 she married Morris Luftig and in the company of this congenial, worldly man discovered a more leisured, fun-loving side of life. The family may have expected that with the appliance business back on a firm financial footing, and opportunities for travel as well as some measure of affluence opening up before her, Goldie would be happy to retire to her comfortable new life. If that is what the brothers thought, they were mistaken.

When the Polk family business roared back to life in 1946, Goldie was among the first to see that the traditional market for furniture, and the ways in which it had been manufactured, were in the process of radical change. Goldie was still doing business at the decorator level, selecting custom furniture from the showrooms at the Merchandise Mart. But even then she recognized a developing market for comfortable, affordable, household furniture with modern styling that could be displayed in the store and delivered directly out of a warehouse. This would become a major merchandising concept of the 1950s.

Those Chicago manufacturers who had survived both the depression and the war also recognized what would become an almost insatiable market for this "good, down-to-earth, inexpensive contemporary furniture." The old-line manufacturers who were able to move with the times, as well as young manufacturers coming into the industry, had at their disposal a palette of new materials with which to work. Traditional upholstered furniture never went out of style. But chrome and glass, plywood, plastics, vinyls and other miracle fabrics were the stuff of which the new American furniture — sectional sofas, reclining chairs, and tubular steel dinette sets — was fashioned.

Goldie sought out the modern designs and the "functional furnishings" that could be mass-produced and sold at popular prices. These styles were a natural for Polk Bros., with its orientation to family shopping and its reputation for offering the best merchandise at the lowest prices in town.

Along the way Mrs. Bachmann, as she was always known in the business, found the perfect right-hand man to help her in her plans to expand Polk Bros.' furniture division. Ernie Kaufer came to work with her on a part-time basis, to help take clients to the Merchandise Mart. Even then, Kaufer, a meticulously dapper man, was considered to be "everything you could want in a furniture salesman, from the white-on-white shirts to the gold cufflinks," Roberta Bachmann Lewis recalls. Over the years Kaufer would be Goldie's principal buyer, store manager, and a trusted friend.

*   *   *

Today Kaufer, like the other furniture salesmen, maintains the friendly rivalry and feigned disdain that existed between Polk Bros.' furniture division and the men who worked major appliances. He remembers that in the early postwar years, before furniture had its own store and showroom, one or another of the brothers would write up a furniture order:

> One day I got called over to the office and got handed a stack of orders this high. I said, "What are these?" They said, "These are orders we promised to fill for customers as soon as we got into the furniture business."
>
> I picked up the first order and looked at it. It said, "One iron table with a burn-proof top and four chairs with plastic covers and a silvery finish." What they meant was a chrome dinette set with a Formica top. The next one I picked up said, "One sofa, brown color, pieces of wood on both sides and something in front." Who knows what they meant by that. So that was the way those boys wrote a furniture order.

The good-natured ribbing went both ways. Edward Stern, an early manager at the 2901 store and later a sales representative for the Chromcraft company, remembers taking a shortcut through the major appliance section one night after closing time, and finding two customers still on the floor. Stopping to ask if he could help, Stern was told by the couple that they wanted a refrigerator; they pointed out the sample of their choice. Stern found an order pad, checked the model number, and wrote up the order.

> I took their money, and I put it in an envelope with the order and a note saying this customer wants such and such a refrigerator and wants it delivered at such and such a time.
> So Harry Polk comes up to me the next day and he says, "Stern, you're stupid."
> I say, "What's the matter?"
> He says, "You want a refrigerator or you want a freezer?"
> I say, "A refrigerator, can't you read?"
> He says, "Well, you sold them a freezer."

"So," Stern now says with a shrug, "What do you expect? I'm a furniture man. I don't know anything about appliances."

* * *

Even as the furniture division grew and prospered, Sol and the brothers had difficulty seeing furniture and carpeting as a major profit center. They were happy enough to indulge their sister's wishes but they were slow to commit energy or capital to expansion of the furniture lines. Roberta Bachmann Lewis comments:

> She [Goldie] had her world and the brothers had their world. Furniture was a complete mystery to them. To give Sol credit, he did go to the markets

occasionally and tried to understand the carpet business. But he never really got into it. Appliances were his world, that's where he was comfortable, and that's where he was doing well.

Which is not to say that Goldie did not relinquish credit given when the occasion demanded. A 1953 piece in a trade publication heralded **Sol's** foresight in furniture field:

> In the *Chicago Tribune* of late Sol Polk has been running a great deal of furniture advertising. Very glamorous copy, too. There is a likelihood that the man who found a chink in the armor of the appliance industry is now swinging into complete home furnishings and in days to come will rival the local Fish Furniture Company.

*   *   *

Goldie was not content to let the mid-range furniture division languish in either success or mediocrity. Responding to suggestions from Polk customers, she developed a juvenile furniture department. When public taste turned to early American, she opened the Colonial Shop. Quality control was paramount, and Goldie was a demanding taskmaster. Roberta remembers:

> She worked with the manufacturers. She went into the factory and saw the frame and the materials used in stuffing. And she knew how to sew a seam. She laid out the specifications for decently made upholstered goods, and then she would go into the factory to see that they were doing what they were supposed to do.

Once furniture was firmly established as a major revenue source for Polk Bros., Goldie pursued her plan to return to upscale lines, offering fine furniture as well as the popular, mass-produced lines. The result was the high-end, contemporary Today store, which she opened in 1952 in a modern two-story showroom with a dramatic glassed-in stairway on the street front. Here she was able to provide the decorator service that she preferred.

"They were way ahead of the times in the Today store," Roberta Lewis remembers:

> She introduced Swedish furniture, with the fine, clean Scandinavian designs. She went out and found Mexican imports that were glorious. The 1950s brought an explosion of creativity to the middle class market. It was the golden age of Bauhaus, and Herman Miller. She placed these designs, with their wonderful, clean lines, on the floor and exposed her customers, who were middle class, to this whole new world of design.

The Today store did not come about without effort. Roberta Lewis remembers that Polk Bros.' ill-deserved reputation as a "discount house" compromised, for a time, Goldie's contacts at the Merchandise Mart. "She found herself hammering on closed doors," Roberta says. "People would not sell to her." She continues:

> I remember going with her to the showroom of a major manufacturer of fine furniture. The salesman is sitting there with his feet up on an ottoman and a cigar in his mouth. Mother went over to speak with him and he never even got up out of his chair. He let her know in no uncertain terms that he was not interested in her business.

The salesman soon changed his tune, and in fact the manufacturer he represented became one of Goldie's most loyal and devoted supporters. Her suppliers over time included the best in the business: Richardson Raymore, Paul

McCobb, Futorian, Douglas, Dresher, Marden, Milano, Stratford, and dozens of other top-flight manufacturers.

* * *

The furniture division at Polk Bros. also played a part in backing young manufacturers who came on the scene in the immediate postwar period. Foremost among these was Interior Crafts, Inc., founded in 1951 by Jerry Seiff and Vito Ursini, both of whom had been employed by the highly respected Tapp, Inc., furniture company.

Seiff and Ursini were well matched for the partnership. Seiff is the business mind and, in the beginning, was a one-man sales force for the company; Ursini, a master craftsman from the Adriatic coast of Italy, supervised factory operations. The two started their business in an unheated loft over a bowling alley on North Milwaukee Avenue, where they upholstered frames purchased from other companies.

On the recommendation of Lester Bachmann, who had gone to school with Seiff, the pair took their samples to Ernie Kaufer and Goldie Bachmann, who recognized the quality workmanship behind their upholstered pieces. Polk Bros. thus became Interior Crafts' first major account and Interior Crafts became Polk Bros.' biggest supplier of upholstered goods.

Over time, sales through Polk Bros. provided Interior Crafts the financial footing that enabled the young company to expand — as Seiff and Ursini had hoped — into the fine cabinetmaking, carving, and wood finishing at which they were uniquely skilled. By 1980 Interior Crafts was recognized as the largest custom furniture house in the country, specializing in reproductions of antique French, English, and Chinese furniture.

Over the decade that Interior Crafts was associated with Polk Bros., Jerry Seiff remembers having no more than two conversations with Sol Polk. Goldie Bachmann, however, was another story altogether.

For some reason, she took a liking to us. I was at the store all the time, and Goldie was like a second mother to us. We got along with Ernie Kaufer, too, but he was relentless. We manufactured all our own pieces, and we were able to give him two-to-three week delivery. But he wanted even better.

Selling to Polk Bros. also meant selling for Polk Bros. Interior Crafts products were shown and sold through Polk's, but the orders were processed, manufactured, and delivered out of the Interior Crafts factory. Seiff says,

For nine years I went to Polk Bros. nearly every night to try to sell my product. I never saw my children grow up. Basically, I showed their salesmen how to sell our furniture. I talked to customers about the features, the fabric, how we stood behind our work.

Ben A. Dahl, who was then a partner in Friedson & Dahl, Inc., an upholstery firm, had a similar experience. He felt the pressure that Goldie Bachmann and Ernie Kaufer put on vendors, but, like Seiff, he remembers the energy generated on a Polk Bros. sales floor. "Goldie," he says, "was a magical person." He continues:

Polk Bros. was an exciting company to sell because they moved a lot of merchandise, but also because they had great sales people there. They had fun. There were a lot of characters, like the salesman that used to go up and down the aisles with a whistle. He was a terrific salesman. And they had talent there. Goldie hired women as interior designers, very talented women.

*   *   *

Roberta Bachmann was in the stores in the period when young suppliers such as Seiff, Ursini, and Dahl were getting their start there. Long before Roberta graduated from Northwestern University, it was understood that she would work in the business. She remembers, "I graduated on a Wednesday, and my mother said, 'You have until Sunday night.' Monday morning was paycheck time."

Like everyone in the family, Roberta did everything. She worked as a design consultant and buyer's assistant during the day, in the evenings she worked the floor as a salesperson, at night she stayed late writing up orders. Roberta also became a favorite among the salesmen when it came time to call in a "turnover man" to help close a sale. As the "T.O." she was known as "Miss Schofel." Roberta says:

> The salesman would call me over and say "This is Miss Schofel, who is our color expert . . . this is Miss Schofel, our merchandiser . . . our interior designer . . . a young manager. . . ." Whatever fitted the situation. And if I could see that the customer wasn't going to buy the item they were discussing, I would move her over to something else. Maybe I would suggest another fabric, or I would bring the price down a little bit.

The furniture division operated on the same business philosophy as major appliances. The theory was that the money a family might save on one major purchase could be used, to everyone's advantage, for additional purchases.

Selecting furniture was an event for a family or for a young couple, and Goldie knew how to maintain the sense of occasion. Roberta says, "They had a good time because they had someone else to visit with. It was social, and in a sense it was an evening out."

*   *   *

By 1955, Polk Bros. advertised that it offered customers "the largest selection of domestic and oriental carpeting in the world," naming all the nationally advertised brands carried at the Polk City and Cottage Grove stores. The company also claimed to be exclusive distributors for nearly a dozen lines of fine oriental carpets. The Today store was described as "setting the style in modern furnishings for all Chicagoland."

In this period Goldie Bachmann took the furniture division far beyond its origin as the stepchild of an appliance and home electronics business. She established a national base with an industrial contract division that processed quantity furniture purchases for hotels, schools, hospitals, and offices. Contract furniture grew steadily, with clients in other states and overseas. But the capital Goldie needed to follow that expansion was not forthcoming from the parent company.

At a critical point, she had an opportunity to purchase a major wholesale furniture company, with a strong anchor at the Merchandise Mart. It would have been a perfect fit, people in the industry believe. But Goldie could not sell the idea to her brothers. Sol, who was reluctant to expand beyond what he could personally control, would not budge. The growth of the furniture division was thwarted, many say, by the brothers' failure to understand furniture as a creative, dynamic industry.

*   *   *

Even while Polk Bros. grew into a major presence on the national retailing scene, Goldie maintained a sense of mission about the company which may be seen as distinctively parochial, but which undoubtedly helped Polk Bros. keep its feet on the ground and sustain its image as your local neighborhood store.

Goldie cultivated that feeling of community by organizing sewing classes in the store, culminating in local fashion shows; cooking demonstrations which went on throughout the day and

evening; and design and home decorating classes for homemakers. "In the small appliances department, there was always something cooking — quite literally," Roberta remembers.

> She felt that the stores were part of a neighborhood,
> and she intended that these classes should be a
> neighborhood gathering place. If someone in the
> neighborhood made a suggestion, she would draw
> on a committee of the women to evaluate the idea. If
> there was a church group active in the community,
> she would help them run fund raisers. The spirit was
> always a sense of neighborhood, and the end result
> was loyal customers.

Personal contacts, in Goldie's side of the business, as with
the brothers, were of the greatest importance. Roberta says,

> I know my mother made a million friends. They all
> made friends. People would bring in homemade
> cakes and cookies at holiday time. It was almost a
> small town thing. That's the way it was in the stores
> in the 1950s. It's so different now. I mean, how many
> friends do you have at Wal-Mart?

As progressive as Goldie Bachmann was in her thinking,
she was also a product of her immigrant European heritage
and her experiences as a young wife and mother in the years
of the Great Depression.

Goldie, for example, never drove a car. Even when the
brothers would have been glad to have had a car and a driver
sent for her every day, she insisted on taking the bus to and
from work. A cab would be too costly, she insisted.

When she and her husband, Morris Luftig, moved from his
apartment on West Jackson to a lakefront high rise, Goldie insisted that the new address would have to be on a bus line. The
apartment they chose at 330 West Diversey Parkway fit her re-
quirements perfectly. No matter how cold the day, one could set

his watch by Goldie's arrival by bus at the corner of Diversey and North Central. Going home was another matter. The furniture vendors looked out for her, and would take turns waiting for her to leave the store at 10 or 11 p.m. to offer her a ride home.

*   *   *

The 1950s and 1960s were a creative period in furniture design. Although the weight of the furniture manufacturing industry began to shift in this period to North Carolina and other southern states, Chicago remained an important design center.

Goldie Bachmann, not only as a high-volume buyer but also by virtue of her daily contact with the buying public, became a force in molding decisions on furniture design. By bringing in the new generation of designers, she captured a new generation of consumers. This, Roberta believes, was Goldie's special genius. Roberta remembers:

Polk Bros. began as a working man's store. But what you must realize is that the wartime generation, those who grew up after World War II, were the first in their families to go to university, the first to leave the neighborhood, the first to leave the influence of their traditional homes.

This generation, as consumers, were no longer content with the Waterfall designs and overstuffed furniture that their parents had bought in the 1930s. They had seen the world. They wanted new designs in furniture. My mother brought these designs into her stores.

*   *   *

In 1973 Goldie suffered a massive stroke. While she would outlive all five of her younger brothers, and would retain her regal demeanor even in her ninetieth year, after 1973 she was no longer able to participate actively in the daily operations of the business. Polk Bros.' furniture and carpeting division continued to prosper, but without Goldie's influence the innovative custom designs she supported were sacrificed to tried-and-true styles.

10

Let's Make a Deal: Polk's Super Salesmen

"The one thing everyone talked about when they mentioned Polk Bros. was the salesmen. The store's salesmen seemed to know every piece of stock the chain carried. They spent time with every customer."

— ***Pioneer Press***
June 24, 1992

"There was no place in the world where such action took place!"

— Aaron Ginsburg
Polk Bros. store manager

Making the sale — closing the deal. That's what it was all about. At Polk Bros. the salesman was king. Over the years, their numbers rose into the thousands. Polk salesmen were known for their tenacity, their garrulous manners, and their crisp white-on-white shirts. Above all, they were known for their willingness to negotiate a better price, if that's what it took to make the sale. "We were the car salesmen of the appliance industry," some have said. But the comparison pales. Polk salesmen were not like anyone before or since. They were one of a kind. And they were the best in the business.

The Polk Bros. sales floor was the setting — the stage — upon which these super salesmen created the exuberant atmosphere summed up in the slogan, "You haven't shopped until you've shopped at Polk's." Day and night Polk Bros. stores pulsed with a vigorous, urgent activity. Customers remember the sales floors as having a life and vitality of their own. It was a scene that, even beyond the perpetual carnival of Polk promotions, captured all the senses.

At Polk Bros., uncarpeted floors and bare ceilings reverberated with the throb of washing machines, the blare of stereo systems, and the clamor of shouted conversations. Vendors demonstrated their lines, competing for the attention of circulating knots of shoppers, while Skippy the Clown handed out balloons or Good Humor bars to the children. If a case of Washington apples or a box of Hawaiian pineapples was the promotion of the week, the air in the store would be pungent with the smell of fresh fruit. "There was always hustle and excitement at Polk stores," *Crain's Chicago Business* columnist Joe Cappo recalls. "They always seemed crowded and hectic."

Above the cacophony on the floor, the excitement was heightened by the persistent voice of the loudspeaker system summoning support from throughout the store by means of an internal Polk Bros. code. A call for "Mr. Otto," for example, could mean "send a turnover man to air conditioners." "Paging Mr. George Morris" called Morrie [Morris George] Polk to the front of the store. A call for "Mr. Greenleaf" could be a security alert in small appliances.

*   *   *

Polk salesmen came from every walk of life. Like Chicago itself, they represented a melting pot of European origins: Jewish, Polish, Italian. What they had in common was a love of selling and a zeal for the deal. For them, there was no better arena for their talents than the hurly-burly climate of the Polk Bros. sales floor. Nor, in their minds, will there ever be such a place again.

John Szilagyi was one of them. Szilagyi (known in the business as Johnny Silagi) went to work for Sol Polk in September 1946 with a short-term assignment. His job was to sell eighty cartons of army surplus flashlight batteries, packed two hundred to the carton. To make the calls, Sol loaned him the company car — David Polk's new Oldsmobile, one of the first automobiles to come out with "Hydra-Matic Drive." In two days, Szilagyi was sold out. He took home two hundred dollars.

"You're one hell of a salesman," Sol said. "Stay on with me, and I'll pay you fifty dollars a week plus one percent. Seventy-five dollars guaranteed." Szilagyi said he'd try it for a couple of weeks. He stayed thirty-six years. In his best month, he delivered $110,000 in sales, working on a five percent commission. By the time he retired in 1982, John Szilagyi had worked in or managed every store in the chain.

Szilagyi is typical of the Polk Bros. sales force. He worked hard, he talked tough, sales were in his blood. He measured his success in terms of the numbers of repeat customers who asked for him by name, and who then sent their friends to him. He is fervently loyal to Polk Bros. and, like dozens of other Polk salesmen, he gets together with the old gang for alumni dinners.

*　　*　　*

Like Szilagyi, Polk salesmen cultivated their own clientele and built personal followings of loyal customers. Sol Polk liked it that way. He made sure that salesmen carried their own business cards "so the customer will know who to come back to." (An exception was a salesman in the Central Avenue store who parodied the line when he handed his card to "just looking" shoppers, saying "so you'll know who you didn't buy it from.")

Some salesmen were exceptionally enterprising. Colleagues tell the story of the fellow in the Skokie store who wore a chain around his neck with a mezuzah on one end and a cross on the other. The emblem that showed was that of the assumed affiliation of whatever customer he was dealing with at the time. A co-worker remembers, "This guy would change his religion twenty times an hour. What we liked most was when he went into Muslim. He had it all down. He also made a heck of a good living."

"Personality was the difference between Polk Bros. and the superstore competitors," Morrie Polk's son, Howard, says. "You could walk into our store and talk to a Polk. You might know your salesman personally. It was the difference between going to your local Chicago hot dog stand and talking to the guy behind the counter and going to the drive-up window at McDonald's."

Long-time manager Aaron Ginsburg says, "People would come back to Polk Bros. even after they had moved somewhere else because they were comfortable shopping at Polk's. The salesmen were the same people they had dealt with before." *Crain's Chicago Business* commented in 1992 on the phenomenon: "Two, even three, generations of customers have done business with the same salesman, something few other stores can boast."

Customers were never dissuaded from the commonly held belief that the way "to get a deal" on a major purchase was to have a personal acquaintance with a Polk salesman, or better yet, with one of the brothers themselves. Ginsburg jokes, "If every customer who came into the store claiming to have gone to school with Sol, or Morrie, or Harry, actually had, it would have been the world's largest graduating class."

But the salesmen played that game, even to the point of placing a dummy phone call to the front office to "verify" claims of a connection. "Right, OK, yeah, that's him, from the old neighborhood." Then turning to the customer, "Mr. Polk told me to take real good care of you. He says to say hello to the wife and kids."

* * *

The spirit of the sales floor was fanned as much by the founder's patriotism as it was by a profit motive. Sol Polk preached an elementary faith: "The economic standard of America depends on mass selling to keep production lines working." The pursuit of volume sales was seen as a sacred mission. Sol's most succinct statement of this creed echoed a fear from the era of the Great Depression: "We're not suffering from over-production," he claimed. "We're suffering from **under-consumption.**" (A *Saturday Evening Post* writer once added a whispered aside: "If so, it's no fault of his.")

The first commandment at Polk's was "nobody walks." Sol didn't want to lose a single sale. Long before Sam Walton began stationing greeters at the door of his variety stores, Sol Polk had closers at his door. These were employees charged with asking anyone leaving the store: "Were you taken care of all right?" If not — if the sale had not been made — the customer was skillfully guided back inside, usually into the hands of the "turnover man," or "T.O.," described earlier. The T.O. held out the promise of a sweeter deal or an unexpected premium. Bill Hamilton, Polk's well-known television announcer, frequently did door duty in the evenings before he went on the air with Polk's "Night Owl Movie." Irv Lewis says Sol Polk himself sometimes manned the front door of the Melrose Park store. "But God forbid," Lewis adds, "if we ever let anyone know who he was."

The T.O. had an important role in the drama that was played out daily on the sales floor. A salesman encountering customer resistance was trained to call in a T.O., saying something like "I want you to meet the man who's in charge of our refrigerator section," or "Let's talk to the store manager — we'll see what he can do on the price." *Chicago Tribune* columnist Ron Grossman remembers that as a part-time Polk Bros.

salesman during his college years, he was often called on to play "Mr. Otto," the code name for the T.O. mentioned earlier. Grossman likens the role to that of a relief pitcher. At one time he would be introduced as the "buyer," at another, he would be the "interior designer." The spiel would fit the occasion. "For whichever of us answered the call, it was like stepping on stage," Grossman recalls. At the 2850 North Central store, the salesman might say, "You're in luck, the owner's here in the store today," and a call would be put out for Harry Polk — who was there every day.

The "nobody walks" policy was rationalized in a company slogan that promised: "We're not here to sell you, we're here to help you buy." Irv Lewis explains the thinking:

> The philosophy, before we were in shopping centers, was that you came into our stores for a purpose. It cost us so much per dollar to bring you into the store, and once we got you there, we wanted to sell you. So if you came into our store, we were going to do our darndest to sell you what you came for. Or help you buy it. After all, you don't buy a refrigerator every day like you buy bananas.

*   *   *

Making sure that nobody walked, and that no salesman gave away the store, was a personal mission for Morrie Polk. Morrie personified the Polk brothers' tough-talking style. His brusque manner was not so much a source of terror on the sales floor as it was a cause for guarded amusement. As one veteran recalls, "If you gave away five dollars on the floor, he'd be ready to fire you, and then he'd turn around and buy you dinner. But he had such a gruff personality that people were afraid to laugh."

Morrie in the 1950s and 1960s was a roving troubleshooter. He tried to "make" all the stores every day. Once in a store, he roamed the sales floor, always on the lookout for a customer whose needs, he thought, were not being attended to. Spotting one, he would close in on the nearest salesman and demand to know who was taking care of that customer. He often became so heated that he jumped into the action himself, seizing the initiative from a startled salesman. Just as often he would yank a sales order out of a salesman's hands to scrutinize the paperwork.

Irv Lewis notes:

> Sol was always the boss. He was the powerhouse. When Sol walked through the store, everybody trembled. That was **his** management style. Morrie only pretended to make people tremble. The guys all loved him. He was one of them.

Customers liked Morrie too. Howard Polk remembers:

> People would come in and ask for Morrie. He was the guy that everybody knew. The salesman would say, "Well, I take care of Morrie's customers, and I'll give you a good price." And he quotes a price, say fifty bucks. But the customer would say, "I gotta see Morrie." Then Morrie himself might come along, and he'd say, "What do you want? It will cost you fifty-five bucks." And the customer would take it — because he was talking to a Polk.

While Morrie worked the several stores in the middle years, Harry stayed put as the brothers' anchor man on the sales floor at 2850 North Central. He was the brothers' in-house man and the one closest to the day-to-day operations of the major appliance section at Polk City. In the first years at 2850, Harry set up an "office" at the back of the store, pulling a folding chair up to the automatic ironer he used as a desk. There, every night, he personally and meticulously went over every line of every invoice.

Harry was seldom seen without a big cigar in his mouth.

After hours, Harry was the brother who could be counted on to join the salesmen for a Scotch or schnapps at the Sparga Restaurant around the corner from Polk City or at a nearby hangout called the One-Two-Three. As often as not, the group might be invited to Harry's own "favorite club" — his home in nearby River Forest.

* * *

The Polk brothers' tough-guy style defined the culture of the sales floor. "It was a male-dominated society," Aaron Ginsburg recalls. "It was a man's world. Nose to nose, rough and tumble, negotiated price." Salesman John Beyer comments on the sense of fraternity that bonded Polk Bros. salesmen.

> What I miss to this day is going in there with that group of men — and I say men because there really weren't any women on the floor selling — you may have had some in the furniture department or the baby department or upstairs in the office, but on the main sales floor, not one in ten or twenty were women. On the main sales floor, it was a man's world, rough language and rough talk. Did you ever see the movie "Tin Men"? Or "Glengarry Glen Ross"? A lot of people say, "Did you really talk that way in real life?" Yes, we did. The difference was, we sold good products at good prices.

* * *

Polk Bros. salesmen fell into a number of categories. There were the inside men and the outside men. There were the old-timers — not an easy crowd to break into. There were the part-timers. These were teachers, off-duty policemen, and college students who played a significant role in Polk's "web of word-of-mouth" advertising. And there were the part-time old-timers, like furniture salesman Bob Zitler, who worked part-time but did so for thirty years. The old-timers remember "Rocco" LaRocco who retired at seventy-five, but stayed on in a token job as a greeter at the warehouse store until well into his nineties. Like most Polk salesmen, he just didn't want to quit.

The old-timers were seasoned professionals. In competition "they would cut your heart out, but then they'd turn around and loan you their last dollar," Aaron Ginsburg recalls. The old-timers had their territories and were intensely protective of their specialties. Internally, they established their own pecking order. White goods didn't mingle much with brown goods. Small appliances were one thing; jewelry and cameras were another; outdoor furniture and sporting goods were something else again. Electronics by the 1960s had garnered its own special cachet.

"You not only battled the public, you battled the other salesmen," John Beyer remembers. "There was a great spirit of camaraderie, but at the same time you had to protect your territory. It was hard going in as the new guy."

Aaron Ginsburg started at Polk as a part-time salesman in small appliances at the Skokie store. Within five years he had moved to the position of sales manager at the 2850 North Central, Polk City, store. Ginsburg managed that store for eighteen years, but still remembers the initiation the old-timers put him through:

> When I got to Central Avenue, I think I was about thirty-two years of age. I was a novice in store management. And somebody threw me on this floor with these guys — these salesmen. I think there were about a hundred of them. And they were licking their chops.
>
> But we had a lot of fun. There were a lot of characters. And a lot of guys who worked well together. It was always a joy to go to work because there was always something going on. It was action.

*   *   *

In Sol's mind, everyone was a potential Polk Bros. salesman. The old-timers, who were proud of their specialties and
their status in the profession, weren't so sure of that. "If Sol
Polk had one fault, it was that he tried to enlist anyone who
came in as a salesman," John Szilagyi says.

Merchandise manager Jerry Unger shared that memory:
"He didn't care if you were a company president or an eleva-
tor operator, he was always giving you a pitch about working
for him." Irv Lewis sees Sol's recruiting efforts differently:
"To Sol, hiring part-timers was spreading bread upon the
water. Every time we put on a part-timer we added more people to our customer list."

Old-timer or part-timer, at Polk Bros. everybody sold.
There was the chiropractor who worked the appliance floor
nights and weekends to earn the money to open his own office; he later ran a highly successful practice but came back to
work at Polk's on weekends. A young company attorney
served his apprenticeship in hard goods. Top management
manned the corporate offices in the daytime and returned to
the store after supper to sell appliances. Even Chief White
Eagle in all his regalia, a favorite at Polk promotions, was a
sometime salesman. Doctor, lawyer, merchant, chief. They all
worked the floor at one time or another.

The children of Goldie, Sam, Morrie, Harry, and David
Polk were no exception. From an early age the boys worked
summers and weekends as stock boys; the girls were posted to
the office or worked behind the record counter.

David Polk's son Richard remembers that his first summer job, at the age of twelve, was assembling bicycles at the
Four Seasons store. He, like his cousins, remembers friendships with the salesmen and some confusion about roles:

> It was hard to know if I was going to lunch with the
> boys, or if they were baby-sitting me. But they gave

me the sense that I was really contributing. That I was really at work.

Howard Polk remembers that salesman "Rocco" LaRocco was the one to taught Howard and his sister Linda how to ride a bicycle.

The Polk children, however, received no special treatment in the stores. The only concession made to family connections was that, once graduated from the stockroom, the Polk kids, like the uncles, were given thinly veiled pseudonyms when called through the intercom system. Electronics buyer Howard Polk, who one day would oversee the closing of the retail stores, was "Mr. Howard." Bruce Bachmann, who ran the Four Seasons store, was "Bud Bruce."

*   *   *

Many of Polk Bros.' innovative sales techniques had their origin in the earliest years of the business. For example, back in the days of the first store at 3334 North Central, Sol kept a refrigerator stocked with Coca-Cola. If the small sales staff was tied up, Sol would hand an arriving customer a bottle of Coke and said "Have this on the house — I'll be with you in a minute." This strategy —"Have a Coke on Polk" — was utilized in innumerable ways over the years to keep the customer on the floor until the sale was made. Irv Lewis says these gestures were good ice-breakers.

> The customer comes in wary because he doesn't know anything about refrigerators, he thinks maybe someone's trying to take advantage of him, and he's afraid he's going to spend more money than he wants to spend. Our psychology was to get the customer settled down, to let him understand that we are trying to help him.

"Try Before You Buy" was another Polk Bros. hallmark that had its beginnings at the first store. "It was a very small

place," John Szilagyi recalls. "All we had on the floor in terms
of saleable merchandise were some refrigerators, a couple of
wringer washers, and the first Bendix automatic, mounted on
a concrete block." He remembers going out into the neighborhood to invite housewives to bring their laundry baskets
into the store and look through the machine's porthole window to see how well the new automatic machine whirled the
soil out of the family wash. "It was a hard sell," Szilagyi recalls.
"They wouldn't believe that this automatic thing could do a
better job than a wringer washer."

Despite the demonstration being a "hard sell," it was suc-
cessful. Not all demonstrations were as successful. Lester
Bachmann remembers that a salesman named Callahan talked
Sol into putting a washing machine out on the sidewalk in
front of the entrance to the new store at 2850 North Central.
It was a sure-fire means of attracting customers into the store,
Callahan promised. Sol remembers:

> We thought it was a little tacky to do something like
> that, but he [Callahan] was a great salesman. So we
> put a new Maytag washer out there. One night we
> went out to lock up, and the washing machine was
> missing. Somebody had stolen it. The next day I told
> Mr. Callahan that we couldn't put a washing ma-
> chine out there anymore. He was a little down-
> hearted because it was his idea. But he bounced back
> a couple of days later with another plan. "We'll fill it
> full of water. Nobody will be able to move that," he
> said. Well, another Maytag, filled with water, was
> out front for a few days. Then we went out one night
> to lock up, and again, the washer was gone. But the
> sidewalk was awash with water.

By 1955, the company had sales-floor demonstrations
down to an art. When the 60,000-square-foot store at 85th
and Cottage Grove Avenue (Polk City South) was built in the
early 1960s, it was equipped with enough plumbing and elec-

trical outlets to keep literally dozens of washers filled with water. *Fortune* reported:

> On the floor for all to see are as many as 125 refrigerators, 75 freezers, 150 washers, dryers, and combinations, 85 air conditioners, 300 television sets. TV sets, washers, and dryers are connected and operable. Polk customers may even plunk their own laundry into Polk's washers and dryers to test them.

When it came to demonstrating a product, Polk salesmen knew how to do it; they knew their stuff. Polk Bros. salesmen were considered by their competitors to be the best in the industry. Mandatory training sessions, often conducted by factory representatives, went on fifty-two weeks of the year, usually after 10 p.m. or before the stores opened. A salesman was expected to know how to take a General Electric range apart and put it back together again, but he also had to know how to "stitch up a little thing" on a Necchi sewing machine.

"That was one of the great secrets of Polk Bros.," Jerry Unger says.

> To sell something, you have talk about it, and the more people you talk to about the product, the more sales you make. We were constantly being taught product knowledge. Not only product knowledge but how to sell the product.
>
> We had to sell against the competition — and that was not always the people who sold the same product we did. The competition was Sears, because they had a private label and they had more stores than anybody and they sold more than anybody.
>
> Some of our sales people would go to Sears and get their pitch. Then they'd tell the customer, "If you go to Sears, they'll tell you this and they'll tell you that." Many of our customers had already been

to Sears, and they'd say, "Yeah, they did tell us that." The impression left was that maybe the Sears pitch was a con job.

Many of Polk's specialist salesmen, including John Szilagyi who had once sold electrical equipment to the industrial trade, continued to call on industrial purchasing agents, making sales for Polk Bros. Conversely, many manufacturers' representatives and vendors worked the Polk Bros. sales floor, training salesmen in the specialized features of their products and demonstrating them to customers.

*   *   *

In keeping with Sol's own early experience as a door-to-door salesman, the in-house sales force in the 1950s and 1960s was supplemented by a group of outside men, called "captains," who scoured the city for prospects. As *Fortune* observed, "Any moderately prosperous home that has a clothesline in the yard is reasonably certain to be visited and lectured on the wonders of electric dryers." Another group of salesmen manned the expanding Home Shopping — or catalogue sales — branch of Polk Bros.' operations.

*   *   *

Polk salesmen also were said to be the best paid in the business. "They come to work in Cadillacs," *Fortune* observed in a 1955 article. Aaron Ginsburg agrees that "they were the highest paid salesmen in Chicago without a doubt."

In the early 1950s, Polk salesman were getting a fifty dollar per week draw plus a one percent commission on sales. Layered on top of that were "spiffs," or bonuses, of a few dollars per item on merchandise that the company or the manufacturer wanted to move at a particular price. Jerry Unger left the women's wear industry in 1954 to work at Polk Bros. on the advice of a friend who promised that "at Polk Bros. you can make one hundred and fifty dollars a week just trying to get away from people." That was probably an understatement. Tom Blackburn, writing for *Electrical Merchandising* in the same period, commented that "men making $10,000, $15,000, or even $20,000 a year are not rarities at Polk Brothers."

In 1955 *Fortune* pegged the average annual income of a Polk Bros. salesman at $8,700, adding, conservatively that "some salesmen are hitting $15,000." (As a point of comparison, a young executive working in Manhattan in 1955 typically was making about $7,000 a year, a substantial salary for the time.) By the mid-1960s, when the commission was raised to five percent, a top salesman in hard goods might take home $30,000 to $35,000. As a point of reference, in the 1960s an associate professor with two doctorates under his belt might make $10,000 a year at Northwestern, a private university in the Chicago metropolitan area.

Later, Polk Bros. went to a straight commission basis. "That's when the Polk salesmen really started to make tons of money," Aaron Ginsburg says. John Beyer estimated that top salesmen were making $40,000 to $50,000 in the early 1980s. The standard commission at that point was five and a half percent.

> Twice yearly they paid another one-half percent of your own gross sales. So, effectively, you got six percent, paid July 30 and January 30. Then you could pick up spiffs of a few dollars, three dollars, four dollars, five dollars, on things they wanted sold at a particular price. If you sold something off the floor, damaged or dented goods, there was something on that.

Store managers did not fare as well, financially, as their top salesmen. Managers, like buyers, made their own deals with the boss. And Sol Polk drove a very hard bargain when it came to compensation of management and executive staff.

Some, it is said, were so intimidated by a negotiation with Sol, that they never came back to push for better pay.

But even for the top earners, life at Polk Bros. was never easy street. The men who made good money were survivors. Tom Blackburn, who conducted an exhaustive series of interviews in the early 1950s with people both inside and outside the organization, gives a picture of the salesmen's working conditions:

> The men have to be big money makers or they would not endure the pace Sol sets for them. Sol saves money on heat — most of his places are glorified warehouses — and the salesmen have to wear long underwear in the winter. When not selling they help with stockkeeping, cleaning up, and other physical chores.
>
> They get on the job at ten in the morning, and leave at ten at night (unless there is a sales meeting) seven days a week. General merchandising manager Jack Pettersen disputes this, but it comes from the mouths of the men themselves. It is a common joke that Polk salesmen either drop out because of pneumonia or ulcers.

For every twelve-hour day worked by the salesmen, the brothers put in fifteen hours, with Sol Polk setting the pace. Ernie LaSalle, who in the early years was a one-man service department, remembers the day, shortly after the end of World War II, that he was hired by Sol Polk.

> We settled on a weekly salary, but stupid me didn't ask about the hours. For years I went in early in the morning and never got home before eleven or twelve at night. My wife said at one point, "Ernie, I haven't seen you in three years. You might as well go back into the army and stay there."

(Sol's sense of urgency gave rise to another of the salesmen's unending stock of in-house jokes. "If Sol ever marries," they would say, it will be to some widow expecting a baby within two months — 'to save time.'")

"There were a lot of good men who left because they couldn't get along with Sol," Aaron Ginsburg comments.

> Sol was impossible to get along with. But he understood human nature and he understood people. He knew who he could yell at, who he could take apart, in front of people. Sometimes he would yell at a guy who he knew could take it in order to get to two other people who couldn't take it. He was better at that than anyone I've ever seen.

The late-night meetings that Sol Polk called to rally his sales force took a heavy toll. A vendor, soured by his experiences working Polk Bros.' sales floor, has this memory:

> Even when the salesmen had worked from early morning until 10 p.m., they were expected to come when called into these meetings. Sol would harangue them until midnight or sometimes two in the morning. He preached the virtues of family life: "Bring the kiddies, have a family experience at Polk Bros., give the wife a dishwasher." But, for the salesmen, what kind of family life was that?

John Szilagyi says, "Sometimes Sol would stand up on the balcony over the sales floor and lecture us until after midnight about how the customer had to be taken care of. Sure enough, we'd be leaving at 2 a.m. and there would be some customer out there thinking the store was open and wanting to come in."

One furniture salesman claims, "We worked eight days a week, and when we didn't, we heard about it." He recalls being confronted on a Monday morning by his man-

ager who asked, "Where were you on Sunday?" The salesman replied, "I was home with my wife." The manager's re-
buttal was to the point: "Your wife doesn't sign your pay
check."

The Polk brothers asked no more of the salesmen than
they required of themselves. On at least one occasion Sam
Polk's wife, Thelma, made her feelings on the matter of family time publicly known. It was the year that Sol decided to
keep the stores open on Memorial Day. Aaron Ginsburg remembers that a managers' meeting had been scheduled at the
Melrose Park headquarters store on Memorial Day morning.

> I was standing there in a candy-striped jacket and
> straw boater hat when Thelma Polk came in and
> pulled Sam out of the meeting. She pulled him right
> out. "You don't work on a holiday," she said, right in
> front of Sol. "This is crazy." Then she looked at me
> and asked, "Do you have children?" I said that I did.
> She said, "You go home, too." And that was it. I went
> home.

*   *   *

No matter how rough working conditions became, Polk
salesmen stayed on the job. Employee tenure at Polk Bros.
was remarkably long for a retail business, averaging ten years
or more. Salesmen went to Polk Bros. because sales were their
life and the money was good. But they stayed on, often for a
lifetime, because they knew that management, however ec-
centric, ultimately was fair.

Tom Blackburn observed in *Electrical Merchandising* that
"while manufacturers sometimes discover that Polk Bros. does
not always pass along spiff money, Sol scrupulously sees that
men always get what is coming to them. One ex-employee interviewed had just received a check more than a year after
leaving the company." He notes that "Sol sees to it that his
men's earning potential holds up. When a slump occurred not

long ago, he laid off salesmen until those remaining were doing their regular ratio of business."

The practice extended to the brothers' personal relations with the sales staff. The stories of brothers looking the other way when a salesman dared to have a personal life, if only for a moment, are as common as the Polk family's stories of television sets being whisked out of their living rooms and returned to the sales floor.

For example, there was the carpet salesman who reported in sick so he could take his son to the circus — where he had the misfortune of running into David Polk. David later said to him, "I know I didn't see you at the circus, but I hope you enjoyed it." There is a similar story about Morrie who, on one of his rare trips to join Marion and the family while they were vacationing in Miami, took the family to a popular restaurant for dinner. There he ran into a Polk Bros. manager who had called in sick the day before in Chicago, with a companion. "The manager turned green," Morrie's daughter, Linda Cutler, recalls. "Dad didn't say a thing to him. He just bought them dinner."

Memories of Sol's personal but very private gestures of concern for the employees are equally common. Salesman Al Schwartz speaks of the day that his father, a representative for Bassett furniture, suffered a near-fatal stroke while working alone in his small office at the Furniture Mart. At the moment, he was on the phone with a fast-thinking Polk Bros. buyer, who picked up another line and called back to the mart to get help to the stricken man. "Sol Polk came to the hospital immediately," Schwartz remembers. "He said to me, 'Do you need any money, kid?' and then asked if my father would like to have a television set installed in his hospital room." Ernie LaSalle says that when he had open heart surgery in the 1980s, Sol, who was not well himself, came to the hospital regularly to check on Ernie's progress.

John Beyer says, "You'll find probably as many stories of great kindness as you will find people saying 'I'll never forget what that bastard did to me' or that kind of thing. I think the give and take of what took place at Polk Bros. was really unique in business and was what made a person love the action as much he might hate some incident."

"I don't think they ever fired anybody, as long as you did your job; you didn't have to be the best or anything," says Eddie Stern, a manager in the furniture stores. Joe Vitale, who worked from a wheelchair, recalls that his multiple sclerosis began to manifest itself shortly after he began working for Polk Bros. "Morrie Polk came into the store one day and saw me stumble. He made me see a doctor — he took me himself. I stayed on with Polk Bros. for thirty-five years, with MS, as a salesman, as a manager, and as a buyer. They treated me great."

When John Szilagyi came to Central Appliance and Furniture in 1946, he was one of three full-time salesmen working out of the little store at 3334 North Central Avenue. The others were Chester Stan and Max Miller. Monroe Singer came in on Saturdays. They shared the space and the duties with Sol, Sam Polk, Lester Bachmann, and Irv Feuerstadt. At its peak, Polk Bros.' sales force was a virtual army, numbering at any given time more than five hundred men and women working out of as many as seventeen stores.

When the stores closed in 1992, Mel Closius, who had been with the company for thirty-four years, was among the many employees interviewed by Chicago media. "Polk Bros. meant integrity and honesty in business," he told a reporter for the *Pioneer Press* chain of community newspapers. "When Polk Bros. said something, the chain meant it. We stood by everything we sold. If that weren't the case, I wouldn't have been here all these years." Salesman Lou Rociola summed his experience up this way: "It was like a tight-knit family group and the salesmen were the front-line troops."

Irv Lewis, speaking to a group of salesmen who met regularly for dinner after the stores closed for the last time in 1992, said, "I'll tell you, what we experienced is never going to be duplicated. It was a skyrocket — it was part of retailing history. You can be very, very proud to have been part of it."

11

Ask for the Polk Price

"The great bazaars of eastern Europe were re-created by the Polks. Polk Bros. was the place to go if you wanted to haggle."

— Jeffrey Polk

"It was a circus, but don't forget: They ran a serious business."

— Earl Lifshey
Home Furnishings Weekly

S ol Polk was the master when it came to keeping the circus going. But standing behind all the razzle-dazzle raised around Polk Bros.' stores was a group of strong-minded businessmen pursuing a sound and deceptively simple business plan. The formula now seems obvious: Lower your markup but earn more in the long run from higher volume. The genius of Polk Bros. was in the execution. In this, the Polks educated a generation of retailers.

The hallmark was Polk's celebrated price negotiation, summed up in the widely advertised invitation to shoppers to come in and "Ask for the Polk Price." It was a tantalizing concept, holding out the promise of a bargain and carrying the aura of the open market place where a clever buyer could match wits with the seller in negotiations over the price of an item — and come out well when the bargain was struck.

Perhaps nowhere in America was this spirit of the marketplace practiced more expertly than in the clamorous environment of the Polk Bros. stores. The brothers themselves, only a few years removed from the street markets of Chicago's Maxwell Street district, thoroughly understood that price competition was the determining factor for a customer shopping for big-ticket items; moreover, they knew how to make bargaining for a better price seem like fun.

One point of difference between Polk Bros. and Maxwell Street, and between Polk Bros. and the discount houses that proliferated after World War II, was that Polk Bros., in its major stores, did not deal in seconds or discontinued or inferior quality goods. Polk Bros. carried top-of-the-line, nationally advertised brand-name merchandise. The company's byword was the best for less.

The famous "Polk price" depended on the invention of merchandising methods guaranteed to draw the traffic needed to propel volume upward. The intense push for volume, which in turn required rapid turnover, was the factor that gave Polk Bros. its tremendous buying power with suppliers of nationally advertised merchandise. That buying power gave Polk's the pricing edge over traditional retailers.

In the early years, with the exception of specials and small appliances, Polk advertisements and merchandise tags did not show prices. If the manufacturer's list price was printed on Polk's bright orange three-by-five-inch tag, there would be a bold slash through it. Polk Bros.' reputation for price cutting was so well known that advertisements frequently gave more emphasis to the Polk name than to the attributes of the product advertised. An ad for a Hotpoint washing machine, for example, declared:

All Porcelain Enamel Finish inside and out gives lifetime beauty. This is the real answer to all your laundering needs. AND IT'S POLK PRICED!

* * *

Fortune writer Daniel Seligman describes a typical trans-action as it might have occurred in the mid-1950s, when fair trade practices were still in place:

> The first price a Polk customer encounters is on a tag bearing the list, or "manufacturer's suggested" price. The only products for which this tag means business are those of companies with rigorous fair-trading rules. On other merchandise the Polk customer ignores the list (or the salesman tells him to), and inquires what the price is.

The ensuing negotiation may begin with the salesman in-quiring whether the customer has an old appliance that he wishes to trade in. Polk's trade-in policy was heavily promoted in advertisements promising that "A Polk-size trade-in on your old washer or dryer will bring the net price way down."

While only the manufacturer's suggested price would be shown on the tag, Polk salesmen knew to the penny how far the company was willing to go in discounting the list price. The amount offered on the trade-in was gauged accordingly. The usual deal at Polk Bros. might consist either of a very long trade-in or a discount of as much as twenty percent off the list price. The discount might be pushed a little deeper if the customer balked or if the trade-in was judged to have some resale value. At that point, Seligman writes,

> A customer who continues to register deep doubts, or who starts to walk out, will probably find that Polk's can be reasoned with. The salesman himself may invent some reason why a slightly larger trade-in is feasible; or, more likely, he will flag one of the store's T.O.'s (takeover men), who will try to close the sale with a final concession. Perhaps a few more dollars or a great big teddy bear for the kid.

These negotiations were serious business for the salesman, who walked a fine line. His job was to keep the discount
as slim as possible, to hold onto any spiff, or bonus, he might
earn on the sale, and to satisfy the house (or the ubiquitous
Morrie Polk) while at the same time making the sale and let-
ting the customer win enough concessions to be seen as a hero
by himself and his family.

The code words "Work United" were the salesmen's secret and the key to Polk's real price on an item. Each letter in
that phrase had a numerical value, from one to ten (zero).
"W" was "one"; "O" was "two"; "R" was three; "K" was four;
and so forth up to the "D" in "United" as ten. A combination
of those letters on a tag was a cryptogram for the Polk price.
A tag that bore the letters "WEE," for example, told the salesman that the price established by the house was one hundred
ninety-nine dollars. "OWE," to take another example, was the
cryptogram for two hundred nineteen dollars. As word got
out, the key phrase would be changed; it might also vary
among departments. In the 1970s, for example, the code word
in major appliances was "Microwave."

*   *   *

Volume was so important to Polk Bros. that when the
brothers eye-balled the balance sheet they judged profitability
by the number of transactions rather than the number of dollars. In the early period, the company knew where it stood financially from month to month, but not from day to day.
Lester Bachmann explains:

> The real formula was the number of people you
> sold. The barometer was the number of major sales
> made in a given store on a given day. For many years
> that number was not related to dollars. It was related
> to units, number of people, number of transactions.
> The idea during the growth period was that if you
> made enough sales, there would be enough profit.

From the earliest years of the business, the company nurtured its reputation as the place to go to get a deal. Sol Polk, Chicago columnist Mark Miller notes, "was the original I-can-get-it-for-you-wholesale guy." In the 1940s and 1950s, Miller adds, "the only way to get a good price was to know someone, and he was the guy everyone knew." Sol himself frequently declared, "I want to do everything I can for my customers. I want them to have the biggest bargains in Chicago."

Bruce Bachmann, who literally grew up with the Polk Bros. stores, reflects on his uncle Sol Polk's evolution from neighborhood retailer to the originator of the modern volume discount store:

> He would always preach that he wasn't selling merchandise, he was making friends. Before discount came in with such force, the idea was that if you knew someone or had a relative in a particular business, you would go to him and say, "I want to buy that refrigerator, or that car. Can you give me a special price?" Sol's philosophy was he would treat all of Chicago as family or friends. He would give them all a special price, and he would sell a lot of merchandise. And that is exactly what happened.

The mystique woven around the promise of "knowing someone who can get you a deal" fit Polk Bros. perfectly. The Polks encouraged the game, and usually it worked, although not always the way the customer expected. One shopper approached a tall, balding salesman on the floor saying, "I know Morrie Polk; what can you do for me?" He was told, "I'm Morrie, and I've never seen you before in my life. But I'll give you ten dollars off for making a good try."

The Polks were ingenious in finding ways to qualify a customer for a discount. Courtesy cards, passed out by the thousands, were a draw. If a customer did not come in bearing one of these cards, he would be asked if this were his first visit to Polk Bros. If so, he might be offered a twenty-percent discount on his purchases that day. Similarly, a police badge, a teaching affiliation, or a connection from the "old neighborhood" could entitle the customer to a special deal.

A union card was always good for a discount. Chicago was a union town, and working men and their families were close to the hearts of the neighborhood-based Polk Bros. stores. In the 1940s Sol Polk personally courted the blue-collar trade, attending union meetings and promising members a good deal and ready credit in Polk Bros. stores.

* * *

The magic of the Polk brothers, it has been said, was that "they were real smart people who figured out what motivated people to buy." The delicate balance between low price and rapid turnover was only as good as the company's ability to draw the levels of store traffic needed to sustain a high volume. It is not coincidental that Polk Bros. was as well known for the perpetual carnival of activity generated in its stores as it was for its deep price cuts on nationally advertised merchandise.

Polk Bros. knew that one of the best ways to convince shoppers that they were getting good value was to give them something for nothing. Polk regularly used giveaways to send customers home happy and to generate the word-of-mouth advertising that the company cultivated. Some of these free offers, like the roasting pans and coupons good for free Good Humor bars, were invitations to come into the store. Others were given as an inducement to buy: If you choose this washing machine, we'll throw in a six-month supply of laundry detergent. Some were humorous: Buy a Ronson electric knife and get a five-pound salami free. Still others were surprise gifts: A salesman might acknowledge the purchase of a color television by suggesting that the customer stop by the record department on his way out and choose an LP album, on the house.

Polk probably never lost a dollar on a big-ticket item, but

the company was an innovator in the use of loss leaders, meaning items advertised and sold at deep discounts as a means of bringing crowds into the stores and creating a buying atmosphere. Polk Bros., for example, generated tremendous business on its annual Fourth of July sales by offering Weber barbecue grills at cost or close to it. Small appliances, which were big sellers at Polk Bros., were often offered at distributor's prices or as a premium given out for a token price with a major purchase. "Sometimes we'd use the whole small appliance department as a loss leader," Howard Polk recalls.

What was good for the goose was not always good for the gander. Sol Polk believed that the Chicago market belonged to Polk Bros. He intended to keep it that way. When a national discount store, such as the Korvette chain, opened Chicago outlets, Sol regarded the newcomer as an invader. When these stores advertised loss leaders, "Sol would send every one of his managers and employees out there to buy up the loss leader — in effect, to clean the competition out so that when people came in to get the item it would not be available," Howard Polk says. The merchandise would then be resold in Polk Bros. stores. Sometimes for a profit, sometimes not. That didn't matter.

When the situation was reversed, Sol turned the occasion into an opportunity. It was well known that small dealers, the few remaining "mom and pop" appliance retailers, often bought at Polk Bros.' low prices and resold the merchandise in their own stores at the standard industry markup. This became a point of pride for Sol Polk, who sometimes added the line "Dealers Welcome" to his advertisements. The impression given was that at Polk's the shopper can get merchandise at wholesale prices. In the same way, coupons were sometimes printed in advertisements advising "one to a customer" or "one to a family." The salesman would let a customer know, in a confidential manner, that limit did not apply to him.

Sol saw any event as an opportunity. Lester Bachmann recalls Sol's response when a major Chicago manufacturer of small appliances dropped its fair trade policies — opening the door to an advertising price war:

> I had gone home for dinner and was returning to the office one night when on the car radio I heard that this company had dropped fair trade. This was a startling bit of news, and it hit us at seven at night. I rushed back to the office to tell Sol and everybody. "Hurry up," I said. "Get an ad together, put an ad in the paper."
> Sol said, "Wait. The first guy doesn't have a chance. The next day somebody will be in there a nickel or a dime cheaper." Sure enough, the ads started appearing right away. A couple of days later Marshall Field and Co. joined in. And we still hadn't run an ad. Finally we ran our ad, and, of course, our prices were the lowest anywhere. Suddenly everyone else stopped advertising that brand.

*   *   *

A critical factor in the Polk pricing equation was the company's cost of doing business. Here the Polk brothers excelled. The motto was "watch the pennies and the dollars will take care of themselves." In the later years of the business, Polk Bros.' penchant for penny-pinching caught up with them, as physical plants deteriorated and out-dated control systems lagged far behind newer technologies. But in Polk Bros.' growth years the manifest plainness of the Polk stores undoubtedly reinforced customers' perception that this was a no-frills operation. The company put it this way:

> Because we buy in such vast volumes, because of our low, low overhead and efficient operation, we can afford to pass these savings on to you. This unique merchandising plan can save you money on established prices on items you see advertised every day.

The locations of Polk stores (more than two dozen over the life span of the company) were inexpensive by downtown standards, particularly in the first wave of expansion in the 1960s. Polk City, for example, was built up on the comparably distant Northwest Side of the city. But Polk customers had cars, and Polk Bros. offered unlimited free parking.

With the exception of the Today store, store decoration was kept to a minimum. "Polk Bros.' ambiance was that they had no ambiance," Bruce Bachmann comments. "You didn't want to go into a Polk Bros. store in the 1950s and 1960s and see plush carpeting and fancy walls. That would make you feel that you were going to pay more for your merchandise."

The older Polk stores were all uncarpeted. Exposed pipes and bare ceilings were standard at Polk's decades before Chicago's trendy River North district discovered the warehouse style. Heating and cooling costs were rigidly controlled. Salesmen remember that Morrie Polk personally set the thermostats in stores each morning, and turned them down every night. A standing joke among insiders was that at Polk Bros. "remodeling" meant getting out the duct tape and perforated board.

Administrative salaries were notoriously low by industry standards. The salesmen, in effect, paid for themselves. Their compensation by the 1960s was pegged to commissions on sales. But executives had to negotiate their own salaries with Sol, as did store managers and buyers. Their arguments tended to fall on deaf ears. "Sol didn't understand why he had to pay people," Bruce Bachmann observes. "People's time was not valued because it was not out of pocket."

Sol Polk's philosophy of the relationship between time and money was colored by the higher value he placed on leverage. Say, for example, Sol started an executive at one dollar a year and the executive later asked to have his salary raised to two dollars. By Sol's reckoning, the dollar he might give in the raise would be put to better use if it were invested in inventory. The inventory, Sol reasoned, might be turned ten times in that year, making the dollar worth ten dollars.

Irv Lewis, who ran Polk Bros.' massive warehouse operation, remembers the day he approached Sol to ask for secretarial assistance. Sol responded by suggesting that Irv calculate how many refrigerators could be bought with the salary he would pay a secretary, and how many times that merchandise could be turned in a year. "Should we have the money for refrigerators, or should we have you a secretary?" Sol said.

"How can you run a business without a secretary?" Irv asked.

Sol replied, "You work a little harder."

Polk Bros. knew their suppliers better than the suppliers might have liked. Whenever possible, Polk buyers waited until the point in an accounting cycle when distributors, to make their own quotas, were most willing to bargain. Not surprisingly, Polk Bros. also had a keen eye for a vendor in distress. Even in these circumstances, Sol Polk and Lester Bachmann had a standard inquiry to make of a buyer coming in to them with a great deal. "See if you get it for less," they would say.

*   *   *

Polk Bros. shaved overhead and used capital in ways that were far less obvious and far more creative than the general public might imagine. Many of Polk's mechanisms to use money to make money and to shift costs from the retailer to the manufacturer were new to their time, although they would be considered textbook strategies today.

Even when volume sales and overnight delivery depended on Polk Bros.' gigantic warehouse operations, the company nonetheless kept inventories lean, pioneering the practice of "just-in-time" buying that is now standard in the industry. "We bought what we needed when we needed it," Howard Polk explains. "We did that from day one. Now just-in-time buying and just-in-time inventory is a major trend in the industry."

By keeping the amount of capital tied up in inventory to a minimum, the company maintained a powerful bargaining position with vendors who were willing to lower the sheet price of merchandise in return for a cash payment. Polk Bros., however, preferred to maintain their strong cash position by selling the merchandise before they had to pay for it. This was a common practice, but Polk Bros.' ability to stay on top of demand with just-in-time buying and inventory control enabled the company to turn the product as many as three or four times before the bill from the vendor became due, picking up a small margin of profit on each transaction.

Polk Bros. never missed a payroll, never bounced a check, and never failed to meet its obligations to its suppliers. "Sol was real proud of that," recalls Bill Platt, a manufacturer's representative and long-time friend. "If he had $10 million in inventory, he would tell you every goddamn cent is paid." But the company did not pay any sooner than they had to. "They always paid my bills on time. But if there was a mistake on an invoice, they would hold it forever. As long as they were justified in not paying it, they would sit back and hold it," Platt says.

The Polks made creative use of cost-shifting — or "squeezing," as manufacturers sometimes describe the practices. Advertising, for example, was virtually all cooperative, with half the outlay, if not more, recovered from the distributors. Manufacturers' representatives and vendors provided a deep pool of free labor for Polk Bros., which often tied its business to the requirement that representatives work the sales floor as demonstrators or salesmen.

*   *   *

Polk's King-Size Trade-In policy was used initially as a means of negotiating list price. But as truckloads of old appliances began to pile up, Sol saw opportunity knocking. Polk Bros. soon turned appliance cast-offs into a cash cow.

In the early years, when Central Appliance and Furniture was still operating out of the little store at 3334 North Central, Ernie LaSalle was the service department manager. In fact, Ernie was the service department. "In the morning I'd be in the store and I'd take the calls; in the afternoon, I'd go out and do the servicing myself."

In 1950, after Polk Bros. established its King-Size Trade-In policy, the service department became the reconditioning department. In its second year, the reconditioning business brought in more than a million dollars, LaSalle recalls. "Reconditioning was the biggest money maker Polk had," LaSalle believes.

Fortune magazine estimated that in the mid-1950s Polk Bros. was taking in enough secondhand appliances on an average weekday to fill two trailer trucks. Many of these appliances were serviced and sold directly to customers out of the Polk Surplus Store at 3500 West Grand Avenue. The majority, however, according to *Fortune*, were sold, as is, overseas. The Dominican Republic was a major buyer in the 1960s, as was Israel. Ernie LaSalle made several trips to the Dominican Republic to set up reconditioning shops there.

The most widely publicized use for Polk Bros.' trade-ins, however, was as donations to schools, prisons, and other institutions where they were used in vocational training programs. Edward Barry wrote in the *Chicago Sunday Tribune Magazine*:

> When your television — or refrigerator or washer — goes out the door as a trade-in on a new model, don't think it's on its way to the junkyard. It may be going to prison — where it will start a second life fully as useful as the first. Appliance dealers such as Polk Brothers send truckloads of trade-ins to Stateville penitentiary (as well as other institutions). The beat-up machines are used in vocational training classes, where prisoners take them apart, learn how

they work, test and repair the parts, and put everything back together again.

Dozens of similar newspaper articles, and letters from
twice again as many schools, acknowledge Polk Bros.' gifts of
automatic washers, refrigerators, air conditioners, radios, television sets, freezers, typewriters, and electric irons. When
they were available, Polk included service manuals with the
shipments.

*   *   *

One aspect of Polk Bros.' business that was not as
amenable to negotiation over price was the Home Shopping
Service, established in 1950. The service began as an out-
growth of a Polk campaign to sell television sets by offering to
demonstrate them in the home. This branch of the business
was at one time characterized as a service intended for shut-
ins. It later grew to a full-scale catalogue sales operation. By
the mid-1960s Home Shopping employed twenty-five people
and accounted for ten to fifteen percent of the company's
gross sales.

The 1954 Home Shopping catalogue carried hundreds of
products. These included all of Polk Bros.' lines of major appliances and furnishings plus a cornucopia of other items. The
catalogue index entry for "T," for instance, included as diverse
a listing of products as tables, tea kettles, television, timers,
toasters, toys, trains, and typewriters — all arranged by the
brand name of the manufacturer.

Polk Bros. also established one of the first short-term
rental and rent-to-own programs. The idea was to encourage
customers to "try out" low-saturation products as they came
into the market. These altogether new products, such as dishwashers, which were considered an unnecessary luxury, often
were a hard sell. For six dollars a month — twenty cents a day
— Polk Bros. would deliver a top-loading portable dishwasher
for the lady of the house to use for as long as it pleased her. In

nearly all cases, the dishwasher stayed on in the home as a purchase.

The rental program, which dealt primarily in dishwashers and compact washers and dryers, was a profitable one. Polk Bros. kept an appliance on rental status until the manufacturer's service contract expired, and then, at the customer's option, replaced the unit with a newer one still under warranty. A major appliance salesman estimated that Polk Bros. made their costs back within the first year or two. By 1967, the company had placed 20,000 rental units in Chicago homes.

*   *   *

Polk Bros. always was secretive about its financial activities, and as a privately held company it never released profit and loss figures to the public. It is probable that even those closest to the family were never fully informed about the full range of the company's business.

Daniel Seligman, writing for *Fortune*, acknowledged that "there is great confusion about Polk's gross margin," which was variously estimated at anywhere from ten to twenty-five percent. There is little doubt, however, that Polk Bros. — true to its promise — did cut its margin of profit on sales very close to the bone. *Fortune* calculated in 1955 that Polk Bros.' gross margin ran about eighteen percent — well below the thirty percent levels of traditional department stores. Operating costs were estimated at sixteen percent of sales, leaving a profit of two percent, before taxes.

In 1963 the *Saturday Evening Post* pegged Polk's profit at a little more than one percent of total sales. "But the price differential enables Polk to sell more appliances than all the great department stores on State Street put together," the writer noted. It should also be noted that as fair trade regulations were abandoned in the mid-1960s and price competition became acute, Polk trimmed its gross margin even closer, knocking it down to perhaps sixteen percent of sales.

*   *   *

Polk Bros.' basic business plan was to move the merchandise as quickly as possible from the factory to the consumer. Their style was to buy by the carload, push volume, and float a fortune. In the growth years of the business, however — sooner than others expected — the driving force in the appliance industry would not be availability of product. It would be price competition.

Competitive pricing — a concept perfected by Polk in the 1940s, 1950s, and 1960s — was rediscovered by American retailers in the 1980s and 1990s. The superstore electronics chains that burst on the scene in the late 1980s adopted the practice with a vengeance. Silo stores promised to "Beat Any Price — Guaranteed." Fretter responded by claiming that "It's Automatically Ten Dollars Less at Fretter!" Even Montgomery Ward's Electric Avenue promised to "Do Whatever It Takes To Earn Your Business."

By the early 1990s Madison Avenue was following suit. "Value marketing" was the new buzz word in advertising. Value marketing in most cases meant price cutting. Price cutting worked for firms, such as running shoe manufacturers, that were able to follow the Polk Bros.' model: Absorb lower profit margins by boosting volume. It did not work so well for other industries, such as airlines, where even higher volume generated by lower fares could not offset fixed costs.

Value marketing in other cases meant giving more for less. This became a popular strategy in the early 1990s, especially among packaged goods manufacturers, who, for example, could offer a ten-ounce bottle of suntan lotion for the price of eight ounces, advertising that the customer was getting "twenty percent more" free. Polk Bros. had been doing just that for decades.

In the rapid growth years that followed the end of World War II — the years when Polk was perfecting its more-for-less pricing policies and promoting its image as the place to go to get a deal — the company could not have asked for a more timely event than the arrival on the scene of commercial television. The medium in its infancy was an ideal vehicle for an opportunistic and imaginative retailer like Sol Polk.

12

The Twenty-One Inch Screen

"We didn't know who ran Sears, Roebuck or Monkey Ward's, but we knew who Sol Polk was because he brought television to Chicagoans."

— Joe Cappo
Crain's Chicago Business

"[By 1958] Sol Polk . . . whose high voltage imagination has brought to life a $60 million housewares chain in Chicago was selling TV sets at the rate of 1,000 a day."

— **Sports Illustrated**
"Two Minds with but a
Single Thought on
Marketing"

The Golden Age of Television has been dated from 1948, the year that commercial television finally became a viable possibility. This was the beginning of yet another Golden Age for Polk Bros. as well. The two were made for one another; television was the medium, and Polk had the message.

In the late 1940s very few families had television in the home, and the commercial potential of the new medium was still being debated. Programming was irregular, both in quality and quantity. A ratings war — had there been such a thing — would have been won hands down by the familiar Indianhead test pattern. But Sol Polk wasn't about to wait for the verdict on TV advertising to come in.

Polk Bros. was one of the first retailers in the country to leap into the embryonic television advertising market. Sears, by comparison, did not even begin to test-market television advertising until 1950. By that time Polk Bros. was already part of communications revolution in the making.

* * *

Lester Bachmann recalls the day in 1949 that Sol Polk and Georgia Rice, then director of advertising for the company, returned from a visit to the Chicago Loop with an announcement that surprised even the unflappable Mr. Bachmann. He says,

> They came in and Mr. Polk said, "We've got to get together some commercials. We're going on television."
>
> Now, these were the early days, when, as I used to say, you had to look in the paper to see if television was even going to be broadcast that day. Mr. Polk said, "We're going to go on Saturday night on WBKB."
>
> I asked, "What are we going to advertise?"
>
> He said, "We're going to advertise television sets."
>
> I was thinking, you've got to be out of your mind. Anyone that would be watching television would have bought the set within the last six months, because television was brand new. "How in the hell can we sell **them**?"

He patted me on the head like the little boy that I was, and he says, "I'm not going to advertise to those people who just bought a television set. I'm going to advertise to all those neighbors and friends who are sitting around these people's living rooms watching this miracle of communication."

That Saturday night the first Polk TV ad was aired from the skeletal WBKB studios at the 190 North State Street building in the Chicago Loop. With that first commercial, Polk Bros. became a pioneer sponsor on Chicago's first television station.

WBKB began as an experimental station run by the U.S. Navy during World War II. The station was purchased by the Balaban and Katz entertainment conglomerate in 1947, which kept former submarine commander W. C. "Bill" Eddy on as director of television. WBKB was then an independent. In the 1950s it was taken over in a merger and became one of the five stations wholly owned by the American Broadcasting Corporation.

Sterling "Red" Quinlan was program manager at WBKB when Sol Polk decided to jump into television advertising. Quinlan, a trail-blazing television broadcaster and author, recommended that Polk Bros. take on the sponsorship of the late-night movies:

That became Sol's main staple. He sponsored the movies. Endless movies. Old movies. The best we could find for the cheapest price. The trade-off, I told him, was you don't even mess with any other stations. Stick with us, and I will put you in with all the creative things, the extra things, that I have.

Polk Bros. did stick with WBKB and soon became Chicago's biggest television advertiser, sponsoring as much as twenty-five hours of television a week. In 1958 Chicagoland was saturated with more than fifteen hundred Polk Bros. TV spots. By 1965 Polk had earned a reputation as the nation's longest sustaining sponsor of television programming, surpassing even the perennial "Kraft Music Hall."

*   *   *

A home in the suburbs, an automobile, and a television set were the three things Americans seemed to want most in the years following World War II. Polk Bros. had the television sets and was among the first retailers to use to the fullest extent both television programming and television advertising to bring people into their stores to see and buy the appliances and housewares that people wanted for those new homes.

From the day the new television set came through the door the household was transformed. Evenings were planned around the TV schedule. Family life, once centered in the kitchen, was reoriented to the living room, around the black-and-white television with its tiny seven- or ten-inch circular screen. In 1949 the nation set its watch by Milton Berle's Tuesday night "Texaco Star Theater." The TV tray and then the TV dinner made their appearances. In the 1950s television showed America not only the "Ozzie and Harriet" lifestyle that families hungered for but also the material trappings of that life-style — products that they, too, could hope to own. Television was the link to the new America.

Writer Tedd Thomey is of that generation of Americans who remember the arrival of television and the impact it made in their lives.

While going over some old household receipts recently, I came across what appeared to be an insignificant date. It was October 5, 1950, the day my wife and I bought our first TV set. As I gazed at that faded sales contract, which also marked the first time we had ever purchased anything on credit, something inside me went click. It occurred to me that I held in my hand an historic family document.

From the beginning, Polk Bros. used television to reach all segments of the market. The company sponsored live drama on "Polk's Playhouse" and "Uncle Bucky's Lunchtime Little Theater." It had talk and interview shows such as Larry Attebery's "Private Line," the "Tom Duggan Show," and, at one time, the perennial "Kup's Show" with Irv Kupcinet. Polk Bros. also sponsored the early morning "Chicago Today" show and the two-hour "Morning Show" with Jim Conway, a forerunner to ABC's "Good Morning America."

Polk Bros. sponsored innumerable children's programs, including "The Blue Fairy," which won a Peabody Award for outstanding children's programming. Polk's "Night Owl Movie" was an entertainment standby for late-night viewers and for Chicago's legion of shift workers. Over the years, Polk Bros. also sponsored numerous television specials, such as the 1958 six-week "Sports Illustrated Spectacular" and the 1959 "Chicago Pan-American Games."

*　*　*

The bonding of Polk Bros. and live television advertising was a natural. Chicago had attracted top-quality talent to radio broadcasting in the 1930s and 1940s. It is not surprising that the city would become an important production center in the early days of television as well, giving rise to what came to called the Chicago school of broadcasting.

When black-and-white television began to develop commercially, Chicago was producing the best shows in the country. Programming, dominated by television pioneer Jules Herbuveaux and the NBC Chicago station WNBQ, was creative, dynamic, experimental, and star-studded. "Garroway At Large," "Stud's Place," and Burr Tilstrom's "Kukla, Fran and Ollie" all came out of Chicago in the early days of television.

These early broadcasters and advertisers had to be creative. They were writing the rules even as they learned them. It was all on-the-job training. As one observer has noted, "Since until now no one had ever tried to do it before, nobody really knew how to do anything. An 'old hand' was somebody who had worked on the show last week."

* * *

Even before they began advertising on television themselves, Polk Bros. had used television to draw people into the store. The original Central Appliance and Furniture store had the first commercially viable set, the RCA 630-TS, with a round tube and ten-inch screen, on display as early as 1946.

Crowds gathered around the little store on a fall morning in 1948 to watch, for the first time, televised national election returns broadcast by WBKB in cooperation with the *Chicago Sun-Times*. The day was memorable for another reason. That was the morning that a famous *Chicago Tribune* headline prematurely proclaimed that New York governor Thomas E. Dewey had beaten Harry S. Truman in the race for the presidency.

When the first network color program, the 1963 New Year's Day Tournament of Roses Parade from Pasadena, was broadcast, Polk Bros. opened its stores and invited the public in to watch the spectacle and the game while enjoying coffee and donuts on the house. "That was how we started staying open New Year's Day," Lester Bachmann says. "It was because of color television. Today that's a tradition across the country. New Year's is a sales day."

The Cerebral Palsy Telethon, the nation's first telethon, originated from the headquarters store in the Polk City complex on North Central Avenue. The Balaban and Katz organization, which then owned WBKB-TV, gave the station and Polk Bros. a free rein in organizing the event, which went on around the clock over a Saturday and Sunday.

Crowds thronged the streets around the store to join in the action and watch the show people and celebrity performers coming and going after the theaters closed at 11 p.m. Polk employees and family members circulated through the crowds outside the building collecting donations.

Sol was careful to be sure that pledges made were collected that night. He made a deal with the Veterans Cab Company to send drivers out to the home of any donor who pledged one hundred dollars or more. The names of these donors were read over the air, but not until the cab driver had returned with the check.

In 1956 Polk Bros. used their new store at 85th and Cottage Grove Avenue as a 60,000-square-foot set for the popular Big-League Bowling television series. The idea came about when Sol and his team were discussing the idea of sponsoring televised bowling tournaments. Bowling was then, and still is, a popular sport in Chicago. The problem was that no existing alley was technically feasible. Then Lester Bachmann had a thought.

> I said, "You know, everybody says that the new store is big enough to be a bowling alley. Why don't we bowl at the store?"
>
> They all looked at me as if I were crazy. But Sol said, "You've got an idea!"
>
> We jumped into the car and went over to the Brunswick office and purchased two regulation bowling alleys. We had them installed in the Cottage Grove windows of the store. The measurement on that side was one hundred eighty feet, so we had plenty of room. Then we bought portable bleachers, and we were ready to go.

Big League Bowling broadcast from Polk Bros.' "Polk City South" store was a tremendous hit. For the first twenty-six weeks the competitions featured professional bowlers. Polk renewed for a second season of playoffs between local teams, offering prizes of cash and merchandise. Bachmann continues:

> The store was open until 6 p.m. on Sundays, so every Sunday evening after the store closed we

would move the merchandise out of the way and set up the portable bleachers. We could seat one hundred fifty to two hundred people inside the store. There were at least as many people outside watching through the windows.

At eight o'clock we went live with the bowling. When we cut to the commercials, the commercials were right there in the store. We'd just turn the camera around and point it over to the sofa, the refrigerator, the washing machine, and so on.

Bachmann remembers that as the playoffs progressed, and public involvement heightened, one local bowler, a tool and die maker, became something of a local celebrity. "He became so popular that his company had to transfer him to their public relations department because so many people were coming into the plant to ask for his autograph."

The grand prize in the elimination playoffs was to be a trip around the world. "This was about the biggest thing you could do," Bachmann says. He recalls the climactic moments of the playoffs:

I had worked with the airlines and the travel people and we had the winner going everywhere from Alaska to Australia and back again. The night of the big affair finally arrived. The suspense had built up over the season. And sure enough, this fellow won. After it was over, he came to me and said, "I can't really afford to take a month off. Could you arrange for a week in Hawaii for my wife and myself?" So that's what we did.

When color television came to Chicago in 1955, Polk Bros. switched much of their advertising to the NBC station, WNBQ-TV. The new WNBQ studios, built for color, were located on the twentieth and twenty-first floors of Chicago's massive Merchandise Mart building. Taking advantage of the location, Polk Bros. created television's first info-mercial: In January every year, manufacturers and buyers from all over the country converged on the Mart for a five-day furniture market. The show was closed to the public, but Polk Bros. managed to bring Chicago shoppers a televised preview. Bachmann tells the story:

> On the Sunday afternoon before the show opened, we ran television cable down the elevator shafts and onto two floors of the Mart. For two hours we visited the exhibits and talked to designers and manufacturers of the various furniture products that were going to be shown to the world for the first time the next morning. They demonstrated their product and talked about how the design had evolved and how it was new or different. Obviously, those we interviewed were all Polk Bros. vendors.

In 1967 Polk Bros., in partnership with WBKB, sponsored the first international satellite transmission to Chicago, taking the signal from the newly orbited Telstar communications satellite. The broadcast, live from the Vatican in Rome, featured the mass celebrating the elevation of Chicago Archbishop John Cardinal Cody and other cardinals.

*   *   *

Back in 1949, when Polk Bros. took to television, their first announcer was a young man by the name of Frank Reynolds who was then doing spot announcing for a radio station in Hammond, Indiana, but who longed to do television news. Red Quinlan had been using him as a standby on the WBKB-TV ten o'clock news. Acting on Quinlan's recommendation, Sol agreed to use Reynolds as the Polk Bros.' announcer. Frank Reynolds went on to become a highly respected White House correspondent and co-anchorman of the "ABC Evening News."

Frank Reynolds was by no means Polk Bros.' only celebrity announcer. Joe Wilson, a sportscaster for WBKB, was well known for his radio play-by-play reporting of Chicago Cubs' baseball and for his televised coverage of the Chicago Blackhawks. He became known as "Whispering Joe Wilson" for his whispered coverage of tense moments in the Polk Bros. Big League Bowling broadcasts. Sports commentator Jack Drees was another favorite Polk Bros. bowling announcer. Pioneer radio announcer and restaurateur Linn Burton began the television career that earned him the nickname "Burton for Certain" when he came on as Polk's late-night TV pitchman in the early 1950s.

But the announcer that two generations of Chicagoans remember as "The Voice of Polk Bros." was veteran radio and television announcer and newsman Bill Hamilton. Hamilton, whose face became as familiar to Chicagoans as the face of the mayor, was Polk Bros.' announcer for thirty-seven years.

In the summer of 1953 in-house ad man Ron Terry was doing all the Polk Bros. TV commercials himself, working seven days and seven nights a week. Hamilton had a cubicle at the 2850 store where he worked editing the coronation film. Sol Polk called Bill into his office and said, "You're gonna start doing the weekend TV stuff." Hamilton recalls, "I told him 'I'm not gonna do television anymore,' and he says, 'You're starting Saturday.'"

And so Bill Hamilton became Polk Bros.' on-air talent for the several Saturday children's programs that Polk Bros. sponsored at that time. Hamilton did as many as three live Polk-sponsored shows on a single morning. "I'd be dressed up in cowboy outfit on one, something else on the second, and a suit on the third," he remembers.

*   *   *

Children didn't buy washing machines, but there was obvious method behind Polk's sponsorship of children's programming. Polk Bros. advertised their promotions as "fun for the family," and much of the activity in Polk Bros. stores was designed to encourage family shopping. There was always something going on in the stores for children, whether it was Skippy the Clown, free Good Humor bars, a Smokey Bear junior ranger certificate, or an invitation to bring mom and dad out to see live elephants in the Polk Bros. parking lot.

"The Blue Fairy" program, featuring thirteen-year-old Bridgid Bazlen, the daughter of Chicago newspaper columnist Maggie Daly, was among the most popular of Polk's children's shows. The program, launched in 1958 on WGN-TV, was broadcast both in black and white and in color every weekday evening from 7:15 to 7:30. This was family time, and Polk Bros. promoted "The Blue Fairy" as a time to "re-create stories our parents used to read to us before bed."

Even Polk Bros. did not realize how big the Blue Fairy's following was until the weekend in 1958 when Bridgid announced, on a Friday evening, that she would be making a personal appearance the next day at the new Polk Bros. store at 5711 North Milwaukee Avenue. On Saturday morning, Lester Bachmann recalls, the crowds were lined up three and four abreast along Milwaukee Avenue and around the block.

* * *

Bill Hamilton soon moved from Polk's Saturday children's shows to the role of full-time regular announcer for the nightly midnight movies. This was live television at its best, and at its worst. Hamilton introduced the films and did six or eight live commercial spots on every show. These commercials were only lightly scripted, and the timing tended to vary to meet the needs of the moment.

Polk's "Night Owl Movie" ads had the impact of breaking news. And, in fact, often were. At 11 p.m. Lester Bachmann collected the early editions of the morning newspapers to scan the print ads that would be on Chicagoans' doorsteps the following morning. "I would read the ads for the next day's paper, and if vacuum cleaners were going for forty-nine dollars that night and Sears had one for forty-eight dollars, I would call Bill at the studio and we would change the price. That was one of the great things about live television."

The company was straightforward about the practice. On the occasion of Polk Bros.' twenty-fifth year in business the Television Bureau of Advertising, with the cooperation of WBKB-TV and WMAQ-TV, produced a thirty-minute documentary titled "The Polk Principle." In one segment, Hamilton tells the viewer that Polk Bros. tries to keep its commercials "as timely as the latest news announcement." He explains:

> We change copy, well, minutes before going on the air. In fact, in the control room there's a phone, and every once in a while, a couple of minutes before the commercial is due to go on, that phone will ring and it's a late news bulletin from Polk City. Something new has arrived, or a new idea has come forth, and this is put on television then and there.

The flexibility of live television was a natural for Polk's shoot-from-the-hip management style. It got them out before the public with advertised specials days before the print media could catch up. If the weather changed, and the temperature shot up, ads for ranges and kitchen appliances were scrubbed on a moment's notice and replaced with ads for air conditioners and electric fans. When a severe snowstorm hit Chicago, Polk Bros. was on the air with ads for snowblowers while the storm was still in progress.

On one occasion, sweltering Chicagoans were offered a deal on circulating fans that surprised even seasoned Polk customers. Those who responded by phone to a "Night-Owl Movie" commercial, had fans in their homes before the film was over. To make the midnight deliveries, Polk's had stationed Home Shopping Service salesmen throughout the Chicago area, their private cars packed with the merchandise. These salesmen called in from pay phones for the addresses of orders from their vicinity. In no time the Polk man, with the fan, was ringing the customer's doorbell.

The flexibility that Polk Bros. demonstrated in its use of live television was characteristic of the company's approach to any problem. In late January 1967 Chicago was paralyzed by the heaviest snowfall in the city's history: twenty-five inches fell overnight. The city and all its business and transportation systems were literally shut down, buried in massive drifts. At Polk Bros.' Melrose Park warehouse, a four-wheel-drive truck was fitted up as a snowplow and loaded with snow blowers for transport to the Four Seasons store at Polk City. Any salesman or manager who lived within hiking distance of the store was told to come in.

"People had to walk in the middle of the street. There was nothing moving," Howard Polk remembers. "We were the only place in the world that was open." Bruce Bachmann, manager of Polk's Four Seasons Store, was glad to see the snow blowers trucked in from the warehouse. Business was brisk. "We'd give people a tank of gas and start up the snow blower, and they'd just drive it off down the street," Bachmann recalls.

*   *   *

By 1950 production of television sets had caught up with demand, and competition among retailers was heating up. The rectangular twenty-one inch screen had replaced the round seven- and ten-inch models. Over the 1950 Christmas season Polk Bros. advertised that for the price of a phone call, a salesman would come out to the customer's home "within an hour" to demonstrate a new twenty-one inch model and quote a trade-in on the spot for the customer's old set. Customers interested in the new top-of-the-line Admiral console could have the use of a set "free of charge and with no obligation to buy" for the duration of the Christmas season.

Polk Bros. used television both to build their store image and to generate sales for the brand-name merchandise that they carried. In this, Polk Bros. used television tie-ins lavishly and creatively, linking brand-name national advertising campaigns with product demonstrations and Polk's own promotions.

For example, when the Ringling Bros. and Barnum & Bailey Circus came to town, Polk Bros. bought up blocks of tickets and offered them free to Polk customers making a major purchase. The announcement of the circus promotion coincided with a series of commercials for Sunbeam electric lawnmowers. The tie-in was obvious to Sol Polk. It is unlikely that anyone else would have thought of it. He brought a Ringling Bros. elephant and her trainer into the studio. As Bill Hamilton went into his spiel for Sunbeam and his invitation to Chicagoans to "be our guests" at the circus, the elephant lumbered around the set pushing a Sunbeam electric lawn mower.

Live commercials were often more suspenseful, and inadvertently more entertaining, than the program itself. It was not at all unusual for Sol Polk to buttonhole a vendor or manufacturer's representative in his office and say, "Come on, I want you to go on television tonight and tell people about this product." The vendor usually did, sometimes with unexpected results.

Lester Bachmann recalls the singular appearance of H. U. Mann, a representative for a company that manufactured washing machines and dishwashers. "Ham the Man," as he was known, was a salesman of the old school, and he had a passion for his product. "A real pitchman," Bachmann says.

> He would get so excited talking about dishwashers that one day Mr. Polk said to him, "Why don't you go on television and tell this story?" We got Ham up to the studio, and cut to him at commercial time, and he started his pitch. And he just talked and talked and talked.
>
> The floor director gave him what we call "the fist," which meant wind it up. And Ham just kept

talking and talking. Finally they gave up and cut back to the movie. The director was mad as a hornet. He said, "When I gave you the fist, why didn't you stop? Why didn't you cut it off?"

Ham said, "I thought you were cheering me on. I thought you were telling me, 'Give 'em hell! Give 'em hell!' "

A representative for RCA television was equally enthusiastic about his product. Sol put him on an afternoon show to talk about the product, which featured a safety glass protecting the picture tube. Bachmann remembers:

This guy got so wound up that he took his foot and he kicked the television set to show how strong the glass was. Nothing broke, but the switchboard lighted up at NBC with parents calling in to say, "The kids are kicking the TV set. Please stop that!"

A local sales manager for Eureka vacuum cleaners had a gimmick that he wanted demonstrated on the air. The idea was to fill a child's sand pail with marbles and let the viewers see how fast the powerful Eureka vacuum could suck the marbles out of the bucket. Most of the time the demonstration worked fairly well. The time that it didn't was the night Hamilton invited the sales manager to come on live and do the demonstration himself. Hamilton recalls:

Sam always had a cigar in his mouth. I introduced him and he stuck the vacuum nozzle down in that bucket of marbles and the camera moved in for a close shot. Nothing much happened. Sam was so nervous that he bit his cigar in two. The last thing the viewers saw was that half a cigar falling into the bucket of marbles. That was the end of the commercial. But people loved it, and they came out to buy those vacuum cleaners.

As Hamilton can attest, it was not the guest but the announcer who usually bore the brunt of the bloopers, foibles, gaffs, and faux pas that were part and parcel of live, unscripted TV.

Hamilton remembers the commercial he did for Bruce Bachmann when Bruce was managing the Four Seasons lawn and garden store. The item being promoted was a lightweight aluminum chaise longue with plastic webbing. Hamilton was to sit on the recliner, demonstrate that it could also be used in a supine position, and give the price. "You can sit like this, or you can just lean back and lie down," I said.

> As I leaned back, the chair legs just gave out on that slick studio floor, and I ended up with my feet up in the air, and my head way back here on the floor. I looked over at the camera, and the cameraman was gone. He was laughing so hard that he ran out of the studio.
>
> Well, the camera was running. I was lying there on the floor. What could I do? I gave the price. But the price I quoted was a dollar under what Bruce had told me to sell it for.
>
> That was a Saturday night. Bruce called me the next morning and said, "Hamilton, there were seven hundred people waiting in front of the patio shop when we opened up this morning, and you cut the price a dollar on that lawn chair! Your goof-up cost us seven hundred dollars. Do it again tonight."

"Bruce was laughing almost as hard as that cameraman," Hamilton recalls. When he did the commercial Sunday night, Hamilton did not repeat the fall, but he did improvise an even better line:

> I got all kinds of trouble from the boss today because I misread the price on this chaise longue. But I'm going to do it again, and here it is. I'll be in trouble

In 1936 Polk Bros. opened its first Chicago store, Central Appliance and Furniture Co., in a sliver of space at 3334 North Central Avenue.

The first store was superceded by the 2850 North Central Avenue store around which the "Polk City" complex was built.

Sam Polk during the early years checks out the kitchen appliance department of the original Polk Bros. store.

Sol Polk, the driving force behind Polk Bros., in his jeep during World War II.

When oriental carpets were introduced into the Polk City store in the early 1950s, the promotion featured carpets carried into the parking lot on the back of a camel. Later advertised as Polk's magic flying carpets, the product was airlifted into Polk City by helicopter. Here David Polk supervises the planning.

In celebration of Polk Bros.' 25th anniversary, Bill Hamilton (left) invites Polk's customers to the Ringling Bros. and Barnum & Bailey Circus.

Sol Polk (right) with Jack Leonard are surrounded by lighted, plastic "Jolly Super Santa Clauses" in one of Polk's most spectacular holiday promotions.

Another popular Polk promotion featured Christmas trees purchased by Sol Polk and brought into Chicago by the carload. Morrie Polk (shown here) and Sol scouted Nova Scotia and other areas to buy up the trees that were given free to customers with the purchase of a major appliance.

In the 1950s and early 1960s, national advertising fanned demand for the "all-electric kitchen," and the accessory products that went with it. Polk Bros. sold them all, with the help of its staff of "super salesmen," who produced legendary volume appliance sales.

Sales floors in the larger Polk Bros. stores were the size of football fields. They were stocked with hundreds of products from two hundred brand-name manufacturers. A collaboration between Sol Polk (shown here) and famed adman Leo Burnett resulted in the long-running "lonely Maytag repairman" advertising campaign.

Among Sol Polk's many motivational signs and slogans, this message was always foremost.

at POLK BROS....
EVERYBODY
THINKS RETAIL!
ACTS RETAIL!

In matters of home furnishings, the Polk brothers (from left) Sam, Sol, Morrie and Harry, listened to their big sister, Goldie Bachman Luftig. As a family in business, they got along fine. Goldie explained: "We argue, we reach a decision — and then nobody says, 'I told you so!' "

Helping a Polk Bros. promotion, Illinois Governor William Stratton (center) became a Smokey Bear junior forest ranger. David Polk (left) presents the governor with his own Smokey Bear. Irving Cohen, the bear's manufacturer, watches.

(From left) Bruce Bachmann, Morris Luftig, Goldie Bachmann Luftig, Roberta Bachmann Lewis and Irv Lewis attend "The World's Largest Birthday Party" at Chicago Stadium, a celebration of the 20th anniversary of the opening of the first Polk Bros. store.

Taking part in the ribbon cutting ceremony at the opening of a Polk Bros. store on the South Side are (from left) Sol, Lester (bow tie), Goldie, Sam, Morrie, Marian (David's wife, in profile), Marion, Morrie's wife, and Pearl, Harry's wife.

with the boss again tomorrow, but this is the price I
read and this is the price you can get it for.

Sometimes Hamilton was the victim of his own enthusiasm for the job. When he demonstrated a convertible sofa-
bed with plenty of room inside for storage of blankets and
pillows, it was Bill's own idea to climb inside.

I had the stage hands fold me up in the sofa. I was
going to emerge, on air, and begin my description of
how roomy the storage space was. For some reason,
I couldn't get out. I was down inside this sofa with
the microphone on, and I'm saying, "Help me, help
me out of here." The stage hands could not go on
camera, so the only thing the viewers saw was my
hand sticking up out of the sofa. That was the commercial. For some reason, this sold sofas like they
were going out of style. People thought it was a gag.

*   *   *

Sol Polk himself never appeared in any of the many thousands of Polk Bros. commercials broadcast over the years.
Nor did any of the other Polk brothers. They didn't believe in
that kind of personal exposure. Lester Bachmann explains that
although Polk Bros. was created in the image of Sol Polk, Sol
himself was loath to see the business identified in the public
mind with a single personality. Sol took his lead from the example of Jim Moran, Bachmann says. Moran had built up the
Hudson automobile dealership in Chicago in the late 1940s.
He and Sol Polk moved in the same business circles. In fact,
the building that housed Polk Bros.' outlet store at 3500 West
Grand had been purchased from Moran, whose Hudson dealership was across the street.

When Moran began television advertising in the early
1950s, he, like many other automobile dealers, appeared in all
his agency's commercials. To the public, he was "Jim Moran, the

Courtesy Man." He also sponsored an interview show, "The Courtesy Hour," on WBKB, which he hosted himself. This kind of visibility had a decided downside, to Sol's way of thinking.

"When Jim went on vacation, it affected his business." Bachmann says.

> People expected to go out to his lot and talk to Jim Moran himself. At one point when he was out of town, they put a big cut-out photograph of Jim on camera and then played audio tapes of his voice saying something like: "This is Jim Moran, speaking to you from Florida." It just wasn't the same thing.

* * *

Although Sol Polk was not willing to go before the cameras himself, he did not hesitate when it came to taking bold steps in the programming he sponsored.

In the mid-1950s, WBKB-TV was said to be the most creative station in town, known especially for its documentaries and special events' programming. The aforementioned Red Quinlan, WBKB program director and, later, vice-president and general manager, says, "A lot of that reputation was due to Sol's help in backing long shots." Quinlan frequently took off-beat programming ideas to the conservative ABC bosses in the New York offices.

> I did a lot of things that New York didn't like, but they couldn't really kick too much because my bottom line was better than the New York station. If I said, "Sol Polk is sponsoring it," they had to shut up. What they didn't know was that I was practically giving it away to Sol, because he was a buddy of mine. He was helping me, and I couldn't charge him what I might someone else.
>
> Another spin on this was that because of Sol's total support of WBKB, we sort of became the re-

tailers' station. State Street merchants, car dealers, they all came to us first. But none of them got the deals that Sol Polk got, because he was the first one in, and he deserved it.

Sol had always believed in the future of color television, even in the years when that future looked more gray than rosy. He also believed in the RCA Corporation's all-electronic, black-and-white compatible system, as opposed to the competing spinning disk system developed first by the Columbia Broadcasting System.

(In the hard-fought battle over color systems the Polk brothers could easily have identified either with RCA chairman David Sarnoff, founder of the NBC network, or with William Paley, who founded the rival CBS network. Sarnoff, of the two, was more like Sol. The son of immigrant Russian Jewish parents, he began his entrepreneurial career as a newsboy on the streets of New York. Paley, however, while not a contemporary of the Polk brothers, had in fact been raised in the same West Side Chicago neighborhood as the Polk boys.)

Polk Bros. had a long-standing relationship with RCA. Television was only one product in their line. RCA console and table model radios and RCA phonographs were in demand after the war and RCA had been a faithful supplier for Polk Bros. Lester Bachmann says that Sol Polk from the beginning bet on RCA in the color wars.

By 1950 television had become a consumer product; it was very big at Christmas that year. RCA had big plans to sell us a lot of merchandise, and we met them at the Knickerbocker Hotel to talk about the deal.

I remember asking Mr. Polk to step out in the hall with me, and I said to him, "Sol, don't get excited about the quantity of sets they want to sell us because no matter how many you buy it will be difficult to make a profit." RCA sets were low margin and they were discounted. This was not a profitable item.

Mr. Polk said, "That's all right. Someday there will be color television and when there is, I expect that RCA will be in the forefront. I want to be on their band wagon." We went back into the room and gave RCA a huge order for black-and-white sets. It might have been a million dollars.

Sol Polk was right. In late 1953 the Federal Communication Commission ended the long, enormously expensive, and acrimonious standoff between CBS and RCA by adopting the Radio Corporation of America color system as standard. The battle was won but not the war. The FCC decision marked only the beginning of an uphill struggle to win public acceptance of color TV.

The next two years were spent working the flaws out of the system and setting up production lines. CBS and NBC had both tried color on some special broadcasts, sporting events, and occasional spectaculars. But as late as 1954, color broadcasting averaged only a slightly more than one hour a week. For a time after the FCC decision, CBS discontinued color broadcasting altogether, and a multitude of electronics companies poised to manufacture color television sets withdrew from the market.

Sol Polk, however, kept the faith with color TV. Lester Bachmann remembers "the first and only vacation that I ever knew Mr. Polk to take":

He went to Miami Beach. He called me two or three times a day from down there. He had lined up maybe half a dozen Miami hotels to buy color television sets for their lobbies. And it wasn't until he came home that they realized that they didn't have color television in Miami. At that time, CBS had broadcast color from New York to Washington, D.C., but it didn't get down to Miami. He totally sold those hotels on the idea that color was coming.

By 1955, RCA estimated that it had spent $70 million on developing color television. The stockholders were becoming impatient to see some return on their money. Manufacturers were ready to roll. But the public was skeptical and resistant to buying a product that it viewed as far from being perfected.

Michael E. Porter, who surveyed the U.S. television market in this period, notes that RCA's tremendous investment not withstanding, "sales of color TV proved to be dismal." He continues:

> Only 20,000 or so color TVs were bought by consumers in 1955. High cost, poor and dim picture quality, and lack of color programming were the key reasons.

The price of a color set then ranged from seven hundred to a thousand dollars or more. It would take mass production to bring the price down, and there simply was no mass market. David Sarnoff needed three things: He needed color programming; he needed a market for that programming; and he needed to sell enough color sets to create that market.

In a gesture of extraordinary confidence, Sol Polk flew to New York to meet with General Sarnoff. Polk placed an order for one thousand RCA color consoles to sell for one thousand one hundred dollars each. On the strength of that deal, Sarnoff agreed to make the Chicago NBC station the first all-color station in the nation. Chicago quickly became the nation's leading color market, and Polk Bros., the leading color TV dealer.

On April 15, 1956, Chicago station WNBQ, the local NBC outlet, became the world's first all-color station, transmitting all of its locally produced programs in color. It was said at the time that the entire RCA color TV development program hung on the acceptance of color television in Chicago. In fact, it hung on the ability of Sol Polk to sell color television sets to Chicago.

Polk Bros. was on the air with color commercials the moment local color broadcasting became available. To support color programming, Polk Bros. switched their own TV advertising to WNBQ. Polk Bros. thus became the first retailer in the country to regularly produce television commercials in color.

*   *   *

Even so, color television was a hard sell. In the beginning, retailers, other than Polk Bros., typically did not promote it. "When you walked into a department store to buy a color television, you probably wouldn't find one on the floor," Bachmann says.

> They didn't display them. The salesman would say to you, "They're not perfected yet." They had black-and-white sets which were selling like popcorn, for four hundred dollars or less. Color was selling for a thousand or fifteen hundred dollars, and then on an "if," "when," and "maybe" basis. Other stores didn't promote color because it was easier for them to sell black and white.

Polk salesmen, however, did promote color. The primary resistance to color, Polk merchandise manager Jerry Unger remembers, was price. But the relatively high price of color sets also worked as an incentive to Polk Bros. salesmen, whose commission was a percentage of sales. Unger recalls customers' reactions to color television:

> Instead of saying "that's too expensive," customers would say, "So that's color? What's so great about that?" That was their excuse for not buying it. But you can't sell anything unless you talk about it, so we just kept talking.

Polk Bros. — as they had done with the earliest black-and-white sets — promoted color television by advertising it in color commercials. They also used a wide network of word-of-mouth advertising. As a means of getting enthusiasm for the product out on the sales floor, the company gave color television sets to its key department managers. (They would later do the same with microwave ovens.) When churches and local charities sponsored a raffle, Polk Bros. would contribute a color TV as a prize. "We exposed it wherever we could — at any public affair we could get to," Lester Bachmann remembers.

*   *   *

In 1947, there were fewer than one thousand television sets in the Chicago area. Ten years later, Polk Bros. was selling television sets at the rate of one thousand a day. By 1960 color had taken over the market. In the mid-1960s, Polk Bros. was airing nearly four thousand commercials a year on Chicago television stations.

In the late 1950s and early 1960s, television accounted for fifty to sixty percent of Polk Bros.' advertising dollars. As Chicago area television reached the point that it priced itself out of the market for the local retail advertiser, Polk Bros. began shifting its ad budget back to print. The company did not resume television advertising on a large scale until the late 1980s. By that time live TV was a thing of the past.

13

Where Else but at Polk Bros.?

"So far as promotional ideas are concerned, Sol needs help the way Winston Churchill needs a speech writer."
— "Chicago's Red Hot Merchandiser"
Fortune, September 1955

"Combine the evangelistic fervor of a Billy Sunday with the promotional acrobatics of a Barnum and you see why Polk Bros moves more . . . appliances than any other dealer in the world."
— **Hotpoint News**, 1960

Chief White Eagle in full regalia, an ice rink in the parking lot. Free balloons and ice-cream bars. Bathing beauties and Davy Crockett wandering the aisles. It's just another ordinary summer day at Polk Bros.

For sheer drawing power nothing equaled the excitement and the fun and the ballyhoo that Polk Bros. generated around its spectacular promotions and imaginative giveaways.

Sol Polk was a merchant by trade, but at heart he was the consummate showman. The idea was to draw people in droves into Polk Bros.' stores, to make shopping fun for the family, and, not incidentally, to send them home with a purchase from Polk Bros. The result was far bigger and better than that. Polk promotions and premium tie-ins were marked by extraordinary inventiveness and enthusiasm.

Polk events included blockbuster extravaganzas such as circus elephants parading through the Polk City parking lot, Polk's buy-out of the premiere showings of Michael Todd's long-awaited film "Around the World in Eighty Days," and All-Star bowling televised on-site from the sales floor of Polk Bros.' Cottage Grove store.

The company shined in staging headline-grabbing stunts such as the gift of a half-mile of red carpet laid for Queen Elizabeth on her arrival at Chicago's Navy Pier in 1959. That carpet-trod-by-royalty was later used in Polk Bros. stores, where, Polk's proclaimed, "We Treat Every Woman Like a Queen." Two years before the queen's visit, Sol Polk had made news in Chicago's predominantly Irish Bridgeport neighborhood by offering a job to the unemployed lord mayor of Dublin.

Polk promotions were designed to be seen — and talked about. Over a three-year period in the early 1960s, Polk Bros.' famous lighted Santa Claus and its partner, the lighted snowman, popped up on the porches, lawns, and rooftops of nearly a quarter of a million Chicago area homes.

Another goal was to keep customers coming back to Polk Bros. stores. From time to time Polk's gave away five, ten, or twenty-five cases of king-size Coca-Cola with a major purchase. Sol Polk figured that no average family could store twenty-five cases at any one time, so he suggested that customers pick up their free cases of Cokes as they needed them. Each Coca-Cola run, of course, required another trip to a Polk Bros. store.

For other promotional campaigns, Sol Polk roamed North America to bring home to Chicago massive giveaways of giant Georgia watermelons, crates of Washington Apples, Florida oranges, Hawaiian pineapples, and Scotch Pine Christmas trees shipped in by the freight car load from Nova Scotia.

Whether it was certificates for free car washes or a brand-new Nash Rambler; a state-of-the-art antenna to take home with your new television set or a free two-hundred-twenty-volt home rewiring with the purchase of an electric range; a Good Humor bar or an entire set of encyclopedias — the impact of Polk Bros. promotions and premiums was pervasive and powerful.

The philosophy behind Polk promotional activity was simple: Make Polk Bros. stores a destination for shoppers, create visibility, kindle word-of-mouth advertising, and clinch customer loyalty. To these, Polk Bros. added the additional goal of using promotions to celebrate America and Americanism.

Polk used all of the traditional types of promotions — premium promotions, seasonal promotions, fad promotions, tie-in promotions, price promotions — and added to these a carnival atmosphere that was all its own. "The point of all these premiums and promotions was to build up traffic," Howard Polk says. "To get people into the stores and create the buying frenzy."

The success of this strategy can be assumed from the sheer numbers involved. Polk Bros. averaged a new promotion every fifteen days from the mid-1950s through the mid-1980s. The number of items distributed to Chicago shoppers ranged from the tens of thousands to the hundreds of thousands. Each premium given out represented at least one customer passing through the store, and in many instances a major purchase as well.

Take the Good Humor ice-cream bars, for example. Beginning in 1958, Polk Bros. began the practice of giving out coupon books to customers, good for ten free Good Humor bars. In the first year, Polk Bros. ordered the equivalent of nearly three million Good Humor bars. By 1963 they had upped the order to five million. One Good Humor vendor set up shop, permanently, in front of the main entrance to the store at 2850 North Central Avenue, as did a hot dog vendor. Both, it was said, had a very comfortable retirement.

* * *

Generating store traffic was the objective, but one suspects that there was yet another point behind it all: Promotions were fun and nothing was too zany for Polk Bros. Polk announcer Bill Hamilton remembers that "it was crazy, but we just had more damn fun!" Polk vice-president Lester Bachmann adds, "We were never afraid to have an idea fail because there were always a dozen more coming along right behind it."

A day in the life of a Polk Bros. store was said to be a "circus." From time to time, that was literally true. On Polk's thirtieth anniversary, the company distributed thousands of free tickets to the Ringling Bros. and Barnum & Bailey Circus to Polk customers. Between shows, circus acts performed in the Polk Bros. parking lot.

In 1983 and 1984 Polk Bros. sponsored the Circus Vargas, billed as "The Biggest Big Top Circus in the World," by giving out free tickets with a major purchase. Cliff Vargas was a friend of Lester Bachmann. Polk employees were astonished, and amused, to see Lester, who ordinarily cut a very conservative figure, riding atop an elephant in the circus parade. "Cliff sort of conned me into it," Lester explains. "I was talking with him at intermission, and the next thing I knew I was on top of this elephant."

Polk's definitely was midway minded. Skippy the Clown could often be found standing on the corner outside the entrance to the main store, handing out lollipops. Or he could be found leading a parade of children through the aisles, giving out Polk Bros. helium balloons.

* * *

Sol Polk instinctively knew that people like to shop at a store where there is something going on. And he made sure that there was always something happening at Polk Bros. stores. Even in the earliest days of the business, the Polk brothers created action by inviting housewives to bring their laundry into the store and try out the new Bendix automatic washer. Before television became commonplace, Polk's set up viewing rooms so that people could come in to the store to watch the big game, or whatever else might be on.

By design, Polk Bros. stores teemed with activity. Polk used demonstrators of merchandise of every description to keep the action moving. Demonstrations of appliances themselves added to the din and sense of perpetual activity. Washing machines were hooked up to a full plumbing system, dryers whirred, and sewing machines clattered away. There were cook-offs, model airplane contests, costume shows.

Chicago has always been a celebrity town, and Polk Bros. attracted celebrity visitors. Famous faces and all-star entertainments in turn drew customers into the store. Ella Fitzgerald stopped by Polk Bros.' record department to promote her latest LP album. The Polks brought Minnesota Fats in to demonstrate pool tables. Movie doyen Joan Crawford appeared at Polk Bros. during a Pepsi Cola tie-in promotion. Singer Eddie Fisher came to Polk's with Coca-Cola promotions. Mr. T and Chicago mayor Harold Washington were frequent visitors.

Movie mogul Michael Todd, who, like the Polk brothers, hailed from Chicago's West Side, came to Chicago with his bride, actress Elizabeth Taylor, to see Sol Polk and help plan Polk's promotion of Todd's film "Around the World in Eighty Days." Not surprisingly, Mike Todd and Sol Polk were great friends — not only by virtue of their old West Side connections but because, as Todd explained it, "We're both in show business."

*   *   *

Polk Bros. was famous for stunts and extravaganzas, but the company also built promotions around surprisingly simple premises. Even back in the beginning, at the little Central Appliance and Furniture store, Polk Bros. used the invitation to "Have a Coke on Polk" to keep customers happy until a salesman was available. A 1955 variation on that theme was the distribution of colored cigarettes during a color TV promotion. Recipients were invited to "Have a Smoke on Polk."

Polk offered a free wash 'n wear suit with the purchase of a washing machine. A supply of ice cream was given away with every home freezer. On George Washington's Birthday one year, Polk Bros. sent a cherry tree home with everyone who bought a Hotpoint appliance. Azalea bushes and shrubbery were offered as premiums with the purchase of garden equipment or lawn furniture.

Polk tied a promotion for the Mr. Coffee drip coffee maker to a Folger coffee campaign by packing a pound of Folger's coffee with every Mr. Coffee machine. Sol once mailed thirty thousand pairs of inner-sole shoe liners out to fellow retailers, exhorting the recipients to "put the bounce back in retailing."

While Sol Polk claimed "to do the common, uncommonly," many of the Polk crowd-pleasers were anything but common. Shortly after the Korean war, Polk Bros. set up a short-wave radio station in the window of the Polk City North store. With licensed amateur radio operators manning the board, Polk's and Polk customers sent out holiday messages to servicemen around the world.

For a time in the mid-1960s, Sol had a financial interest in a helicopter company. He used it imaginatively. When Polk Bros. bought a supply of Oriental carpets, they launched the Magic Carpet campaign, delivering rugs to the Polk Bros. parking lot by helicopter. Similarly, when Polk's was giving away 250,000 Hawaiian pineapples, the reigning Miss Hawaii was flown in to emerge with fanfare from a helicopter landing in the Polk lot.

Some of Polk Bros.' promotions were simply kooky. A favorite was an elongated string instrument with a crooked neck called the "Polk-a-Lay-Lee." Polk Bros. advertised this as "a beautiful musical instrument, handmade of solid wood by American instrument craftsmen." Ads suggested that the owners of a Polk-a-Lay-Lee could "enjoy a music fiesta at home — fun for the whole family." Alternatively, "Be the life of the party — Be a Polk-a-Lay-Lee performer!" Fifty thousand Polk-a-Lay-Lee's were distributed. "It was a horribly ugly thing," Roberta Lewis remembers. "But every kid in Chicago wanted one."

Some opportunities were missed, but not many. Bill Hamilton, the Polk Bros. television announcer and himself a private pilot, urged Sol to have the Polk Bros. name painted on the roof of the mammoth Polk Bros. warehouse in Melrose Park, which lay directly under a main approach lane to Chicago's O'Hare International Airport. That was one that Sol never quite got around to.

* * *

Polk Bros. — although its stock-in-trade was hard goods — for some reason had a continuing interest in agricultural products, at least when it came to fanciful promotions. It began with Florida oranges. From January through March of 1959, Polk Bros. gave out 158,000 cases of them. The orange promotion is a good example of Polk's integrated approach to its advertising campaigns.

The orange promotion was launched in the dead of winter with the promise: "Polk Bros. Gives You a Box of Sunshine From Florida." It featured crates of Cypress Gardens Temple oranges "picked and packed for Polk Bros." as a giveaway with any purchase of twenty-five dollars or more.

This promotion employed the full media mix that might be used by a sophisticated advertising agency today.

Taking as its musical theme, "You Are My Sunshine," the campaign integrated television, newspaper, radio, outdoor board, and direct mail over a ten-week period. Polk Bros.' checks to vendors were written on oversize sheets imprinted with a large image of an orange. The campaign even included airline and package-tour tie-ins, with winners of Florida vacations chosen in weekly drawings held in Polk Bros. stores.

But this campaign was not done by an ad agency. As was typical of Polk Bros., it was planned and executed entirely in-house. The Florida sunshine promotion was literally redolent with Polk Bros.' unique touch: "Where else but at Polk Bros." would the orange ink used by the *Chicago Tribune* in the "Box of Sunshine" advertisements be chemically treated with a substance that gave off the fragrance of oranges?

While the genius behind Polk's mile-a-minute promotional ideas was Sol Polk himself, and while it might appear that these schemes popped up out of the blue, in fact there was a good deal of planning behind them. Sol was always on the lookout for a good promotional idea. Part of his singular ability was a serendipitous talent for seeing opportunity in the ordinary.

Such was the case with Polk Bros.' Black Diamond watermelon giveaway. When Sol saw a whimsical newspaper item reporting that Georgia was having a bumper crop of sixty-pound watermelons, he flew to Georgia and bought the whole crop. A watermelon was given away with every major purchase that summer. But not just any watermelon. These were truly monster watermelons, some weighing as much as ninety pounds. Sol's theory, as he explained it, was:

> It's too big to put in the refrigerator, and so you give part of it away to the neighbors. In so doing there's a thirty-minute conversation telling how it came from Polk Bros. That's the best kind of advertising — word of mouth.

Sol was right. That summer, neighborhoods all over Chicago buzzed with conversations about Sol Polk, his watermelons, and his stores.

The watermelon promotion was followed in another year by the gift of a crate of Washington apples to customers who made a twenty-five dollar purchase. Polk's sent their own trucks out to Washington state to bring back the apples, and the governor of the state publicly thanked Polk Bros. for the huge boost that Polk's gave to the state's orchard industry.

The 1962 "Rose Garden of Your Dreams" promotion was a collaboration of Polk Bros., the "World's Largest Center for Brand Name Appliances," and Jackson & Perkins, the "World's Largest Rose Growers." Polk Bros. made a gift of one dozen two-year-old Jackson & Perkins rose plants with a major purchase. Some 65,000 Polk customers took advantage of the offer. Polk donated another fifteen hundred packages of rose plants to a veterans' hospital.

The way the plan worked was that the customer was given a coupon, imprinted with Sol Polk's signature, to be mailed to Jackson & Perkins for redemption. Lester Bachmann recalls that this simple certificate seemed to lack the drama of, say, a sixty-pound watermelon giveaway.

> Sol recognized right away that there wasn't enough glamour in that presentation. So he rushed out the first or second day and bought thousands of large, colorful plastic watering cans — pink, yellow, green, blue. We took the coupon and put it into a watering can and handed that to the customer.

Polk's overlooked just one other small factor. The rose promotion took place in February. The promise was that the rose bushes would be shipped from the Jackson & Perkins nursery at the appropriate time for planting. But many Chicago customers lived in apartments, without gardens. As the Polks soon discovered, some of these people sent their coupons to friends and relatives living as far away as Florida, Texas, and California, the rose growers' southernmost zone. Jackson & Perkins fulfilled in a timely way. "So we had Polk Bros. rose gardens all over the south before they ever showed up in Chicago," Bachmann says.

In the spring of 1973, Polk offered customers a package of seventeen seed packets, with the potential, they said, to grow one hundred fifty dollars worth of vegetables. Polk Bros. ordered fifty thousand of these seed packages from Vaughan's Seed Company. The rationale, according to the Polk advertisement, was:

> The cost of living is on everyone's mind now. The average household is concerned with the cost of food. This seed promotion is a beautiful way of beating inflation and staying healthy.

Unlike most Polk premiums, the seed package lacked immediate visibility, but that was all right with Sol. He called it a "post-point-of-purchase reminder" of Polk Bros. stores.

*   *   *

Polk Bros. promotions often were public-spirited and tied to civic activities. In these cases, Polk Bros. might ride the coattails of a larger campaign, to commercial advantage, as it did in its brand name cooperative advertising programs. But the effort should not be viewed with cynicism. Polk Bros. put cold hard cash behind these campaigns. Their promise of support for a cause was literally as good as gold.

Illinois Governor William G. Stratton launched Polk Bros.' Smokey Bear campaign, which was organized by David Polk in 1953. The idea was to "spark" fire prevention by enrolling 100,000 Chicago children in the U.S. Department of Agriculture's Junior Forest Ranger program. Application forms were given out in Polk Bros. stores; shoppers making a twenty-five-dollar purchase were given the Smokey Bear doll manufactured by the Ideal Toy Corporation.

When the Chicago Transit Authority and the suburban Regional Transportation Authority launched a campaign to conserve energy and build ridership for public transit, Polk Bros. jumped on board with its "Fare Deal" promotion: Polk promised shoppers who rode the bus a $1.20 cash refund — the price of a round-trip ride with transfer.

The *Chicago Tribune* announced: "Polks to pay CTA fares for shoppers." A *Sun-Times* editorial paraphrased the 1950s line, "What's good for General Motors is good for America," proclaiming, "What's good for Polk Bros. is good for the Regional Transportation Authority." Congressman Frank Annunzio took the idea to the floor of the U.S. House of Representatives. The *Sun-Times* summed up the Fare Deal idea as "a great way to draw customers for Polk Bros. and a great way to draw rides for public transit. Other stores should follow the Polk Bros. 'Fare Deal' example."

Polk's commitment to the plan included $100,000 budgeted for advertising that would encourage people to save energy by using public transportation. Sol was candid, and characteristically expansive, in discussing his intent. He told participants in a press conference, "If this doesn't increase my business by twenty percent, I'll give everyone in this room a free smoke alarm." He told reporters that he was not concerned by the possibility that non-shoppers might come into a Polk store just to collect a refund.

> This is a great country and what you've gotta do is take chances. I believe that if you come to a Polk Bros. store and just look at our merchandise, we'll show you something there you need.

When Alaska and Hawaii joined the Union, Polk Bros. gave Chicago business leaders fifty-star flags that had flown over the U.S. Capitol Building. When the U.S. launched its first earth-orbiting satellite, Polk Bros. offered customers world globes as a premium. When American astronaut Neil Armstrong stepped onto the moon, Polk Bros. distributed forty thousand Rand McNally maps of the moon.

Polk Bros.' promotional activities often were directed toward educational ends. On one occasion, Sol Polk took one hundred Chicago high school seniors by train to the Air Force Academy near Colorado Springs, at his own expense, to inspire them to complete their education and formulate goals for the future.

When he heard of plans for the John F. Kennedy Memorial Library, Sol bought several thousand recordings of the president's speeches and made them available to clubs, churches, and civic organizations that would give or sell them to individuals who pledged a one-dollar donation to the library building fund.

In 1981 Polk's paid for the publication of 200,000 copies of the script of the CBS-TV special "The Marva Collins Story" to be distributed to Chicago area schools. Lewis Lazare, reporting the plan in his *Crain's Chicago Business* column, wrote, "Sol Polk is out to save our country. . . . God bless him, he means it."

The same year, Polk Bros. offered a complete set of the *Random House Encyclopedia* for ten dollars with a major purchase. Seventy thousand sets were distributed, because, Sol said, "I figure every American family should have one." A gilt bookplate affixed to an inside front cover, and signed by Polk Bros., was addressed to "Young Americans Who Explore This Knowledge Source." It informed readers: "We want you to be better able to experience the American dream of prosperity and a better life, just as we have over the years."

The American Heritage Dictionary, another premium, also carried a message from Polk Bros.: "The power of words properly understood and used is mankind's most precious gift."

Sol did not have much time to read himself, but he valued books, particularly those that had an inspirational, motivational, or patriotic message. Sol bought books by the tens of thousands and sent them to friends, business associates, and civic leaders, usually with a letter containing a motivational message of his own.

The books that Polk Bros. gave away over the years were as varied as Sol's tastes were eclectic. The first was *This I Believe* by Edward R. Murrow. He distributed books written by Chicago friends such as advice columnist Ann Landers and radio personality Wally Phillips. His choices were as heterogeneous as the *Better Homes & Gardens Cookbook* and *The Story of the F.B.I.* A small inspirational book, *The Precious Present*, by Spencer Johnson, M.D, was perhaps Polk's most popular gift book.

Sol Polk wore his patriotism on his sleeve. As Sol often said to his friend, advertising executive Jack Leonard, "Aren't you glad our parents didn't miss the boat?" Facsimile copies of the Declaration of Independence were a favorite giveaway. In 1963 Polk Bros. packaged facsimiles of historic documents — including the Declaration of Independence, the Bill of Rights, and the Gettysburg Address — as a gift set they called "The Liberty Collection." The accompanying message from Polk Bros. read in part:

> These basic documents form the cornerstone of the American way of life and guarantee to every citizen the greatest freedoms of any country on earth. Nowhere in the World does a person have a better opportunity to pursue his goals and achieve his ambitions.

In 1981 Polk Bros. joined the U.S. Chamber of Commerce in a campaign inspired by the Reagan Administration, urging American business to a new spirit of enterprise. The theme was, "Let's Rebuild America in the '80s — We Can Do It Together."

Polk Bros. spent $25,000 on two hundred "Rebuild America" billboards to be placed throughout the Chicago area. Sol sent out four thousand letters to suppliers and other retailers urging support for the campaign. Polk Bros.

stores were saturated with banners and signs bearing the "Rebuild" theme and the stars and stripes logo. Polk Bros. staffers breathed a sigh of relief when those signs went up. As Howard Polk says, "We knew we wouldn't have to change those signs for another ten years." He adds, "And, by god, that is what happened. They didn't come down until January 1, 1990."

For some reason, known perhaps only to himself, Sol chose to promote the theme with a beach towel premium and imprinted tee shirts. In 1981 he gave out twenty-thousand beach towels printed with the "Let's Rebuild America in the '80s" message. Non-swimmers, he pragmatically suggested, could use the towel as an exercise mat.

*   *   *

Polk Bros.' first really big promotional offer was Christmas trees. The idea came about in 1953 when Sol Polk and Morrie Polk acquired freight car loads of lush and fragrant Scotch pine trees from a Canadian grower. The concept was brilliant, linking the excitement of a family Christmas-time purchase of a major appliance to the ceremony of selecting the tree, courtesy of Polk Bros.

That year, and during the holiday season for several years thereafter, every Polk Bros. parking lot was turned into a Christmas tree lot. When the customer and his family had made their purchase from the Polk Bros. sales floor, they were invited to step outside to select their ten-foot Christmas tree. It goes without saying that these families were only too happy to tell neighbors how they got their tree at Polk Bros.

In the late 1950s aluminum trees became the vogue. Polk entered into an agreement with a partner in a company called Tomar Industries to manufacture them. In 1960, Polk Bros. distributed thirty thousand of these trees within a one-month period. The aluminum tree retailed for seventeen dollars. Polk customers got theirs for five dollars as a premium with a major purchase. Aluminum trees became so popular so quickly that the following year Chicago nurserymen reported a glut in the market for live, green trees.

In 1965, when the pendulum of public taste shifted back to green, Polk was ready with the Imperial Christmas Tree, a seven-foot plastic, flameproof, imitation balsam, complete with stand, and offered it for five dollars with a major purchase.

But for sheer staying power, not even Polk Bros. could match again the effect on the buying public of its mid-1960s Santa Claus promotion. Thirty years after their first appearance, Polk's lighted plastic Santa Claus figures still emerge from the attics at Christmas time to decorate lawns and rooftops throughout the Chicago area.

This promotion was launched in 1962 when Polk Bros. rolled out sixty-thousand "Jolly Super Santa Clauses" (and two hundred thousand more in years come) as a premium available for five dollars to customers who made a major purchase at Polk Bros. This "Holiday Special" was widely advertised in newspapers and on television, but was made even more visible by the fact that the Santa figure, at five feet, three inches tall, was never boxed or delivered. It had to be hauled home, as is. The same was true of the red-capped Polk Super Snowman that came along a year or two later.

Saturday Evening Post writer Roul Tunley wrote in 1965 that "the sight of people all over town lugging king-size Santas is one which Chicago could not easily ignore." He adds:

> Its impact on the city can be summed up in the remark of a girl of six whose father had taken his Santa Claus home, put a light in it and set it up on the front lawn. When he had finished, he turned triumphantly to his small daughter and asked, "Do you know who that is?"
>
> Without hesitation, the girl replied, "Sure! That's Sol Polk!"

14

Advertising

"What we need is more advertising, more promotion and better distribution to bring prices down, down, down, and customer interest up, up, up."
— Sol Polk

"I can't tell you if Sol Polk was about enhancing the world or manipulating people. But he invented the idea that you're not selling dishwashers — you're selling time to be together. This today is a cornerstone of marketing."
— E. Richard Polk

Television made Polk Bros. a household name. The spectacular Polk promotions drew shoppers to Polk stores by the tens of thousands. But the glue that held it all together was the relentless tide of ink that Polk Bros. poured into newspaper advertising.

Polk Bros. went into print advertising in the early 1940s with a few small items placed in the classified pages of neighborhood papers. In 1963, when the company opened its eleventh and twelfth stores, Polk backed up the expansion program with 1.1 million lines of advertising. By 1967, the company was running more than two million lines of newspaper advertising annually, carried in the four major Chicago papers and any number of suburban and community newspapers.

When the century-old *Chicago Daily News* said farewell to the city, Polk Bros. saturated the last edition — Saturday, March 4, 1978 — with full-page Polk Bros. advertisements. Sol Polk's reasoning was that it gave more bang for the buck. The last edition, he figured, correctly, would sell out and would have long shelf life as a collector's item.

Print was the perfect medium for Sol Polk to preach his basic message. The themes remained consistent over a period of more than fifty years: Labor-saving appliances and the wonders of home electronics strengthen the American family, and mass sales of these products support the American economy.

Slogans used and reused over the years were variations on these themes: You Haven't Shopped Until You've Shopped at Polk's; In Our Business, the Customer is King; Shopping at Polk Bros. Is a Family Affair; People Who Have Are Happy People; and Strike a Blow for America.

The primary purpose of newspaper advertising, of course, was to draw customers into the store and keep the merchandise turning at a high velocity. Students of communications and the advertising arts today might groan over the content and style of Polk Bros. display ads. But no one could argue with the bottom line. The fact remains: they worked.

Polk's frequently made use of long-copy ads, with an editorial quality. Many of these are memorable. The standard Polk Bros. advertisement, however, was a big, cluttered display ad, featuring the Polk logo and the logos of famous name manufacturers. Sol made sure that as much information as possible was packed into these full-page ads. "Why would you want 'white space' in an ad," he argued. "We're **paying** for that space!"

The basic pitch was built around the promise of the famous "Polk Price," and the formula seldom varied. Polk Bros. ads promised the **lowest prices** on the **largest selection** of nationally advertised brands. To add value, "Polk Extras" were always cited. These included king-size trade-ins, double warranties, free overnight delivery, free installation, free removal of old appliances, and special premiums with a major purchase.

*   *   *

Easing the housewife's work load was an article of faith for Polk Bros. and a recurring theme in Polk advertising. Long before McDonald's restaurant chain urged Dad to "Give Mom a Break Today," Polk Bros. equated labor-saving appliances with precious time saved for the homemaker to spend with her family. The gift of a new appliance, Polk Bros. did not hesitate to suggest, was a gift of love.

Nowhere was this more evident than in Polk Bros.' promotion of the automatic dishwasher. Dishwashers were an altogether new product when they came onto the market in 1947, and Polk Bros., with the first General Electric model, was the first Chicago dealer to carry it.

Manufacturers and retailers alike soon found that dishwashers were a hard sell. Consumer research conducted by Westinghouse indicated, according to journalist and historian David Halberstam, that "women were wary of buying dishwashers because the modern kitchen had become so automated that they feared if they stopped doing the dishes by hand, they would lose their last toehold in the kitchen and husbands would start wondering if they needed wives at all."

On a more practical level, women were reluctant to make a major purchasing decision in favor of a dishwasher because they were skeptical about the technology. They believed, with some justification, that an automatic dishwasher could not get dishes really clean. Polk Bros. addressed that concern by placing portable dishwashers in the home on a month-to-month rental basis.

Manufacturers' own advertising of electric dishwashers had disappointing results. Market saturation remained low through the mid-1950s. And prices remained relatively high, ranging from three hundred twenty-five dollars to more than five hundred dollars for the GE, Hotpoint, and Westinghouse models that Polk Bros. carried. To move dishwashers, Polk's fell back on a tried-and-true strategy. Their own ad campaign targeted not Mrs. Consumer but her loving husband.

Copy created by Polk consultant Dwight Bombach tells the story. The headline itself was a grabber:

Free: Two Weeks A Year

Experts in such matters say the average homemaker spends two hours a day washing dishes by hand.

But they also say that the lucky lady with an electric dishwasher spends just half as much time. (And doesn't have to worry about dishpan hands, either!)

Let's see — one hour a day saved makes thirty hours a month, makes 360 hours a year. That's about two weeks' worth of hours a year, saved for mom by an electric dishwasher.

At this point we might say, "Give mom a two weeks' vacation from dishes with a new dishwasher from Polk's." But we won't. Because actually you give her a lot more than that.

Dishwashing time usually falls right in the middle of **family** time — when the kids are home and during the few hours when dad is around. The dishwasher gives a woman an extra hour a day with the people she loves most — her family. And vice versa.

"Giving Mom a Break," in the minds of the Polk brothers did not offer women complete emancipation from household duties. Moms still had their traditional roles. A 1957 pitch for portable television sets, for example, reminded dad: "It's sort of comforting to know mom can cook dinner and patch clothes while watching TV with the family on the patio. All she needs is an electric outlet and a few portable appliances." (Returning to a familiar theme, the copy reminds readers: "We're all for anything that holds the family together, even if it's only an extension cord.")

Similarly, an ad for automatic washing equipment promises to ease the homemaker's wash day burden, but adds this rationale: "She can do a big washing and still look fresh and pretty when Dad comes in the door. (Chances are, he gets a better supper, besides!)"

Sol articulated his philosophy in a 1955 profile in *Fortune* magazine:

> It should be unlawful for women to work in the home when they can have mechanical appliances! It is definitely unfair to our future generations to take a woman today and have her, when she finishes her washing, go into the back yard in the mud and hang up clothes. It is wrong because it weakens her body! It tires her! It doesn't give her the necessary time that she must spend with her children!

It may stretch a point to suggest that the image of his own mother, Yetta, laboring over a coal stove to heat water and cook for a family of eight, haunted Sol. But the point is not stretched very far. Polk Bros.' ads returned again and again to the theme of rescuing the mother from hard, emaciating labor. References to an older generation often were quite explicit:

> Our great-grandmothers — even our **mothers** — worked like drudges in the kitchen. No wonder they were worn out every night. A modern kitchen must add years to a woman's life.

*   *   *

Earl Lifshey, a long-time friend of the Polks who became known as the dean of the home furnishings columnists, commented in print from time to time on the ideological underpinnings of Sol's passion for appliances, including the ideas that popped up so often in Polk advertising:

> Sol Polk is convinced that anyone in the home electronics and appliance business should take the greatest personal pride in what they are doing, not from a monetary standpoint, but rather in the contribution they are making in providing people with the things that help make for a better life.

"I am a vendor of happiness," Sol himself often proclaimed, "enabling people to enjoy their American heritage." Sol was never embarrassed by his unabashed patriotic fervor, sometimes describing himself as "the corniest guy around."

In this respect, Polk Bros. ads often were quite topical, riding the publicity attached to a local or national newsworthy event. And they often were quite political. Sol, particularly in the later years, seldom missed an opportunity to make a patriotic comment or a pitch for the free-enterprise system.

These ads, however public-spirited, did not lose sight of the point — which was to promote Polk Bros. and the merchandise it offered. For example, when the United States launched its first orbiting satellite, Polk Bros. congratulated the Chicago electronics' firms that had contributed to the research, adding this note:

> There's nothing from Polk Bros. out there in space. But at least we are selling the brands that help hire the scientists who make the parts that go into the rockets that launched the satellite. A small and distant claim to fame perhaps — but we're proud of it.

Even before Richard Nixon confronted Nikita Khrushchev in the highly publicized Moscow "Kitchen Debate," Polk Bros. came up with the idea, cleverly phrased, that our refrigerators might "end cold wars" and our ranges "melt the iron curtain," if only "Mrs. Russky of Moscow" could see for herself the selection of appliances that American housewives had to choose from when they shopped at Polk Bros. The ad suggested:

> We're so intrigued with the diplomatic possibilities, we'd like to volunteer our services. If someone in the State Department can arrange it, we'll charter a plane to bring a load of Soviet homemakers in for an eye-opening weekend in Chicago. And we'll pick up the tab.

When fears of a "runaway inflation" such as that which accompanied the Korean conflict swept the country, Polk Bros. rushed into print with an elaboration of Sol Polk's favorite economic maxim:

> **Buyers must shop wisely** — getting the most value possible for each dollar. And **sellers must sell more efficiently**, so we can sell more good products at the lowest possible prices. Greater efficiency in government . . . in production . . . and in marketing. These are tools we all must wield together, to make America strong in defense **and** in economy.

A Polk commentary, re-printed frequently, made the point more succinctly:

> Buying doesn't bring inflation, it brings prosperity. What brings inflation is **buying at inflated prices**. . . . So, in our humble way, we believe we are helping combat inflation, at Polk's, by **deflating** prices.

*   *   *

A remarkable aspect of Polk Bros.' advertising is that even when the budget ran into the millions of dollars annually, almost all of the company's advertising and public relations activity was created, coordinated, and sold in-house by regular Polk Bros. employees. Despite the striking success of their efforts, the people who did Polk's advertising continued to claim over the years that they were mere amateurs still "learning on the job."

Chief among these were Lester Bachmann, who coordinated creative work and negotiated cooperative advertising contracts and media buys, and Georgia Rice, who managed the small ad department staff and supervised production and scheduling of the literally hundreds of Polk Bros. ads aired or printed every week. Georgia also handled the advertising budget, including payments and co-op billings, and headed up the very active direct mail department. This was only part of Georgia Rice's responsibilities. Like Lester Bachmann, she wore many hats. Her title, insofar as anyone at Polk Bros. had a title, was Assistant to the President.

Georgia Rice spent virtually all of her forty-year business career with Polk Bros. As one of Sol's first non-family employees, she filled a multitude of roles as the business grew, including establishment of Polk Bros.' customer service department and its huge order department. Known as "Miss Rice" in the business world and as "Georgie" in the office, Georgia had been talked into taking a job as a secretary at Central Appliance and Furniture when Sol returned from the service in 1946.

Georgia's affinity to Polk Bros. seemed almost foreordained. She was a native-born Chicagoan, of Ukrainian descent like the Polk family. For business reasons, she changed her name from Hrycyk (the "H" was silent) to its phonetic equivalent "Rice" soon after she started working at Polk's. Like Sol, Georgia was a night person, ambitious, enormously capable, career-driven, and seemingly disinclined toward marriage.

A 1962 newspaper profile, in a reference to Polk Bros.' advertising budget, described Georgia Rice as "one of the few women in the nation who spends more than a million dollars a year." It continued:

> As assistant to president Sol Polk, she is the American counterpart of Roberta Lund, the English "Girl Friday" to Paul Getty, the world's richest man. Georgia takes care of many details for [Sol] Polk that have nothing to do with advertising. She is always in touch with him, either by phone or in person.

The writer, somewhat suggestively, went on to describe Georgia as a trim, blue-eyed, brunette "bachelor girl" who dressed conservatively in the office but preferred "more feminine fashions for social occasions." The slant of the article was appropriate for a time when strong, independent women in business were supposed to take on the coloration of "the woman behind the man." When asked to comment on her business philosophy, Georgia played the part: "Always be willing to let the men in the company take credit for accomplishments. Any girl in business who hasn't learned that is headed for disaster."

This kind of copy, however, could not have done much to quell rumors within the company of a romantic liaison between Georgia and Sol. That may have been the appearance, but it very likely was not the fact. There is no doubt, however, that the association was a devoted one. In the last decade of his life, Georgia allowed Sol to move into the downstairs unit of her two-flat apartment. This period, when she took care of his meals and tended to some of his medical needs, was stressful for both of them.

*   *   *

Polk Bros. had good reasons for producing its own advertising and doing its own media buys. Not the least of these was cost. Sol would see no advantage in paying an agency creative fee and service fee, plus commission, if, in the Polk tradition, "we can do it ourselves." All that was needed was a small group of talented, dedicated people willing to make heroic efforts and able to drive themselves to the point of exhaustion.

Another reason was far more practical. Polk Bros. was a fast-paced and promotionally aggressive business. The constantly changing strategies and management directives, together with the need to move quickly to gain competitive price advantages and to take advantage of such factors as changes in the weather demanded rapid response with virtually no turn-around time. This was particularly true for radio advertising. As was the case with its live television ads, Polk radio scripts often were written or rewritten hours, even minutes, before air time.

Sol recognized that potential economic and accounting advantages could be gained when media buys were placed through an agency — provided Polk Bros. owned the agency. At this point, he created a dual-purpose division called Incentive Planners which functioned as both an in-house advertising agency and an outlet for Polk Bros. corporate gifts and premiums department.

*   *   *

An incidental advantage accrued to Polk Bros.' "do it ourselves" policy. The excitement and spontaneity generated around the company's eleventh-hour, shoot-from-the-hip advertising style attracted an informal brain trust of highly skilled, for the most part unpaid, advisers.

Among these was the fabled Leo Burnett, founder of the company that in the 1950s became the hottest advertising agency in the country. Polk Bros. was never a Leo Burnett client, but Burnett himself was a close friend to Sol Polk.

The two shared many traits, including the determination of both to keep their multi-million-dollar businesses based in Chicago. Like Sol, Leo Burnett worked seven days a week and took only Christmas day off. He eschewed the highbrow sophistication of his New York counterparts and kept a file on his desk called "Corny Language" in which he collected the colloquial Americanisms that characterized Burnett copy.

Whether Leo Burnett picked Sol Polk's brain or the other way around is an open question. Clearly, Burnett, who once said, "I like to imagine that we Chicago ad-makers are all working stiffs," openly admired the Polk brothers' blue-collar, down-home style.

The Lonely Maytag Repairman — the longest running advertising theme in television history — was a product of Leo Burnett's personal relationship with Sol Polk. Lester Bachmann relates the circumstances:

> Leo Burnett called Sol and said they were making a bid for the Maytag account but they didn't know anything about washing machines. Leo had a psychologist on his staff, and he said, "I want you to put him on the floor as a salesman, but don't let anyone know who he is. I want to find out how and why women buy washing machines."

Maytag, Bachmann notes, had an excellent reputation for their wringer washers, but the company was one of the last of the major manufacturers to go into automatic washers. This gave them the benefit of others' experience — and they used it.

> The man they put on our sales floor turned out to be a hell of a good salesman. I wish we could have afforded him. What he learned was that women's primary concern about automatic washers, either from their own experience or from a neighbor's experience, was service problems.

Lester Bachmann recalls that Leo Burnett came back to Sol Polk and asked him what was the most expensive model Maytag made.

> He said, "I'll pay you double whatever that machine costs if you'll guarantee to keep it running, with no service problems." And that's where "Old Lonely," the Maytag repairman, came from.

The Old Lonely claim was a valid one. In a sample of 76,000 washing machines purchased between 1955 and 1962, *Consumer Reports* identified two brands with a significantly lower number of service calls than all other major brands. One of these was Maytag. The other, Sol would have been loathe to acknowledge, was Kenmore, the Sears brand. The character actor Jessie White, who played the Maytag repairman, was not at all lonely, Bachmann recalls. White was a frequent visitor at Polk Bros.

At least two members of the advertising brain trust were employed intermittently by Polk Bros. Alan Kent, a Leo Burnett writer from New York, worked nights selling hard goods at Polk as a way of learning how a retail business worked. Jack Pettersen, a veteran of advertising campaigns done for General Electric Supply Corporation, Motorola, and Norge, worked full time for Polk Bros. in 1954 and 1955 in the capacity of merchandising manager.

Lester Bachmann explains the company's informal association with top advertising talent in this way: "We had made friends over the years with people in advertising agencies and from time to time they would come in and sit around and talk." Even after Jack Pettersen left Polk Bros. to establish his own agency, he continued to advise and consult on Polk campaigns. "Sometimes I would go down to his office, but usually he came in to see us. Sol depended on Jack to be our sounding board," Bachmann remembers.

> Jack and [copy writer] Bob Moore and I would kick ideas around on a Saturday morning or a Sunday

morning. One of them would come up with a headline idea and they'd try out some rough copy. We'd
get half a dozen ideas in a day. Five we would throw
out, and one we would use.

Leo Burnett writer Dwight Bombach moonlighted five
years for Sol Polk and never sent a bill. And Bombach was
high-priced talent. In the same period, he served as creative
director for such stellar Burnett agency accounts as All State,
Motorola, Chrysler, the Harris Bank, and Brown's Shoe Company, which manufactured the Buster Brown and Air Step
lines.

Bombach wrote a series of anecdotal, conversational
columns for Polk Bros. that began running in the *Chicago
Daily Tribune* and the *Chicago Daily News* in the fall of 1957 as
paid advertisements. Bombach calls the series the "One By
One" columns, a reference to the Polk promise that, while
merchandise was bought by the carload, customers were
served "one by one."

The format was engaging. The columns typically were
headed with a cartoon and a catchy headline, such as: "Don't
let rugs throw you!" (followed by copy explaining how Polk
Bros. "carpeting tailors" measure a home for carpeting) or
"old family retainer" (reminding readers that a third of the refrigerators in America were ten years old or older).

Bombach, who lived in a northern suburb and worked
out of the Leo Burnett headquarters in the London Guarantee Building in Chicago, wrote the popular column while riding the commuter train. ("It was just the right length to write
between Barrington and the downtown station," Bombach
says.) A number of these columns were so successful — or so
close to the heart of Sol Polk — that they were re-run from
time to time over the years. One such classic Polk pitch was
headlined "Wanted: Railroad Presidents":

Every boy should be a railroad president. And every
father should be a Chairman of the Board. One of

the surest ways we know to get a boy and his dad on
the track to lifelong partnership is to give them both
an electric train . . . We've outfitted thousands of
family railroads at Polk Brothers . . .

Dwight Bombach met Sol Polk in 1954 when copy writer
Alan Kent asked Bombach to collaborate with him in developing an ad announcing the opening of Polk Bros.' new store
at 85th and Cottage Grove Avenue. Bombach remembers:

Alan told me about this guy, Sol, and said, "You
know, they are going to open their first store outside
the Central Avenue area. Sol wants to do full-page
newspaper opening ads. He wants something great."

I was kind of scared about meeting this guy, but
actually Sol was running scared, too, in a way. He
was at heart a Central Avenue, West Side, guy. The
new South Side store was a big jump for them.

Kent and Bombach took six layouts and copy for six ads
to a meeting with Sol at the Sparga restaurant, around the
corner from Polk City.

We sat around the table and presented the ads.
When we came to one ad, "The family that just
moved in," Sol's eyes moistened. He loved it so. He
said, "Well, how much do I owe you?" Something
like that. We were prepared for that.

We had an envelope with a note inside. The envelope said that our creative charge for the work
would be fifteen hundred dollars. I think Sol was a
little surprised by that. I remember him holding the
envelope up and showing it to others so they could
share his reaction.

But down at the bottom of the envelope we had
written, "First open this envelope and look inside."
The note inside said, "But we don't want to be paid

at all. This is a housewarming gift to Polk Bros." It just blew him over.

Leo Burnett himself contributed suggestions on the final layout. The ad, with the headline, "Remember when you were the family that just moved in?" was so popular that it was used, with variations, over a period of more than thirty years.

Bombach left Burnett in 1959 to establish his own agency, but he and his family remained close to Sol, Goldie Bachmann Luftig, and Sam and Thelma Polk. Even after his retirement to Phoenix, where he pursued a second career as an author, Bombach stayed in touch with the Polks. Lester Bachmann recalls:

> After Dwight moved to Phoenix, he and I communicated by audio tape. When we had an idea we wanted to use, we'd call Sol in and get on a speaker phone, and the next thing you knew Dwight had roughed an outline of an ad and some words and mailed it to us.

Polk Bros. also had a friend in Herb Baker, president of the Herb Baker and Associates agency. Bachmann asked Baker to brainstorm some ideas for the mid-winter 1961 to 1962 Polk Bros./Jackson & Perkins Co. "Rose Garden of Your Dreams" promotion. The line "Where Else But at Polk Bros.?" came out of the rough copy for that promotion, Bachmann recalls, and Baker's rough layout for the four-color brochure, together with Sol's ringing presentation, sold C. H. Perkins on the concept.

*   *   *

Polk Bros. did not limit its print advertising to newspapers. The company made extensive use of tie-ins with brand-name advertising that appeared in the pages of national magazines, such as *Good Housekeeping* and *Ladies' Home Jour-*

nal. Sol Polk, the former neighborhood newsboy, always had a special place in his heart for the venerable *Saturday Evening Post.* When the *Post* began accepting zoned, or regional, advertising, Polk Bros. took out a series of ads of its own. The first of these long-copy advertisements appeared in the November 26, 1960, issue.

The Polks also had a special relationship with *Life* magazine, and later with *Sports Illustrated,* through a longstanding friendship with Time Inc. executive Jack Leonard. Sam Polk and Lester Bachmann met Leonard when the three traveled on the same train to San Francisco to attend a General Electric sales conference. Leonard at that time managed the huge General Electric advertising account for *Life*, a responsibility he kept even after he was promoted to the post of Midwest manager for *Sports Illustrated.* Jack remembers his own first meeting with Sol:

> Sam had told me to come on out to the store and meet his brother. This must have been 1949. I'll never forget my first sight of Sol. He was coming down the stairs at 2850 North Central. He was wearing a snap brim hat, a jacket with the biggest, widest lapels you've ever seen, and he had cigarettes going a mile a minute. A real West Side kind of guy. Later on, he gave up the hat and ditched the cigarettes and got himself a good tailor. He was sharp, very sharp.

Polk Bros. and *Life* magazine had an understanding over the years that worked to everyone's benefit: Polk's itself never bought a line of advertising space in *Life*. But the national manufacturers whose products Polk Bros. carried did. Polk's used these ads to promote national brands, and the sales volume that Polk Bros. delivered, in turn, sold more ad lines for *Life*.

In his book, *The Time of My Life*, Jack Leonard recounts an event illustrating the way these reciprocal relationships worked. He writes that Sol, headed for meetings at the General Electric headquarters in Louisville, suggested that Leonard accompany him. Sol wanted to support Jack in his role as manager of the GE advertising account with *Life*. Sol's plan was that Jack would "just happen" to pass by the office where Sol was meeting with Chuck Reiger, vice-president of the appliance division at GE, so Sol could call him in. "You know, Chuck," Sol said, "I couldn't live without your advertising in *Life* magazine. . . . At my store from door to door, the place is filled with *Life* logos and posters." Leonard writes:

> That's all I needed. The biggest GE dealer in America is patting *Life* magazine on the back. Obviously, that endorsement from Sol Polk helped to cement *Life*'s relationship with GE for many more years. That's the kind of guy Sol Polk was.

When *Life* magazine celebrated its twenty-fifth anniversary in 1961, Polk Bros. ran a full-page advertisement in the *Chicago Tribune* congratulating *Life* on national advertising placed in the magazine over the years by more than eighty "famous brand" manufacturers whose products were carried at Polk Bros.

The headline read: "Thanks, *Life*, for starting an American Revolution!" The lead copy established the link, as Sol saw it, between the magazine, Polk Bros., and the reader:

> It may seem a bit "cheeky" for a local storekeeper to congratulate America's biggest, most high-powered magazine. But *Life* helped start a **good** revolution 25 years ago that's changed **your** life. **The volume of demand *Life* created helped us cut traditional markups on appliances and furniture practically in half.** As a consumer, that's money in your pocket. So we're proud to have had a hand in the revolution!

The concept was imaginative, declaring that when Polk Bros. opened their first store in 1935 they needed a "Super

Salesman" to help them "sell appliances and furniture at less cost than ever before." Sol said,

> We found our "salesman" at the newsstand. It was an exciting new magazine called *Life*. . . . Every week more new products for the home were introduced by this great new salesman. Every week more people wanted more things.

The long-copy ad has just one illustration, and it is an interesting one. This is a photograph depicting a woman lifting the roof off what appears to be a model of the main Polk City store at 2850 North Central Avenue. The reader is given a birds-eye view into the vast interior of the store, thronged with bustling crowds of shoppers. The hands who held the roof were, in real life, the hands of Miss Georgia Rice. The caption describes Polk Bros. as "A Store As Big As *Life*."

*   *   *

Manufacturers and distributors also made direct contributions to Polk Bros.' advertising budget through the vehicle of cooperative advertising contracts. *Fortune* magazine estimated in the mid-1950s that Polk Bros.' annual budget for advertising was about $1.5 million, against annual sales of something like $40 million. The writer noted, however: "The advertising is virtually all cooperative, with half the outlay, if not more, recovered from distributors and manufacturers."

Cooperative arrangements were not unique to Polk Bros. Advertising expenses were, and are, shared among vendors and dealers in a number of ways. Manufacturers or distributors frequently advertise their brand name products in area newspapers or regional editions of national magazines. This kind of advertising frequently carries the names of dealers that carry the product. In this case, the dealers named may pay some small percentage of the cost.

The terms of a co-op advertising arrangement, on the

other hand, usually are negotiated as part of the sales agreement made between the vendor and the dealer when the merchandise is purchased. Every deal is different, but the general pattern is this: The vendor agrees to commit a percentage of the dollar value of the order to support advertising costs. The practice of giving a percentage, rather than a fixed amount, made co-op advertising deals especially sweet for the high-volume dealer such as Polk Bros. In this situation, the dealer negotiates the highest percentage he can, he then advertises as creatively and efficiently as he is able, and he collects every penny due him.

Generally the media buy is then done through the retailer's advertising agency. The agency, typically, quotes the newspaper's sheet price for the ad. The agency, on its own, however, might negotiate a better price with the newspaper, based on volume of business. Or it might take a standard agency discount offered by the newspaper.

At Polk Bros., co-op advertising agreements were negotiated individually. There was no standard formula. Like all Polk business accounts, the details of these agreements were closely guarded information. It is probable that not even the buyers knew the details of the larger contracts.

Polk Bros. worked through its in-house agency, Incentive Planners. Once an agreement with the vendor was negotiated, Incentive Planners would make the media buys for Polk Bros., take the commissions, and bill the vendors for their share of the sheet price of the ad. Over time, with millions of advertising dollars flowing through the company, the return on advertising contracts could have been considerable.

In recent years, several industries have developed any number of creative variations on the type of co-op deals that Polk Bros. made in the 1950s, 1960s, and 1970s. In some cases, the dealer assumes responsibility for advertising production costs and the vendor picks up the far larger media bills. At the extreme end of the scale — as might be the case with powerhouse retailers such as national chain stores — the manufacturer might pick up one hundred percent of advertis-

ing costs, provided certain conditions are met by the retailer.
Newspapers themselves have even entered into the co-op advertising business, offering to put retailers in touch with co-
op advertisers and handle the paperwork and billing for both
parties.

*　　*　　*

Like other aspects of its business, Polk Bros. never revealed figures indicating what percentage of gross sales went
into advertising. There is little doubt, however, that when it
came to advertising, Polk Bros. always got not only the maximum bang for its buck but also the maximum mix. "We did it
all," says Lester Bachmann. "Radio, television, print, billboards, catalogues, bus placards, word-of-mouth, even sky-
writing."

Bachmann forgets to mention the cartoons. The series,
called "Polk-a-Dots" ran for a short time in *Chicago's American*. Perhaps these were forgettable. A typical panel depicts a
large dog racing along the sidewalk toward a smaller doggy
pal. The caption says,"Oh boy! My owner just bought a big
new famous brand TV set at Polk Bros. He's the swellest
friend a dog ever had!"

Otherwise Polk Bros.' media campaign was persistent
and compelling, spreading out over the metropolitan area like
an omnipresent underground hum. In an average week in the
mid-1960s, Chicagoland was saturated with literally hundreds
of Polk Bros.' one-minute radio spots, carried on ten stations,
plus some seventy-five television commercials.

Polk Bros.' outdoor displays blanketed the Chicago area.
On any given week in the mid-1960s, no fewer than two hundred billboards carried Polk's brand name advertising messages. Similarly, more than four hundred bus placards flashed
the Polk Bros. name up and down every major street and intersection throughout the city and the suburbs, as did the con-
tinuously updated advertising messages displayed on the
panels of Polk's own fleet of more than one hundred orange

and white delivery trucks. Direct mail campaigns, targeted through Polk's own list of more than six hundred thousand names, carried some two million pieces of Polk promotional mail into Chicagoland homes in 1967 alone.

From the day of the first radio ad, run on a small suburban station in 1947, the airways were flooded with Polk Bros. propaganda. One series of ads was called "Happy Folks That Shop at Polk's." For these, on-air talent came cheap. Announcer Bill Hamilton buttonholed customers on the sales floor with questions such as: "What do you like most when you shop at Polk's?" Many of these testimonials were used in TV ads as well, with still photographs of the subjects, snapped by Hamilton, providing the visual element.

Similarly, Polk Bros. was not inclined toward paying professional models. Many Polk employees, and Polk children, even up to the time of the stores' closings in 1992, made their major media debuts in Polk Bros.' print or television advertisements.

A half-century of Polk Bros. print ads constitute a veritable album of Americana in the postwar decades, reflecting changing life-styles, changing styles of dress, and changing values. It's a nostalgic journey, reflecting such domestic milestones as the sectional sofa, the early years of television, the introduction of microwave cooking, and the advent of the VCR.

Polk Bros. ads, together with the stuff of their countless promotions, also represent a catalogue of forty years of American fads and foibles, depicting, as they do, such artifacts as the coonskin cap, the hula hoop, and Hawaiian shirts. Who would otherwise remember such fleeting fancies as that Thor Auto-Magic washing machine which, when the laundry was done, could be reset to wash the dinner dishes? Or the "summer wardrobe" of "miracle fiber" disposable paper dresses? One summer Polk Bros. gave away two hundred thousand of these — twelve to a customer, with the purchase of a Philco appliance or television set.

*   *   *

From the day that Sol Polk hitched his star to nationally advertised brand-name merchandise (at a time when many manufacturers would not even sell to dealers who discounted list prices) he tapped into a virtual gold mine of free (to him) advertising.

National manufacturers and their distributors spent millions of advertising dollars in the postwar period in developing brand-name recognition for major appliances and in building the consumer loyalty that created demand for their products. Polk Bros., by using manufacturers' logos in their own advertising as well as ads produced by the manufacturers themselves, reaped the benefit of this national advertising blitz.

The point was made in a 1955 address to the Association of National Advertisers by *Advertising Age* editor S. R. Bernstein, who used Polk Bros. to illustrate his conclusion:

> Here, I would say, we have the finest flowering of the advertising tree: first the development through advertising of consumer brand acceptance, and then the activation of that acceptance by a type of retailer who is riding the nationally advertised brand's coattails all the way.

Sol was always quick to acknowledge the debt. A statement of Polk Bros. business philosophy that formed the core of many of his speeches states:

> Nationally advertised and nationally known brands have helped build us. Research, engineering, design know-how have given us prestige in the eyes of the potential customer that our name alone could not do. National brands have built us, and we are loyal to those brands that let us use their names.

15

World's Largest Center for Brand-Name Products

"Polk Bros. is the largest independent appliance dealer in the country, with the biggest share of the appliance market in the country."
— **Crain's Chicago Business**, 1981

"Our company was built on the cornerstone of the largest possible selection of national brand products."
— Sol Polk
Home Entertainment Retailing, 1964

The astonishing array of brand-name products found on a Polk Bros.' sales floor ran the gamut from Amana to Zenith. These and most of the famous brands in between, in the words of an editor of *Advertising Age*, were "as well-known as the name of the president of the United States."

Polk Bros. did not hide this light under a bushel. A walk across the parking lot at the Polk City flagship store was a trip into a neon midway where every foot of space over the store's display windows was emblazoned with the logos of Polk's national suppliers: Kelvinator, RCA Victor, Roper, Norelco, Philco, and Necchi, to name a few, all crowned by the megawatt GE emblem blazing over the main entrance.

The parking lot itself was reminiscent of a major league ballpark, where perimeter fences do double-duty as sign boards for highly visible advertising. Instead of beer or auto repair shops, however, Polk Bros.' signs carried the signature names and logos of a multitude of famous appliance and home electronics manufacturers.

*   *   *

The range of brands offered by Polk Bros. was an astonishing accomplishment in its time. The typical appliance dealer of the 1950s and 1960s, limited by traditional franchise agreements, carried the products of no more than one or two nationally known manufacturers. The selection at the giant Sears, Roebuck chain might be even more limited: Sears carried only its own, private label, Coldspot and Kenmore lines.

The Polk brothers, however, by some alchemy of personality, moxie, and sheer buying power, managed in the early years of the business to forge personal relationships and a constellation of franchise agreements that enabled them to link the Polk Bros.' name, in time, to the names and reputations of well over two hundred major manufacturers.

On the face of it, the marriage of brand-name manufacturers to Sol Polk — the father of the modern discount superstores and a leading opponent of manufacturer-supported fair-trade practices — would seem an unlikely alliance. In fact, it was a brilliant match.

The appeal to the customer was apparent. "At Polk Bros.," the company was proud to say, "you'll find every size, every model, every brand of nationally advertised appliances which you can compare side by side." A 1955 advertisement announcing the opening of Polk's 85th and Cottage Grove store summarized the promise. "When we moved in," the ad said,

> We brought the biggest selection of nationally advertised brands ever sold in one store. By anybody. For example, take television. We offer you not just one or two famous brands, but more than fifteen. Take washers, over sixty-six different models. Here at Polk Bros. you can compare the very best brands. All in one store.

Polk Bros. made broad selection a mainstay of its advertising themes, tying the range of choice to Polk's promise of a knowledgeable sales staff offering custom tailored personal service. One ad featured a salesman saying:

> I've got fourteen famous brands of TV here, seventy-six different models. The biggest selection of TV on one floor in America. I don't **have** to fit a family to the set. I can help them pick exactly the right set to fit **them**.

Polk Bros.' aggressive merchandising was equally attractive to suppliers. In the years just after World War II many suppliers refused to sell to Polk Bros., a company that was rapidly gaining a reputation for selling below manufacturers' suggested list price. But it didn't take long for them to realize that this renegade Chicago company, with its garish, even gaudy, appearance, moved product like nobody before or since. Soon enough, even the most rigid holdouts found themselves lining up at 10 p.m. for a chance to meet with Sol Polk and Lester Bachmann at one of their customary midnight buying conferences.

By 1955 Polk Bros. had become the country's foremost dealer in GE, Westinghouse, Norge, Hotpoint, and Whirlpool white goods as well as virtually every major line of television set. In 1964, when fair trade laws were finally overturned, there were nine major brands of washing machines on the market. Polk Bros. already carried eight of them. The ninth was Sears' Kenmore brand.

Polk Bros., in turn, reaped all the benefits of these brand name manufacturers' national and regional advertising campaigns. Polk used manufacturers' advertisements as displays in their stores, they used manufacturer's films liberally in their own prolific television advertising, they jumped aboard manufacturer-underwritten cooperative advertising campaigns, and they participated in brand name advertising tie-ins and promotions.

During a national Frigidaire-Pepsi Cola tie-in, for example, Polk's gave seven cases of Pepsi to every customer who bought a Frigidaire product. Polk's paper dress giveaway was part of a national Philco-Ford promotion. During RCA Victor Week, Polk offered a free antenna set-up to any purchaser of an RCA Victor color television and a ten-record stereo album with the purchase of a Philco home entertainment center.

Polk Bros.' timing was right. Brand names were good for business. They were trusted. People paid more for them. Nationally advertised brands had better margins than private brands. Jeffrey Polk observes:

> Back in the 'fifties, being a consumer was relatively simple. It was a good time for retail, and brand names were very meaningful. If you bought a good brand, you knew it was going to work.

Just as Polk Bros. rode the coattails of national brand-name reputations, so too, friends in the industry looked to Polk Bros., with its command of the important Chicago market, when it came to new product introductions. Sol Polk's support could make the difference between an item that remained a specialty product and an item that had the potential to move into the category of standard merchandising.

When Amana Refrigeration, for example, brought the combination refrigerator-freezer to market in the mid-1950s, Amana chairman George Foerstner came to Sol Polk to seek his blessing. Sol's role, which was definitive, in the introduction of RCA's color television system to American audiences is well known.

Similarly, Polk Bros. was one of the first dealers in the country to carry microwave ovens and to heavily promote the product. Public acceptance came slowly, but by 1985 microwave ovens accounted for one-fourth of all appliance shipments in America. By 1986, microwave ovens had become the fastest selling product in appliance history.

* * *

Polk Bros.' love affair with brand-name products was by no means limited to furniture and major appliances. Small appliances, and other "carry-home" merchandise, had always been a mainstay of the business. Sol Polk, after all, got his start selling Sunbeam electric irons door to door on the Northwest Side of Chicago.

Polk Bros. did a high-volume business in innovative products such as blenders, clock-radios, crock pots, egg cookers, electric knives, hair dryers, ice crushers, popcorn poppers, rotisseries, pop-up toasters, and electric tea kettles. To take the letter "s," as in "sales," as just one example, in the 1950s Polk Bros. sold items as diverse as sandwich grills, scales, sewing machines, shavers, electric sheets, shredders, silverware, slicers, steak knives, sweepers, and soda syphons.

The Polk brothers' cousin Irving Feuerstadt was the buyer for small appliances and gained a national recognition for his work in this field. He managed this department for nearly forty years, from 1945 until his death in 1983. "Irv Feuerstadt was incredibly loyal to the company," Howard Polk says. "He really was 'Mr. Housewares.' He had the reputation of being the top housewares merchandiser in the business."

The company also had an excellent camera department and a quality jewelry department, offering a broad selection of watches, diamonds, sterling silver and high-end gift items. The jewelry department was built up in the early 1950s by Mel Arbeit, whose wife, Diane, was a sister of Irv Feuerstadt's wife, Ruth.

Polk Bros., with its tremendous buying power, was masterful at utilizing carry-home products to generate traffic. In the early years, Polk used its record department for this purpose. The sales floor was arranged with the record department at the back so that shoppers in search of their favorite musical selections would have to pass through the major appliance department to reach their destination.

When theft and shrinkage became a concern, Polk stopped selling records itself and developed the small appliance department as the primary traffic department. Polk Bros.' advertised bargains in small appliances were real; loss-leaders (items sold at or below cost) were common. "When the Mr. Coffee coffee makers came into the market, we sold thousands of them, below cost, to get people into the stores," Howard Polk remembers. Even when small appliances were no longer profitable — with margins squeezed by newer outlets such as catalogue showrooms — Sol Polk continued to devote a significant amount of space to that department.

In the 1980s the electronics department (originally called the radio counter) took over the traffic function. When the video cassette recorder became popular, Polk Bros. generated traffic by selling blank video tapes at or below cost. They later did the same thing with video game cartridges.

*   *   *

Polk Bros.' relationship with its brand-name suppliers was built on mutual admiration. Sol Polk believed that the research and development behind national brand products produced the finest America had to offer. Manufacturers, in turn, saw Polk Bros. not only as the front line of innovative merchandising concepts but as a retailer in day-to-day touch with patterns in consumer demand. It is not surprising that Polk's over the years served as an informal training ground for men who later became leaders in their industries.

Gerald McCarthy, president of the Zenith Sales Co. division of Zenith Electronics Corporation, worked at Polk Bros. nights and weekends during his first years at Zenith. Ross Siragusa, founder of the Admiral Corporation, was a valued supplier and a personal friend to Sol. Ross Siragusa Jr. spent the year following his graduation from Yale University working in Polk Bros.' radio department.

Other future industry leaders established relationships with Polk Bros. in the early stages of their careers. Mark Viken, who worked five years at Polk Bros., became vice-president of the Sony Corporation of America general audio division. Jim Palumbo started at Sony as a sales representative in Chicago, where Polk Bros. was his major account and major training ground. Palumbo later became president of Sony's television division.

In other cases, Polk Bros. salesmen became vendors themselves. Lew Bolus was a salesman and department manager for Polk Bros. before he became a distributor for Fedders. In a more formal way, just as Polk Bros. sent its sales staff to manufacturers' sales and service training programs, manufacturers and distributors often sent promising young executives in groups to Chicago to study Polk Bros.' operations.

Sol Polk also used manufacturers' representatives to great advantage as sales trainers. Howard Haas, a vice-president for Mitchell Manufacturers, makers of window air conditioners, and later president of Sealy Mattress, remembers that a sale to Polk generally meant a stint in the classroom.

> Sol let the vendors do the sales training. It was their job to train the salesmen on how to sell their product. It was well worth the representative's time. When Sol bought something, he bought in great,

great depth. You could count on Polk's word. And they paid on time.

Sol also used vendors as salesmen. The theory was that the vendor would assist the Polk salesman on the floor, demonstrating the product or supporting the sales staff in pointing out special features. Bill Platt, who represented Litton, says,

> If you sold Polk, you had to rep the floor. Sol insisted on it. This way, he had the best qualified people in the world to sell the product. And he didn't have to pay them.

At one time, Platt recalls, the Hoover company had fifty or more people working the Polk Bros. sales floors. The effort appears to have paid off: In the mid-1980s, Polk claimed that "almost half of all households in Chicagoland have bought one or more vacuum cleaners from Polk Bros."

Platt recalls by name more than one salesman who would let the valuable Polk Bros.' business go to other representatives in their company because they didn't want to become forced volunteers on Polk's sales floor. On the other hand, Platt notes, for some representatives, working at Polk Bros. might be a permanent assignment.

> When I was a regional manager for Litton, I had a man who did nothing but work the Highland [Superstores] floor in Detroit, and a man who did nothing but work the Polk Bros. sales floor. We did it for other retailers, but the concept was all Sol's. He originated it in the middle to late 1940s.

*   *   *

As Howard Haas noted, selling Polk Bros. might not have been easy, but it was well worth the wait. The tribulations of getting in to see Sol have been recounted by many vendors over many years. The move of Polk Bros.' headquarters offices out of the old family bedrooms over the store on North Central Avenue to a larger space in Melrose Park did not improve the process. Sol's office, where Polk's million-dollar deals were made, remained chaotic.

Bill Platt remembers:

> Guys would wait in line for days to see Sol and Lester. I once told my wife that if the kids ever asked what their father did, she should tell them he's a "waiter." But this is what you did at Polk's. You did it because the business was good, the volume was excellent, and if you wanted to sell business in Chicago, you had to sell Polk Bros.

Sol didn't do anything without interruptions. There was always a crowd and plenty of commotion. "If you went to a meeting in his office, you could put it on Broadway," says advertising executive Jack Leonard. "The only day that office wasn't cluttered was the first day they moved in."

Physically, the space was crowded and cluttered with memorabilia, samples, posters, commemorative paperweights, and a jumble of potential premiums and the latest promotional items. Portraits of the Polk brothers' immigrant parents, painted from old photographs, were hung behind the conference table Sol used as a desk. Hanging beside them was the Declaration of Independence.

Otherwise, the walls were all but covered with citations and awards, most reflecting Polk Bros.' widespread philanthropic and charitable activities. Among these were the valued Brand Name Retailer of the Year plaques, awarded to Polk Bros. in three separate years by the New York-based Brand Name Foundation; the 1966 Man of the Year award from NARDA, the National Appliance and Radio-TV Dealers Association; and the 1967 Chicago Retailer Merchandiser of the Year.

Sol did not, however, treat his office as a shrine to his own or his company's achievements. Lester Bachmann remembers that "Sol would slap things up on his wall at random, whatever he was interested in at the time. But he always had the Declaration of Independence up there." Sol also plastered the administrative offices and the walls of Polk Bros.' stores with the patriotic messages, motivational slogans, and homilies of which he was so fond. It was a changing panorama, but this one remained: "Work Hard. Think Big. Buy More. Live Better. Shop at Polk's."

Every major deal went through Sol and Lester Bachmann, Polk's principal purchasing agent. Even when Polk Bros.' yearly volume approached the $100-million mark, the company had no more than half a dozen primary buyers: carpeting; furniture; outdoor furniture and seasonal goods; major appliances; small appliances; and electronics, split between audio and video.

The boss did not make the buyers' job easy. Sol's characteristic response to most deals was to send the Polk man back to the table with that standard instruction: "See if you can get it for less." A supplier who did business with Polk Bros. over a period of many years says it wasn't any easier on the vendor's side: "With Sol, working the deal was the main thing: You had to let him beat you to death." In the later years of the business, buyers learned to "leave something for Lester," meaning that they would allow a little negotiating room for the last, final deal.

When the deal was done, the transaction was often made with lightning speed, closed on the strength of a word and a handshake. Sol moved fast. Lester, on the other hand, took a painstaking approach. A prodigious note taker, he had the kind of mind that was able to re-create the details of a conversation years after the fact. If a caricaturist were to do a portrait of the two of them at work, Sol would be a churning dynamo, all words and motion; Lester would be imperturbable, sitting back with his signature bow-tie, a pipe, and a notebook. "They were the perfect team," Howard Polk says.

In the middle of a meeting where a large deal was being negotiated, Sol would toss the ball to Lester. Lester would sit there, drawing on his pipe, not saying anything. The room would fall silent. Sol pumped them up and then turned to Lester to slow the game down. Everybody would be waiting for Lester to speak. He was masterful. Sol needed a guy like Lester to implement.

* * *

Sol Polk was a merchandising genius — on that point all agree. But he could also be a hard man to deal with. A montage of opinion from a cross-section of those who knew him gives a picture of an enormously persuasive, paradoxical, brilliant, and sometimes quite unlovable man:

> Some people loved him, some people liked him, some people hated him. But everybody respected him. . . . What motivated Sol was doing the deal, the excitement of the deal. His brilliance was marketing, but his instinct was for using, for manipulating, people . . .
>
> Crackpot or genius? He was both. Sol was about making a deal, getting an edge, having control. . . . He was definitely on the genius level, but they say Einstein couldn't do simple math. That's where Lester and the brothers came in. He needed them for the mechanics, the process. . . .
>
> He would ask for the planet, the entire planetary system, but he would settle for a piece of the moon. He would ask questions to which only he knew the answer. He made demands of people that could never be fulfilled. . . . If Sol wanted your eye teeth, he'd get them, and you'd end up thinking he'd done you a favor. . . .
>
> To Sol, there were only two classes of people in

the world. You either worked for him or you were a customer. If you worked for him, he controlled you — and he wanted everybody to work for him.

Sol was a hero. There's no question in my mind that he was a hero to the Chicago community. To his peers in the industry he was a hero. And to a nephew growing up, he certainly was a hero. Oh, he did have an ability to intimidate. . . . He was a legendary Chicagoan. The best of the best.

My view of Sol? I always saw him as possibly a harmless maniac. . . . The guy was so alien. There was nobody like him. He might just have dropped down off a space ship. Nobody can prove that he didn't.

Sol Polk was not the kind of executive to unwind at home after work. In fact, he seldom had much of a home. At various times, he lived in a residential hotel; he had a three-room, sparsely furnished apartment; and he had rooms at his club. Frequently he simply stayed at the office, sleeping on a cot in a back room.

But Sol did not spend all his time in the office either. Sol's recreation — an extension of his life at the store — came in the form of business conventions and trade shows, which he attended with zeal, often staying on his feet for twenty hours at a time. Roberta Lewis remembers that "Sol went to all the shows: gift shows, trade shows, builders' shows — anything that was happening. His mind was always working, and he was always collecting ideas."

While administrative staff was trained not to acknowledge or publicize the absence of any of the brothers from the store, Sol, in fact, was a frequent flyer. According to Howard Polk,

One day he'd get up and say, "I'm going to Vegas," or "I'm going to L.A. to see a new store there." And he'd be gone. Just like that. He was single. He was free as a bird. He didn't have to answer to anybody.

Lester Bachmann tells a story about a trip Sol made to the 1960 Democratic Party Convention in Los Angeles. Following John F. Kennedy's speech accepting the party's nomination, Sol made a dash for the airport.

> From Los Angeles, it's all eastern traffic. He went up to the counter with no reservations and asked for the next plane to Chicago. They all laughed at him. He said, "Well, where is the next plane going to?"
>
> And they said, "Hawaii."
>
> He said, "Fine, I'll take it." And he flew to Hawaii, and then back to Chicago. So that's how fluid he was.

People who occasionally traveled with Sol were not eager to repeat the experience. Sol never rested. Bill Platt, a sales representative and family friend who sometimes attended trade shows with Sol, remembers that Sol had a creative way of eluding the crush of vendors eager to meet and do business with him:

> When I traveled with him, he would introduce me as Sol Polk. He'd say, "You ought to come work for this guy here." I don't know if he did this with other people. But he used to pawn me off as Sol.
>
> He'd show me how to work the shows. You get the layout, he'd say, and then you work on the diagonal. So when everybody else was going this way, he would be going that way. He said that was how to beat the crowd around the room.

*   *   *

Sol Polk had two natural enemies. One was the weather, which if it was good kept people outside working in their gar-

dens. Or, if it was bad tended also to keep people away from
Sol Polk's stores. The other enemy was Sears. The weather
Sol could not do much about. Sears was another matter.

In 1967, the trade paper *Home Furnishings Daily* commented: "If it weren't for Polk's, the slogan 'Sears has everything' would be virtually true." When it came to hard goods,
Polk Bros. did have everything. And the company used its
brand-name advantage to put pressure on the giant Sears,
Roebuck conglomerate. The word used to be: "Go to Sears
and look at the Kenmore, and then come to Polk Bros. and
look at everything else."

Sears, with thirty-two stores in the Chicago metropolitan
area, led in market share in seven of nine major appliance categories surveyed in 1966 — but not by much. Polk Bros., with
half as many stores, ran a close second in all these categories,
and surpassed Sears in two others: room air conditioners and
dishwashers.

Being second, even to Sears, in anything, was just not
good enough for Sol Polk. He created a battlefield mentality
among his salesmen, exhorting the troops to go the extra mile
and then some to outsell Sears. As one salesman remembers it,
the situation amounted to not much more than psychological
warfare, but it was motivating:

> Actually, we were peanuts compared to Sears, Roe-
> buck. But in Chicago it was all scream and tussle.
> And so, this was the great enemy — and we were out
> there to show them up. That was the psychology of
> the thing. We've got to beat out Sears.

Sol Polk was scathing in his contempt for private brands
or "off brands" and "ghost brands," as he called them. Conve-
niently, Sears, which he perceived to be his chief competitor,
was a private-label merchandiser. And Sears was not his only
target. Montgomery Ward with its Signature lines also fell
under the umbrella of Sol's umbrage, as did other major re-

tailers. This Polk Bros. advertisement from the late 1950s was characteristic:

> What does your furniture say about you, behind your back?
>
> According to a psychologist friend of ours, it says **plenty**. He says the brand of furniture or appliance you buy is a reflection of your own personality. Some brands tell people you have good taste. Some say you are conservative. Others say you are "daring."
>
> "What about 'off-brands'?" we asked him. (As if we didn't know!) "For instance, what does an off-brand TV set tell visitors about its owner?" Our friend simply raised an expressive professional eyebrow.

Ten years later, Sol was still at it, with heightened invective. Polk Bros. placed a full-page, long-copy newspaper ad in 1967 headlined, "It's time somebody told the truth about 'ghost brand' appliances." The ad read:

> The washer, refrigerator, television set or stereo that doesn't carry the name of a reputable maker may not be the bargain you think it is. Read how certain retailers trick the consumer with pleasant sounding private brands — "ghost brands" that mean little.

"Quality manufacturers," the ad goes on to say, "are proud to put their names on honest products." It should be noted that Sears was a major stockholder in the Whirlpool Corporation and carried its products under the Sears Kenmore label. Whirlpool was also a major supplier to Polk Bros., which did a volume business in Whirlpool laundry equipment. The common source, however, was a fact that Sol chose to ignore in his battle against private label brands.

Over the years Sol Polk's abundant patriotism and un-qualified belief in a democratic free-enterprise system became commingled with his personal advocacy for brand-name mer-chandise. As Irv Lewis explains it:

> Sol, in essence, was a patriot. He really believed in the country, in the system, and he felt that as a con-sumer you had a right to make a choice. It was good for business, obviously, but it was also good for you, as a consumer. And so, we had that breadth of selec-tion.

A Polk Bros. manifesto from the early 1960s, which Sol incorporated into a number of speeches, elaborated that theme. Polk Bros.' philosophy of doing business, the tract states, is: "To build people — and to build their dignity as peo-ple — by making Brand Name production miracles available to them at lower cost." It goes on:

> Polk Bros. knows that any healthy, developing, consumer-based society must be a **democratic** so-ciety. Its members, like those of any democratic so-ciety, must be **free to choose**. Free to exercise as broad a choice as possible in their tools for better living. . . .

> Polk Bros. recognizes that an expanding free con-sumer choice does more than build better products. **It also builds better people**. . . . It gives them a larger measure of responsibility for making free en-terprise and the competitive economy work.

Warming to his subject, Sol proceeds in this statement to equate private label merchandising with "slavery," identi-fying Sears and Montgomery Ward by name, and warning that "slavery" to a single product line begets slavery among consumers: "We at Polk Bros. firmly believe that the private label and the off brand move the consumer away from a fuller participation [in a free society] by lessening his free choice."

Sol Polk was also a fervent booster of the city of Chicago and an advocate for Chicago manufacturers. A Polk Bros. advertisement for Motorola television sets, for example, usually carried the headline "Motorola — **Made in Chicago by Chicagoans** — for all America." A Hotpoint washer ad would proclaim that the product was "American Made in Chicago by Chicagoans!"

Whether Sol Polk's campaign against "ghost brands" actually pierced the steel and glass armor of the monumental Sears Tower in Chicago cannot be known. There is some evidence, in the form of letters of protest from Sears legal counsel, that it did. The fact of the matter is that in the late 1970s Sears did cross over to Sol's side of the fence with regard to brand-name merchandise. In this period Sears and Ward's both restructured their major appliance and electronics outlets into the multi-brand Sears Brand Central and Montgomery Ward Electric Avenue stores.

*   *   *

When Polk Bros. celebrated the company's twentieth year in business in 1955, Sol Polk was just thirty-eight years old. But to the postwar generation of home buyers, it must have seemed that Polk's appliance and home furnishings business had been around forever. A 1957 advertisement addressed that point. Headlined "Meet the Family," the copy read:

> It made us feel like real old codgers the other day to hear a new customer exclaim, "Y'mean the original Polk Brothers are still active in the stores?!"

Honestly, we're not that old!

And you **bet** we're active . . . meeting customers, buying next year's merchandise, helping write ads, training salesmen, taking a turn on the sales floor . . . .

In fact, a second generation of Polk cousins was coming along by the late 1950s. Sol was unmarried, but the four brothers and Goldie among them had twelve children. Polk Bros. reached its maximum growth in the decades of the 1960s and 1970s. In 1967, a peak year, Polk Bros. employed 1,600 people and had sixteen stores, registering sales of over $100 million annually. These were the years when the second generation of Polk sons and daughters, as young adults, came into the business — and most left it.

Goldie's son, Bruce Bachmann, was the first of the younger generation to come into the business. He started working at Polk Bros. full time in 1958, selling summer furniture and lawn equipment at the Four Seasons store on North Central Avenue. "Whatever I learned — and the mistakes I made, and I'm sure there were plenty of them — were on-the-job training," he remembers. Bruce knew, as all members of the second-generation knew or would learn, that there were no privileges nor special favors granted to the Polk kids.

In his ten years with the company, Bruce became the store manager and then the principal buyer for Four Seasons. In 1968, he left Polk Bros. to build his own successful career in real estate development.

David Polk's three boys — Mitchel, Richard, and Jeffrey — were all under the age of ten when David died. Sam Polk, the oldest of David's brothers, moved easily into the role of protective uncle. The boys worked summers as stockboys in the Skokie store, and in their college years all worked as salesmen. Mitchel stayed with the company until after Sol Polk's death in the late 1980s. Richard and Jeffrey made their marks in other fields; Richard in his own specialty footwear business and Jeffrey in real estate.

Morrie Polk and his family moved to north suburban Skokie from their home on the South Side of Chicago in 1964, shortly after Polk Bros.' Skokie store opened. Their daughter Linda worked in the record department at the Skokie store and in accounts payable at the headquarters office in Melrose Park, but her dream was to teach, which she did after her graduation from Southern Illinois University.

Morrie's son Howard, the youngest of the boys in the second generation, ultimately became the only one of the seven sons in the Polk families to move into the top executive ranks of the company. Howard began selling radios at Polk Bros.' Melrose Park headquarters store when he was sixteen, working at Polk Bros. summers and holidays through high school and college.

Howard went on to manage the Central Avenue radio department, the company's leading radio outlet and eventually became an electronics buyer for the entire chain, dealing primarily with high-end audio products.

* * *

The Polk Bros. name was always identified in Chicago with major appliances and home furnishings, but the company was also an undisputed leader in the home electronics field.

By 1954, home electronics, an industry that was born in Chicago in the laboratories of companies like Zenith and Motorola in the pre-war years, had become a five-billion-dollar business in America. By 1964 Polk sales of home entertainment products accounted for nearly a quarter of the company's revenues. In 1985 Polk Bros. was described by *Crain's Chicago Business* as "long Chicago's number one purveyor of discount, high volume electronics wares."

From the beginning, Polk's dominated the Chicago market for black and white television. By 1965 it also held the top spot in sales of color television, with nearly twenty-two percent of the market, compared to Sears' fourteen percent share. A year later, Polk bumped Sears from its perch as Chicago's leading source of stereo-hifi equipment. By that time Polk Bros.' relationships with the leaders of the all-important Japanese electronic industry were well established.

American manufacturers held the lead in consumer electronics until the mid-1960s, when the Japanese began their successful invasion of world markets. Polk Bros. had been among the first mainstream dealers in the country to take Japanese electronics seriously: They started buying Japanese-made products in the late 1950s, when the label "Made in Japan" still carried an aura of tawdry mass production.

Polk Bros. began selling Japanese-made electronics as a lower-priced alternative. The fact was that Japanese electronic products were cheap not because they were cheaply made but because the Japanese in the 1960s were underselling the competition: They were buying U.S. market share by selling product abroad for less than its price at home.

Polk Bros.' association with the Sony Corporation, as with other major suppliers, was built on a personal friendship. This had been the case with GE distributor Dick Cooper, Amana CEO George Foerstner, and RCA chairman David Sarnoff. And so it was with Sony founder Akio Morita.

Akio Morita came to see Sol Polk in 1959 with a six-transistor radio, the first Sony product introduced in America. "Sol bought from Akio Morita, and that was the start of Sony in the United States," Lester Bachmann says. Polk was also among the first dealers to carry the Sony Betamax, the first video cassette recorder, and the Sony Walkman. Friendships made early were not forgotten. In 1985 Polk Bros. recognized its own fiftieth year and Sony's twenty-fifth year with the Polk Bros. and Sony "Gold and Silver" anniversary celebration. Morita, then an international celebrity, honored the occasion and a long association by making a personal visit to Polk Bros. stores. Similarly, Sol Polk was one of the first American dealers to visit Japan in the early 1960s to tour the Matsushita factories.

*   *   *

Polk never relinquished its edge as a leading source for Chicagoans buying home electronics products, but in the late 1970s the retail arena began to assume a new character as sophisticated out-of-town competitors surged into the market. The arrival of Radio Shack with its own brands precipitated a retail battle of mammoth proportions among Chicago-area high-fidelity equipment dealers. The advent of the powerful appliance and electronics superstores would not be far behind. Polk Bros.' response was characteristic: "We're used to competition."

The struggle over foreign competition, specifically in the area of Japanese-made television sets, also was becoming vastly more complicated. Issues surrounding charges that importers of Japanese products were "dumping" in the American market had reached the proportions of a tariff war by the mid-1970s, involving the U.S. Treasury Department and eventually the intervention of the International Trade Commission. But by then Japanese imports had captured a solid forty percent of the American market for color television sets. American manufacturers, including Chicago-based Zenith, were forced either to move their own manufacturing abroad to compete or get out of the color television business altogether.

The terrain in these years was slippery. Momentous shifts in the distribution system created confusion in the industry; the curve of consumer demand for the audio systems of the 1960s and for color television sets had peaked; and retailers were seeing the effects of the 1978 recession on their balance sheets. At this point the home electronics industry was saved, and changed forever, by the introduction of the video cassette recorder.

*   *   *

The appliance and home electronics industries perpetually strive to create that one new product that will create a surge of consumer demand and cause all that came before to be rendered obsolete. The 1940s was the decade of the automatic washing machine. The new products of the 1950s were the refrigerator-freezer and the room air conditioner. In the 1960s it was color television. The innovation of the 1970s was the microwave oven. Polk Bros. had been among the first in the market with all of these items.

The new product of the 1980s was the VCR, followed closely by the introduction of the camcorder. The video cassette recorder was one of those innovations that revolutionize an industry. It was the retailer's dream come true, creating a ground swell of new interest in consumer electronics.

Polk Bros. had carried the first video recording system, an American-made set called Cartra-Vision, introduced in the early 1970s by Admiral. "That was way before its time," Howard Polk comments. When Japan's electronics giants, Sony and Matsushita, came out with competing and incompatible video recording systems in the late 1970s, Polk Bros. carried both.

Polk had introduced the Sony-made Beta system to the Chicago market, but Polk Bros. was also a huge dealer for RCA, and had in fact, backed RCA in the 1950s in the battle over color television systems. RCA was buying the JVC/Matsushita VHS system from the Matsushita factory and, marketing it under the Panasonic brand name. Polk Bros. carried both Panasonic and RCA, as well as Sony.

By 1980 electronics was big again: Video disks, video tapes, and electronic toys were big sellers at Christmas. Polk Bros. led Chicagoland in sales of VCRs that season. The boom was on. In 1985 Americans bought 1.5 million VCRs, and there was no end in sight. On the audio side, the new compact disk player was quickly replacing the turntable. By 1989 home electronics had become the most competitive arena in consumer goods.

Polk Bros. was also the first to carry home video games, beginning in the 1970s with the Magnavox Odyssey and later the hugely successful Atari games. These became the phenomenon of the 1980s and 1990s, linked to the proliferation of the home computer. In the age of Nintendo, Polk backed

Sega, and did well with Sega game cartridges. But the company never sold Nintendo, even though it was far and away the industry giant at that time. Howard Polk shrugs off the lapse, saying, "Nintendo tried to sell us early on, but we didn't buy it." He adds, "We were pretty successful with Sega."

The rise of consumer electronics in the 1970s "changed the whole complexion of our industry," Lester Bachmann noted in 1993.

> Major appliances became a lesser factor. The big chains now are predominantly electronics, and the major appliances are stuck back in the corners. White goods is an orphan.

* * *

Had Sol Polk been born a generation later, he undoubtedly would have embraced the electronics revolution of the 1980s and 1990s with the same fervor that he lavished on labor-saving home appliances in the 1950s. The two words invariably used to describe Sol are "genius" and "visionary." Sol Polk pioneered many of the innovations that began transforming the retail industry in the late 1950s and early 1960s: discount merchandising, just-in-time buying, central warehousing, and cost shifting, to name a few.

But he also foresaw technological advances that would affect the ways in which merchandising would be done in the future. For example, Sol spoke as early as the mid-1950s of interactive marketing through the medium of television. A vision which had become a practical reality by the 1990s and which also was not so far removed from the even bigger phenomenon of the home shopping networks.

Sol Polk's belief in the resourcefulness of national manufacturers played a large part in his forecasts. In a speech delivered in the late 1950s, Sol credited research being done in "Brand Name laboratories" for the development of products that he predicted would someday become commonplace.

He said, for example, that one day we would see a portable television set small enough to be carried in a man's pocket. The same man might have a "walkie-talkie" small enough to fit snugly in the other pocket. He predicted that the day would come when we would see "an entire musical library that will require less space than a flashlight." Sol might well have been describing a sports fan of the 1990s carrying his two-inch Sony Watchman color TV in one pocket, a Motorola cellular flip phone in the other, and the Boston Pops on compact disk in his car.

Sol also prophesied "color television that will appear three-dimensionally in the very center of the living room — like theater in the round — through the miracle of laser beams." That has yet to be seen in everybody's living room, but as early as the 1970s, any visitor to the haunted house at a Disney theme park could see laser imaging in the round. As for bringing 3-D images of actors into the center of the living room, by the 1990s the technology of virtual reality was putting the viewer himself into the center of the action.

*   *   *

Business analysts studying the tight markets of the 1990s and the high failure rate for even well-established retail businesses came back with recommendations that mirror a business strategy that Polk Bros. had practiced for nearly sixty years. The turn-around consultants of the 1990s advised faltering retailers to close the gap between themselves and their suppliers; forge strong ties with manufacturers; build closer relationships with distributors; develop just-in-time buying strategies; and cultivate store and brand loyalty.

Lester Bachmann, in considering the phenomenon of Polk's early and innovative relationships with brand-name suppliers saw the matter more simply:

> The vendors were our friends. They weren't computer files. They were living, breathing, walking-around human beings.

Polk Bros.' post-war rise to a dominant position in the Chicago appliance and consumer electronics market can be summed up in three words: **price, promotion,** and **selection**. Advertised low prices, dramatic promotions, and a staggering selection of merchandise were the face that Polk Bros. put forward to the public. The largest part of the company's work force, however, was employed behind the scenes, in the offices and workshops of Polk Bros.' headquarters store and distribution center, known as "the warehouse," out on North Avenue just west of the Chicago city limits.

16

Behind the Scenes

"The mystical, mythical genie who emerged from Aladdin's magic lamp produced no wonders that could pale the sight which faces the visitor to the Polk Bros. Distribution Center. . . ."
— **Home Entertainment Retailing**, 1964

"When I load my trucks, I'm sending happiness out to thousands of people."
— Sol Polk
Quoted in **Housewares Buyer**, 1967

Backstage, behind Polk Bros.' feast of fabulous promotions and sales-floor superlatives, stood a mechanism so vast and so critical to the company's success that, but for this, the rest would have been little more than a stage set. The beating heart of the Polk enterprise was the distribution center, or warehouse, that operated behind the scenes of Polk Bros.' corporate headquarters and retail store at 8311 West North Avenue in Melrose Park.

Like the bustling complex of tunnels beneath the streets of Disneyworld, Polk Bros.' distribution center was almost a small city unto itself. There the company operated its own garage, its own water system, and its own railway spur. It had its own cabinet shop and refinishing department, its own sign shop, and even its own handsomely fitted Pullman car.

The warehouse was the key to the company's ability to buy massive quantities of merchandise at the best prices and to maintain a constant turnover. The distribution center was the nerve center of the business — the critical link between Polk Bros.' chain of retail stores and the thousands, sometimes tens of thousands, of customers who bought appliances and furniture at Polk Bros. on any given day.

With the exception of carry-home items, the stores themselves stocked no inventory. Customers made their furniture and appliance selections from full-line displays on the sales floors. Orders were carried by a Polk courier service, or telephoned if the hour was late, to the warehouse — on whose massive shoulders rested full responsibility for fulfillment of Polk's promise of next-day delivery.

On an average day in the 1960s, twenty truck loads of furniture and appliances rolled into Polk Bros.' distribution center. The railway dock was large enough to serve nine freight cars at a time. The warehouse itself easily accommodated more than one hundred carloads of merchandise.

Polk Bros. moved its warehouse operations to Melrose Park in the late 1950s when the company bought the old Raytheon warehouse, once used for the distribution of Raytheon's Admiral-brand television sets. Incidental to its primary function as a warehouse, Polk Bros. used the building in a minor way as an outlet for sales of "scratch and dent" merchandise. Over time, a full-line retail store and furniture showroom evolved at the site.

In the early 1960s, the company's over-crowded administrative offices were relocated — one by one and in a typically hodge-podge fashion — from Central Avenue to the larger space at the Melrose Park warehouse and retail store. The store at 8311 West North Avenue became one of Polk Bros.' largest and highest volume locations, but it never entirely outgrew its original appellation. Within the company, the 8311 West North Avenue store was always called "the warehouse."

Jack Leonard, who managed the General Electric account for *Life* magazine, remembers going out to Melrose Park with Sol Polk to look at the property before it was purchased:

> It was becoming vacant at that time. We drove right through the thing. Sol had a very clear concept of mass merchandising out of one center. He visualized that the product would come to him directly from the factory, on freight cars. From this distribution center he would send the merchandise out to the customers on Polk's own trucks.

Sol's vision was twenty-twenty. Polk Bros.' warehouse operation foreshadowed by many years both the "cluster concept" adopted by retailers in the 1970s, where branch stores are serviced out of a centrally located warehouse, and the low-inventory quick-response systems developed by the electronics superstores in the 1980s.

The Raytheon property was ideal for Polk Bros.' purposes. It was just west of the Chicago city limits, between the suburban towns of River Forest and Melrose Park. The twenty-acre site was bounded on the west by the Maywood Park Race track and encircled on three sides by the Thatcher Woods Forest Preserve. The location, at First Street and North Avenue, offered ready access for Polk's fleet of trucks. The railway spur entered the property at the southeast corner, linking the warehouse to the network of rail lines that served the Clearing Industrial District and Melrose Park Yard to the west.

* * *

The distribution center had a presence all its own, but it was run by a team of people who on any given day accomplished the impossible, and then came back and did it again the next day. A guiding spirit behind the smooth operation of the distribution center was Irv Lewis, Polk Bros.' vice-president for operations, and by all accounts one of the most admired members of Polk Bros.' executive team.

Irv Lewis married Roberta Bachmann in January of 1953, less than a year after the two met on a blind date arranged by friends. Although Irv is Goldie Luftig's son-in-law, he describes himself not as an in-law but an "out-law." Over the twenty years that he spent with the company, Irv saw Sol Polk as a creative and merchandising genius but continued to challenge Sol to keep the company's operations and personnel policies apace with the times.

When Irv and Roberta married, Irv worked in the family scrap iron business, was active in civic affairs, and later joined a brokerage firm. Six years later he joined Polk Bros. He says:

> I can remember Roberta and I drove into Chicago, and I had a meeting with Sol. He had all the family there. Sol was a stem winder. He had me ten feet off the ground in around thirty seconds. So we decided I would go to work for Polk Bros. Sol could paint pictures. He was a visionary. He struck the right chord with me. I thought, holy smoke, this is going to be wonderful!

Irv's first job with Polk Bros. was selling summer furniture and lawnmowers out of a tent at the 85th and Cottage Grove store. "As I progressed through the company, there was never a time when I wouldn't spend nights on the sales floor. Sol's concept was 'everybody sells,'" Irv says.

Irv was accustomed to handling heavy equipment, and managing men who did that work. He gravitated naturally to the Polk Bros.' reconditioning, manufacturing, and warehouse operations, locating sites and remodeling properties for the several stores that Polk Bros. opened in the 1960s. He supervised construction for the altogether new store that Polk's opened in the far south suburb of Burbank in the early 1970s, and managed that store in its first year. When chief operations manager Robert Kornblatt left to join a family partner in another business in 1973, Irv moved into the position of vice-president of operations.

Like all the members of the Polk family, Irv worked seven days a week. He seldom left the warehouse before midnight and often was back before dawn to double-check the loading of the trucks. On occasional weekends Roberta, with the three children, would check into the motel on North Avenue next to the warehouse so that the kids could visit their dad.

* * *

The distribution center ran around the clock — a schedule that was not matched even by the gigantic Sears and Montgomery Ward warehouses. "It was a very efficient use of capital assets," Irv Lewis remarks.

> You own the building, you own the trucks, you own the equipment for lifts. You are heating the building and the lights are on. Why work only eight hours a day?

The warehouse work schedule was divided into three eight-hour shifts. Typically, the first shift, which came in at 7 a.m., received merchandise; the second put it away; and the third, the 11 p.m. to 7 a.m. shift, fulfilled orders and loaded the trucks. In high volume periods it seemed that warehouse manager Frank Genatempo (known in the business as Frank Tempo) worked all three shifts.

At night, the vast recesses of the warehouse came alive. Dispatchers analyzed the day's orders and labored over routing sheets, as workers riding forklift carts cruised the aisles collecting merchandise and carrying it to the staging areas. There Polk Bros.' fleet of orange and white delivery trucks were loaded, ready to fan out through the city and suburbs when the drivers arrived at 8 a.m.

The pace was hectic. In peak seasons, the trucks often started their runs before dawn, returning to the warehouse in the late morning or early afternoon for a second load. Irv Lewis notes:

> If you were in one of our stores at ten o'clock at night and you bought a refrigerator that was in our inventory, we could deliver the next day, sometimes by eight o'clock in the morning. That's real turn-around. The character of the business, remember, was **get it done**. It was exciting, believe me!

Exciting indeed, but also harrowing. The dispatchers did what had to be done, even if it meant sending crews out at night to meet an especially heavy delivery schedule. "I used to get pretty tough with some of the drivers," Irv recalls, "but by the same token I knew that these guys were out there hauling iron and that they were the absolute best at what they were doing."

This is not to say that the Polks did not monitor the routes. The cost of labor was high, and Morrie Polk, especially, did not want to see an hour squandered. The company sent out "spotters" to follow a truck if they suspected a driver might be parked under a tree taking a longer-than-authorized lunch break. Woe to the driver caught snoozing by Morrie himself, who did not earn his nickname "Morrie Thunder" for nothing.

*   *   *

The responsibility for working out the delivery routes fell largely on the shoulders of chief dispatcher Gus Galino, who handled the job with the skill of an air traffic controller. The territory served was vast, encompassing virtually all of the metropolitan area known as Chicagoland.

Polk Bros. had come of age in the working class neighborhoods of northwest and southwest Chicago. In the late 1950s, Polk's began following the population in its outward sprawl into the suburbs. The company's decision to move its warehouse and eventually its corporate headquarters to a near western suburb was the logical extension of its expansion plans.

Over the fifty-year period from the beginning of World War II to the day the business closed, Polk Bros. opened more than two dozen stores. That figure would be closer to three dozen if the eleven separate buildings of the Polk City North complex are counted individually. The number of Polk stores at any given time was fluid. Sites opened and sites closed with some regularity.

The company's maximum expansion had been completed by 1967, with seventeen Polk Bros. stores located within the city of Chicago and in the surrounding suburbs. At this time, the Chicago stores included the Polk City complex on North Central Avenue, the two South Side stores on West 63rd Street and 85th and Cottage Grove Avenue, a Near North store in the former Peterson Furniture store building at 1048 West Belmont, and the large northwest Chicago store at 5711 N. Milwaukee Avenue. The Polk surplus and reconditioning center was at 3500 Grand Avenue.

Between 1962 and 1968, the company had an outlet known as Polk's Commercial Tire and Supply Company at 4657 West Madison, on the far West Side, and a downtown site, which remained open through the 1970s, at 600 West Adams in the Chicago Loop.

Polk's first suburban store, on West Grand Avenue in River Grove, was opened in the late 1950s. Within ten years the company had stores in Joliet, Waukegan, LaGrange, Skokie, Arlington Heights, Harvey, Elgin, Melrose Park, and a far South Side store in the Ford City shopping plaza.

* * *

The wonder of Polk Bros.' distribution process was that, up through the 1970s, the warehouse operation depended on manual inventory control. Virtually every transaction was done by hand. When a salesman completed a sale, he would call the order into the order department at the Melrose Park headquarters. Each item in inventory had a card assigned to it indicating, first, the model, style, and color of the item and, second, a sequential number, or "line," that was assigned to each individual unit in that model and style.

When the order was phoned in, the card for that item would be pulled, indicating that the unit bearing that number was reserved for the customer who had just made the purchase. The salesman was given the card and line number to enter onto the sales ticket, and he, in turn, would give the order department the customer's name and the number of the sales ticket. Every evening the company's inter-office courier picked up the day's orders at each store and delivered them to the order department. From there they were hand-carried back to the warehouse where the loading process took place.

Furniture sales were handled in much the same way, except that the furniture inventory was printed on IBM cards with the appropriate storage areas marked by aisle and bay number. White goods and electronics inventory was checked two or three times a week, but the process was largely visual. If a buyer wanted to know what quantity of a particular item remained in stock, he could check the card and line files in the order department — or he could go out back to the warehouse and take a look.

The holiday season, from Thanksgiving through Christmas, was the busiest period in the warehouse calendar, in part because of stepped-up advertising campaigns and increased volume of sales of gift items such as dishwashers, stereo systems, and television sets. The season was busy also because the approach of the holidays prompted people to refurbish their homes with new carpeting and furnishings.

The most chaotic periods, however, were the weeks when Chicago's frequent summer heat waves hit. "When it got hot, people wanted to buy air conditioners — window air conditioners — and the stores just went crazy," Irv remembers.

> You could see the way the sales curve moved. The highest sales were not on the first day of a heat wave, but on the third and fourth days, when people were worn down and couldn't take it any more. That's when they said, "We haven't slept in three days, we have to have an air conditioner."

Polk Bros. made their air-conditioner buys in mid-winter, securing their supply of product before the first days of summer. But it sometimes happened that the stock sold down faster than even Polk's savvy buyer, Lester Bachmann, anticipated. When this happened, Irv says, Polk's scoured the country for replenishment.

> It was a matter of geography. If it was hot in Chicago, it might not be hot in another sector of the country. So that's where we went. I remember one year getting truckloads of air conditioners up from Texas. We unloaded trucks day and night.

People buying air conditioners often were not willing to wait for next-day delivery, or over the weekend if the purchase was made on a Saturday. When Chicago temperatures soared, Polk's stacked cartons of air conditioners out on the sidewalk at the Polk City stores and on the loading docks at the warehouse, ready for customers to pick up themselves. On Sundays, when customers' cars lined up at the warehouse to pick up air conditioners, Polk's sent boys out among them giving away cold Cokes.

*   *   *

If promotions were the draw to customers, the warehouse was the draw to the world. Almost daily, Polk Bros.' distribution center was toured by manufacturers' representatives, dealer groups, and delegations from trade associations. Foreign visitors were commonplace, often traveling in groups sponsored by national economic councils, the international branches of U.S. manufacturers, and international trade associations. French, Swiss, Australian, and Canadian groups were regular visitors, but Japanese delegations were by far the most frequent, a reflection of Japan's growing role in the home electronics industry. When the big trade shows, such as the electronics or housewares or furniture expositions, were in town, Polk Bros. warehouse tours went on almost around the clock.

Jack Leonard was once asked by the head of a major advertising agency if Leonard could get him and a colleague in to meet Sol Polk and see the Polk Bros. distribution center. Sol agreed to meet the party at midnight, which was the time he normally wrapped up his business day. Under the circumstances, that was just fine with them. "Here were three of the top marketing executives in the United States walking around a warehouse at two in the morning," Leonard remembers.

There was a lot to see. The space within the warehouse was vast. The very size of it was momentarily disorienting to the visitor stepping into the warehouse through one of the human-scale doors at the back of the retail store. The railroad tracks ran through the warehouse from the loading dock at the south end right up to the sales floor and showrooms off the retail store on the north side of the huge building.

In every direction one could see stacks of crated appliances, piled like a giant's building blocks. Mattresses and box springs were stored on five levels, along seven aisles, stretching almost the length of a full city block. When bedding ads were running, the Polk stores would sell more than five hundred mattresses a day, all shipped out overnight from the Melrose Park distribution center.

The spirit of hyperbole that characterized all of Polk Bros.' mega-operations was not lost on writers for *Home Entertainment Retailing* who visited the distribution center in 1964. They reported:

> The mystical, mythical genie who emerged from Aladdin's magic lamp produced no wonders that could pale the sight which faces the visitor to the Polk Bros. Distribution Center in Melrose Park, Ill. Stretching over an area covering some 358,000 square feet (larger than Chicago's McCormick Place) are endless rows of color television sets, stereo combinations, radios, recorders, white goods of every type, furniture of every kind, boats, toys and a myriad of other products, stacked as high as the spacious ceilings permit.

* * *

Polk's operated a second warehouse, known as warehouse 77, across First Avenue from the distribution center. This was the location of Polk Bros.' sign shop, run by former Chicago Bears player Lew Posner. Hundreds of bus placards advertising Polk Bros. were made here, as well as multiplicity of signs bearing motivational slogans favored by Sol and sent around to all the stores.

Warehouse 77 was also the repository for the surplus materials and odd lots of odd things that Sol picked up along the way. When Chicago's Hilton Hotel was redecorated, Sol bought up all the chandeliers from the ballroom. When a wave of interest in women's wigs waned in the 1970s, Sol acquired a load of wig boxes that folded flat. Polk's gave them away as carriers for Barbie Doll wardrobes.

Service manager Gerry Bruns remembers the day that Sol turned up with "tons and tons of steel wool." She continues:

I said, what is he going to do with steel wool! Well, we gave it to customers. And we had to make the customer think that a roll of steel wool was probably the best thing he ever got. People really liked the idea of getting something for nothing — even if it was steel wool.

When Sol salvaged thousands of metal milk cans from Illinois farms and dairies in the mid-1960s, he had them cleaned up in the reconditioning shop, "antiqued" in a soft green color, and decorated with the American eagle emblem. The milk cans, in the guise of umbrella stands or decorative accents, were offered as premiums with purchases or one hundred dollars or more.

Ernie LaSalle, who ran Polk's Grand Avenue reconditioning shop, and Irv Lewis both remember the forty-year-old British infantry shovels. Sol had picked 75,000 of them up for a song at a trade show. "When those things started arriving at Grand Avenue, trailer loads of them, I thought I'd just quit," LaSalle says. LaSalle didn't quit. He and his crew sandblasted away thirty years of calcified deposits, stamped the Polk Bros. logo on the shovels, painted them gold, and applied the motto "Dig For More Sales . . . and Profit."

Sol rented a Brink's truck, and the shovels were delivered, in long plastic bags, to business leaders throughout Chicago. They were a great hit with everyone but Ernie LaSalle and Irv Lewis. Irv had to make many of the deliveries. He says, "Here I am walking into all the major downtown offices carrying these shovels. I felt like such a jerk!"

*   *   *

When Polk Bros. took over the Raytheon property, they doubled the size of the warehouse and built a garage for vehicle maintenance. Administrative offices were built behind and over the new store, accommodating the executive offices, the huge customer credit and direct mail departments, accounts payable which also handled rentals, and the payroll and personnel department.

The advertising department with its own layout and typesetting sections occupied space adjacent to the retail store. Two special divisions — Incentive Planners and the Home Shopping Service — also were located in this part of the building. The order department and cubicles for managers and buyers were on the east end of the retail store. The carpet installation section was on the main floor, behind an employee lunchroom. The operations division, which included the service department, was at the south end of the warehouse.

All told, more than five hundred people worked in the complex, spread about equally between the operations and administrative divisions. Characteristically, the offices were far from plush. They were cold in the winter, hot in the summer, and sparsely furnished.

*   *   *

Like all of the Polk youngsters, Sam Polk's daughters, Sandra, Barbara, and Ellen, grew up working in the stores. The boys in the Polk families started as stockboys and moved up to become salesmen; the girls generally started in the record department, or jewelry, or small appliances. Barbara, who had an artistic bent, and Ellen, who later became an interior designer and furniture buyer for Polk Bros., followed that path as teenagers, but both also worked in the Today store.

When Sandra graduated from Wellesley College with a degree in economics, Sam might have expected or hoped that she would follow him into the family business. As it happened, Sandra did discover her future career at Polk Bros. But it wasn't in retail.

While she was in college, Sandra chose to work in Polk's payroll department, one of the company's few computerized operations, because, she says, it was the only office that was carpeted and air conditioned — a requirement of the 1960-vintage IBM mainframe. There she met the IBM people who serviced the Polk Bros. account. Eventually, she was recruited by IBM, where she ultimately served as the director of marketing for the midwest region.

*   *   *

In planning new office space, the brothers perpetuated a habit that had been with them from their youth. They were hive builders, burrowing into a nest of offices like a colony of moles. Even as the 2850 North Central location grew to encompass two city blocks, the Polk brothers and other key staff continued to share a small chaotic office space. At the new headquarters building, Lester Bachmann finally got his own office, adjoining Sol's. But Sam Polk, Morrie Polk, financial consultant Irv Weiner, and personnel manager Howard Pontius — in different combinations at different times — shared one office.

Perhaps, given the chock-a-block nature of the office space, it is not surprising that job descriptions were indistinct at best. *Home Entertainment Retailing* in a 1964 article made the observation: "If you were to call Polk's with a complaint, it is not only possible but likely that your call would be personally taken by one of the top Polk executives — and it would be acted upon promptly." Lester Bachmann, who notes that "much of our thinking and planning was done after the stores closed," remembers one such complaint call in particular:

> We had a small switchboard. After hours, incoming calls would be plugged into Sol's desk. At 3 a.m. one night the phone rang. I picked it up and said, "Polk Bros."
>
> The woman caller said, "Where's my washing machine? You promised to send it out and it's not

·· here yet." I found the paperwork. It was a GE wringer-washer. Believe me, it was on the truck in the morning.

Irv Lewis says,

If I had a call from a customer at five o'clock in the afternoon, saying, "Mr. Lewis, I have been sitting home all day long, you promised to deliver my dryer, and it didn't get here," my posture was that the first truck that came in was going to go back with a drier for that lady. That was an expensive proposition. The drivers loved to work for us because we had lots of overtime.

* * *

When the headquarters was moved from the old offices over the store at 2850 North Central Avenue to the new distribution center, Morrie Polk stayed at the South Side store at 85th and Cottage Grove, and Harry Polk remained at 2850. Harry, who worked his entire career at the 2850 store, managed the white goods department and was the company's on-site deal closer, or turnover man. In the late 1960s, Harry had a series of small strokes, but refused to heed the warnings and cut back on the sixteen-hour days.

In July of 1969 Harry came home and went to his favorite chair in the sun room of the family home in River Forest to rest. He died there, suddenly and peacefully. He was sixty-two. Harry's older son, Michael, stayed in the business, working as a salesman and later as a store manager. Michael was only thirty-three when he died in 1979.

Pearl and Harry Polk's second son, Edward, worked as a stockboy and later became a salesman. But he had no interest in the business after Harry died.

*   *   *

Even in the administrative offices, job descriptions were flexible. Everybody did everything. Barbara Toomey, a niece to advertising director Georgia Rice, was one of several key women working in the administrative side of the organization. Barbara started with Polk Bros. as a young teenager, coming in after school and on weekends to help out in the advertising department. She joined the company full time when she graduated from high school in 1956. Her first job was typing radio and television scripts. Like many Polk employees, Barbara met her spouse at Polk Bros. In her case, it was on the Christmas tree lot, where her husband-to-be was helping customers select trees and tie them to the tops of their cars.

In common with many women in the organization, Barbara worked part-time or intermittently during the years when she was raising her family. Several of the administrative departments ran both day and evening shifts, but office employees were not always limited to that schedule. While Polk's never articulated a flex-time policy, in fact the company, to its own benefit, was generous in allowing women to work part-time or non-traditional hours to accommodate family schedules.

Over time Barbara worked all aspects of the advertising department, including at least one live appearance in a television ad for vacuum cleaners. She served some years as Sol Polk's secretary, and in the 1980s became advertising coordinator, assuming many of Georgia Rice's responsibilities. "Titles," she says, "were just so when you go to the shows you can pass a card around." Barbara's card read, "Special Services Manager."

Polk Bros., like the appliance industry itself, was a man's world. But when it came to business, the brothers themselves were anything but traditional male chauvinists. While the actual number of women in top job slots was few — Goldie Bachmann Luftig being the prime example — the Polks had no hesitation about placing talented women in general management positions.

Georgia Rice was a vice-president of the company. Sophie Goldstein was hired to manage the accounts payable department. Barbara Toomey circulated among several management positions. Annette Bennette, a four-foot-ten-inch human dynamo, headed up and was a buyer for Incentive Planners, Polk Bros.' premium division, which provided specialty merchandise to large corporations.

Barbara Flick was television and radio advertising administrator. Nadine Lacefield was in charge of the rental department, and was the first woman to become a store manager. Sol gave her the coveted job when Polk Bros. opened a store in Glen Ellyn. If the rough-and-ready sales force resented the promotion, they never said a word. She had the boss's blessing.

Geraldine "Gerry" Bruns, who had been village clerk in the suburban community of Stone Park before coming the Polk Bros., was the first woman to head departments in the all-male operations division, and the first woman in the industry to do so. Gerry ran the service department, as well as the appliance, carpet, and television installation departments. Gerry remembers that "Sophie, Annette, and I all came in at about the same time. It really shook the place up."

The ground on which the warehouse stood was familiar territory to Gerry. She had grown up there in the 1940s when the Polk property was a family farm owned by Gerry's father. Coincidentally, Phil Cortese, Polk's air conditioning manager, had lived in the old farmhouse before Gerry's father bought the property.

*   *   *

The women in general management positions worked closely with Sam Polk, Morrie Polk, and Irv Lewis — and sometimes with Sol. The brothers were known in the offices as "Mr. Sol," "Mr. Sam," and "Mr. Morrie." Gerry Bruns worked most closely with Irv Lewis, but had interactions with all the brothers.

> I really enjoyed working for Irv. He always told you when you were doing a good job. We didn't have a whole lot of that after he left. I used to tell him that it would be all his fault if I developed a terrible superiority complex.
>
> Irv Lewis had such a grasp of the whole company and such a sense of where it could go. He did research and development, he would locate new stores for us, he negotiated with the unions. He was involved with everything. When he left, he said it was because his family was growing up without him.

Gerry, like all of the administrative staff, was especially fond of Sam Polk, whom she describes as "a very, very gentle man." She remembers the day Sam asked her to join him for lunch.

> He had taken some papers upstairs for him to sign, and he said, "Have you had lunch yet?" I said I hadn't, and he said, "Come on, I'll take you to lunch." We went downstairs to the employee cafeteria, and he opened this brown paper bag and shared his lunch with me: liver sausage sandwiches on rye.

After Harry's death in 1969, Morrie Polk was the only one of the brothers left in the field. He ran the South Side stores and traveled among all of the seventeen stores acting as a roving supervisor. In 1977 Morrie, too, made a permanent move to the distribution center where he worked with Sam in the business and investment side and with Irv in operations and union negotiations, particularly those involving the Teamsters. Gerry Bruns worked closely with Morrie. She says,

Morrie didn't just have a job. He had a commitment. If it snowed, he was on the roof with a snow board clearing the snow. If we had a lot of business, he was out in the parking lot directing traffic. He traveled to all the stores. He got involved in everything. You couldn't walk by him with a piece of paper without him taking it and looking at it.

Gerry had a good relationship with Sol Polk, but, like others who worked closely with Sol, found him, in the later years, to be a hard man to know, much less love. "I got along with him because I made up my mind that I would never let him see me cry," she says.

He got mad at me for something once, and said "What do I have to do! Get somebody in from New York to handle your job?"

I handed him the phone, and said, "Call him right now, because, so far as the job goes, I don't need it."

He said, "No, no, wait! Do anything you want."

The story Gerry tells is a common one. The people who got on best with Sol were the ones who stood up to him. Sol was accustomed to berating and humiliating managers and buyers in public. He would drive people to the point that they would come to him to say they would prefer to just move on to another situation. Sol would then spend hours, days even, cajoling and pleading with them to stay. Not everyone was persuaded.

*   *   *

Polk Bros. in its last two decades was beset by sales-force and drivers' strikes, organized by Local 1550 of the United Food and Commercial Workers union and the independent Chicago Truck Drivers, Helpers, and Warehouse

Workers union. These were sad episodes in the company's history.

Most but not all of Polk Bros.' salesmen belonged to the United Food and Commercial Workers Union, which primarily represented workers in the grocery businesses. A unionized sales force in the appliance business was almost unprecedented in retailing. "Chicago was a union town, and so they were a union company; it was just that simple," Edward Polk believes.

The last of the sales-force strikes, in August and September, 1983, was the most damaging to the company, and undoubtedly the most difficult for Sol and Morrie, the two surviving brothers, to comprehend. At this time, somewhat over three hundred Polk Bros. salesmen went out in a strike that lasted for twenty days. As a result Polk Bros., which boasted that its stores were open seven days and six nights a week, was forced to close nine of the chain of twelve stores for the duration of the strike.

Salesman John Beyer remembers that during the 1983 strike:

> Sol used to stand at the window of the offices in Melrose Park and look out across the street toward the forest preserve where the salesmen were picketing. He'd tell the ones who were left in the store, "If I see you in a picket line, you're all finished." It was just a very bitter strike. Years later it would still be talked about on the floor. Those people who kept on working were just totally disliked. It was always brought up that they crossed the picket line.

Not all strikes were as debilitating to Polk Bros. as the 1983 salesmen's strike. When the drivers struck in 1966, Sol's first response was almost whimsical. He set up a U-Haul operation in the parking lot at the warehouse store. "People would buy an appliance, and we'd rent them a trailer to take it home in," Gerry Bruns remembers. "Nothing got Sol down for long."

The salesmen's strikes were galling to Sol, but they were for the most part white-collar events and relatively benign. Sandra Polk Guthman remembers that the porters, members of the International Building Workers union, went on strike in the summer of 1961 when she was working in payroll.

> I had been involved in the retail strikes, but somehow this was much uglier. They threw up a picket line around the warehouse and tried to prevent the truck drivers from crossing the line. The president of the International Building Workers was a huge man named Jim Kemp. He was at least six-foot-three and must have weighed two hundred eighty pounds. The first time I ever laid eyes on him was at lunchtime during this strike.
>
> I had gone out to see what was going on. I was very concerned about the strike and about my father. There was a truck in the driveway. My father was standing on the driver's side running board, and Jim Kemp was standing on the other running board. And they were both arguing with the driver, and shouting at each other through the open truck windows. The issue, of course, was whether the driver would cross the picket line.
>
> And I don't recall whether he did or not. What I do remember is that I was standing around behind my father, who at that time, I believe, had already had one stroke. I was concerned about him, and from that angle Jim Kemp, standing up there on the running board, looked bigger than life.

The running board confrontation, as Sandra later learned, may have been more show than fury — a dialogue between men who respected and understood one another. Years later, Sandra and her husband, Jack Guthman, attended the Twentieth Ward annual dinner dance — a political event held in the heartland of Chicago's predominantly black South Side. Sandra explains,

> So we go to this party, the Twentieth Ward party, and just had a wonderful time. I ended up dancing with Jim Kemp! This was the last time I saw him, but that night he gave me a ten-minute lecture about what a wonderful human being my father was.

Polk Bros.' last encounter with the unions no doubt was the hardest to bear. In June of 1987 some two hundred drivers, warehouse workers, and furniture refinishers were displaced by the huge fire that destroyed the distribution center and disrupted all of the delivery operations. The company could not find an adequate replacement warehouse and, after an analysis of the costs, elected not to rebuild the Melrose Park facility. In August Polk Bros. entered into a contract with a delivery firm that used owner-operated vehicles. Polk's delivery and warehouse workers were let go.

In September, the company sold its fleet of trucks. The sale of the trucks, though by no means unforeseen, was fodder to the union, which organized picket lines around Polk's Central Avenue store and two others, urging customers to boycott the stores. The action was a stab in the back to management, which even then was engaged in an expedited arbitration over back pay and benefits for the ousted workers. The union described the untimely picket line as "informational picketing" intended to drive blue-collar customers away from Polk Bros.' stores.

In the early years, Sol Polk had courted Chicago's West Side working class families, often visiting the union halls and offering special discounts to men who showed their union cards when they came into the store. The union leaders, in the old days, got turkeys at Christmas with a card from the Polk brothers. In the end, these old friends turned on them.

17

Making Money

"Chicago retailer Sol Polk last week revealed two more holdings in his growing investment portfolio including a long-time 9.92% stake in Long Island based Gyrodyne Co. of America Inc., which has interests in real estate, oil wells and citrus groves.

"[When Gyrodyne corporate secretary Joseph Dorn discovered the extent of Polk holdings in Gyrodyne, he said], 'I thought Polk Bros. was a brokerage house.' "

— ***Crain's Chicago Business***
September 6, 1982

"They made money in ways that most people couldn't conceive of."
— Howard Polk

Until the end, Polk Bros. remained an intensely private, family-held and managed financial empire where, even with sales of $150 million a year, one or more of the brothers reviewed every invoice and signed every check.

Polk Bros.' retail business — combining high volume and tight margins with stringent control of company overhead —

continued to turn a steady profit well into the 1980s. But retail sales were by no means the only source of Polk Bros.' assets, which in 1994 were valued at over $150 million. Polk
Bros. Inc. may have run a Spartan ship, but the company was
never poor.

Profits from Polk Bros.' retail operation were re-invested
in real estate, publicly traded stock, and a multiplicity of subsidiary ventures, all of which remained closely held and managed by Sol, Sam, and Morrie Polk, and a small inner circle of
advisers. This diversity of business and investment activities
was how Polk Bros. made its money. Bruce Bachmann, a director of the Polk Bros. Foundation, observes:

> I think you'll find that for Polk Bros. itself the sell-
> ing of an appliance could never be very profitable. If
> you buy it for ten dollars and sell it for eleven dol-
> lars, you don't make any money. But if you also have
> a real estate company, and you have a delivery com-
> pany, and you have an advertising company, and a fi-
> nance company. . . .

"They started the business as entrepreneurs, and, no
matter how big it got, that's the way they continued to run it,"
Howard Polk says. "It was one big pot, and at the end of the
year, that big pot made a lot of money."

*   *   *

The most active of the Polk-owned companies was Rand
Investment Company, an unpublicized home mortgage business which by the early 1990s held some $90 million in well-
secured loans. Others were Cafco Builders, a land-holding
company whose name was an acronym for Central Appliance
and Furniture Company; and Wards Enterprises, Inc., a
wholly-owned Polk Bros. subsidiary that for a time served as
an umbrella for a variety of investment activities.

Polk Bros. got into the mortgage business in the early

1970s when the company sold some properties it owned and gave the buyers financing. The mortgage company, Rand Investment, a partnership, was incorporated in 1979. Rand's policies were conservative. It dealt almost entirely in single-family residential properties. It did not advertise or solicit business. It dealt with people the Polks knew or who came to them through referrals. In the beginning Rand undercut the market on interest rates but took a thirty-percent equity interest in the property.

In the mid-1960s Irving Weiner, a friend of Sam Polk's from their days together at Postal Telegraph in the late 1930s, was persuaded to come back into the Polk family orbit to work with Sam in the investment side of the business. Weiner then took over the management of the mortgage business. In the early 1990s, Howard Polk assumed many of these duties. "To this day we have never, virtually never, lost a dime in principal," Howard says.

The Polk brothers began investing in real estate in the 1940s when they started buying land and buildings for the expansion of the business on North Central Avenue, 63rd Street, and Cottage Grove Avenue. Polk's bought and sold real estate, took land in trades, and perhaps acquired other properties in satisfaction of debts. Over time the company acquired large holdings, both for the purpose of establishing new stores and for investment purposes. The real estate activities were not restricted to the Chicago area. Polk also owned land in California, Arizona, and Arkansas.

In the late 1980s, when a reckoning was made, it was seen that Polk Bros., or a combination of Polk Bros. Inc. and one or more of its subsidiaries, owned outright the land and buildings occupied by most of Polk Bros.' stores, which at that time numbered ten. This included the twenty-two acre property in Melrose Park where the new headquarters store was located and where the old warehouse had stood. These were valuable properties. The Polk Bros. store in Schaumburg, for example, stood on nearly ten acres fronting Golf Road, one of the most densely settled retail thoroughfares in the Chicago area.

Among other holdings, the company owned one-hundred-twenty-acre tracts in Schaumburg and in the affluent North Shore suburb of Highland Park. The Schaumburg and Highland park properties were sold after Sol Polk's death for development as residential subdivisions. At the time of the sale, the value of the Schaumburg land alone was estimated at about $75,000 an acre.

Over the years Sol entered into business partnerships with an enormous diversity of enterprises, and made overtures for joint ventures to the principals of as many more. These associations came and went, but the Polks' interest in the stock market remained constant. Sol collected the annual reports of hundreds of companies but left the management of these investments in the hands of Sam Polk and Irv Weiner.

Polk stock portfolios were of a magnitude that attracted the scrutiny of the Securities and Exchange Commission in 1982. At that time Sol was required to disclose that Polk Bros., Wards Enterprises, and Sol and Morrie Polk collectively owned nearly ten percent of the stock in the Long Island-based Gyrodyne Company of America. Gyrodyne at one time made helicopters for the Navy but later diversified into investments in real estate, oil wells, and citrus groves.

The Polk group also had holdings exceeding the five percent threshold requiring disclosure to the Securities and Exchange Commission in several Chicago companies. These included Weiboldt Stores; Goldblatt Bros.; Ero Industries; Advance Ross; and Dynascan Corporation, then a manufacturer of citizens' band radios and telephones.

Dynascan was not a casual investment. Polk Bros.' shares in that company were the product of a long-standing relationship that over the years had involved ingenuity, enterprise, and considerable financial risk: the paradigm of the American free-enterprise system so earnestly admired by the Polk brothers.

Carl Korn, the president of Dynascan, and the Polk family had been friends since the 1950s. In Polk Bros.' growth years, Korn and Sol Polk became partners in the Central Service Company, an appliance service and repair company that was used exclusively by Polk Bros., but which also did business with a number of other dealers.

Korn branched out to establish the Dyanscan Corporation in the early 1960s, and Sol Polk backed the venture. Dynascan's principal product at that time was a CB radio, marketed under the Cobra brand name. The company later diversified to manufacture telephone answering machines, cordless phones, and radar speed detectors.

When the telephone industry was deregulated in the early 1980s, Dynascan was one of the first companies to offer a telephone instrument as a consumer product. Polk Bros. bought tens of thousands of these Cobra phones as a premium offer. For five dollars, with a major purchase, a Polk customer could, for the first time in his life, own his own telephone.

Dynascan later redirected its efforts into the manufacture of electronic industrial control systems. When the company went public, Polk Bros. invested heavily in Dynascan stock. They backed a winner. *Crain's Chicago Business*, in early 1981, identified Carl Korn as one of six Chicago businessmen who "possess the million dollar touch." Korn, *Crain's* reported, earned $2.7 million in 1980 from dividends buoyed by a one-hundred-sixty-seven-percent surge in Dynascan stock. Sol Polk, a director and the largest shareholder in Dynascan, earned $2.5 million in the same period, according to *Crain's*.

*   *   *

Sol Polk had a knack for spinning off profitable subsidiaries that were directly or indirectly related to the retail business. These included Polk Bros.' own advertising agency, Incentive Planners, through which the company created and managed in-house virtually all of its own radio, television, and newspaper advertising. Under the same name the company operated the Incentive Planners Premium Division.

In 1969 Polk Bros. established Polk Revolving Charge (PRC), an in-house consumer credit operation. By underwriting and administering customers' time-payment accounts themselves, Polk Bros. was able to cut the interest rates formerly charged by outside financing contracts. PRC was a significant business for Polk Bros. Depending on the time period under consideration, as much as forty percent of Polk's retail sales were financed on time-payment plans.

The Appliance Credit Corporation was a Polk-owned finance company of a type known in the industry as a "floor plan" company. Polk used the Appliance Credit Corporation as a means of refinancing its own purchases to take advantage of certain manufacturer discounts and, when it was expedient to do so, as a means of moving cash to take advantage of the prevailing cost of money.

A floor plan company is essentially a finance company which guarantees a dealer's contract with a manufacturer, extends long-term credit to the dealer, and negotiates, on its own behalf, a discount from the manufacturer for full payment of the account within a specified period of time, usually ten days. The discount allowed by the manufacturer might be as much as five percent. The amount of money involved could be considerable, given the size of Polk Bros. purchases which often were in the range of a million dollars or more.

Polk Bros. might choose to "floor plan" a major buy in a situation where the manufacturer was squeezed for cash and willing to negotiate a better discount than Polk could earn, at prevailing interest rates, from a comparable short-term investment in more traditional financial instruments. The more common use of the re-financing mechanism was an accounting matter. The full amount of Polk's contract with the manufacturer was charged against the retail operation's cost of goods. The difference, that is, the "profit" earned by the floor plan company, would then be made available to another Polk operation.

The company handled the bookkeeping side of Incentive Planners, the advertising subsidiary, in much the same way. The full cost of advertisements placed under cooperative advertising agreements was posted as a charge against the retail operation. Any difference realized through agency discounts and creative space buys was credited to Incentive Planners.

Polk also had financial interests in companies that provided ancillary services to Polk Bros. Polk, for example, had a stake in Tomar Industries, which manufactured Polk's famous lighted Santa Clauses and, later, the aluminum Christmas trees, which were marketed nationally. Similarly, Sol Polk backed friend and associate Jack Hendrickson in Hendrickson & Sons, an appliance installation service which worked under contract to Polk Bros.

Polk Bros. discovered and exploited off-shore markets for reconditioned American-made appliances. Tax write-offs related to Polk's numerous charitable activities and donations of new and used appliances to churches, schools, and other institutions were not neglected.

The company was able to utilize subsidiaries such as the Appliance Credit Corporation in the way that it did because it had the financial means to do so. Polk Bros. was cash rich. It never had to borrow to finance its inventory. On the contrary, Sam Polk, who had a keen sense for the velocity of money and the uses of other people's money, frequently turned inventory and the short-term debt it represented to financial advantage. For example, the company might negotiate thirty-day terms before payment was due on a major purchase. Polk Bros. might sell that inventory within ten days. Sam would then invest the money due the supplier for the twenty days remaining on the contract.

It is notable that the brothers' financial activities, with very few exceptions, were handled entirely within the family circle, without benefit of intermediary money managers or investment consultants. They did not need any help. But even if they had not had the benefit of Sam Polk's financial acumen, the brothers would have been loathe to pay commissions to anyone, much less relinquish any measure of control over their financial business or closely held financial information.

*   *   *

A ritual grew up around the signing not only of the merchandise checks that Polk issued to its suppliers but any check dealing with an expenditure of company funds, with the exception of payroll. This ritual was a tangible symbol of the brothers' concern that every part of the financial aspect of the business remain within their immediate control.

Sam Polk, quite properly, regarded the personal review he made of every expenditure as an auditing function. The difficulty was that as the company grew, the task became one of mammoth proportions. Sam's daughters remember that when he came home from the store at night, he would be carrying stacks of these checks, each one accompanied by all the backup paper related to the transaction. After supper, Sam would retire to his desk in the basement where he could concentrate on the checks, away from the tumult of the office.

In Sol's mind the check-signing ritual represented power: Whoever signed the checks controlled the money, whoever controlled the money held the power. Sol, Sam, or Morrie would sign a check only after it had been signed by Lester Bachmann, the company's chief purchasing officer. Bachmann would sign only after the check had been audited by the buyers, or other employees, responsible for the expenditure. Sol might require six or seven signatures on a merchandise check before it was released.

The only signature that meant anything, so far as the bank was concerned, was that of Sol, Sam, or Morrie. But internally the process was very meaningful. It was also inordinately burdensome. Irv Lewis remembers staying at the office until "nine, ten, eleven o'clock at night" initialing checks and feeling the full weight of the responsibility.

*   *   *

The brothers recognized a problem faced by every retailer: employee theft. In the early years they adopted policies that stayed with the company to the end, which can be summarized as "no one touches the money except family, and fam-

ily must be there to see the merchandise going out the door."
The checks were Sam Polk's responsibility; Harry Polk, at the
headquarters store on North Central Avenue, was in charge of
keeping an eye on the door.

The irony of Sol Polk's concern over theft is that the
brothers themselves were honorable to a fault in their own
business dealings. As was often said, their word was their
bond. When a store manager embezzled money from Polk
Bros., it disturbed Sol greatly. Sol had placed his trust in the
man and that trust was betrayed. Family members say that Sol
was never able to get past his feelings over the incident. The
amount of money involved was insignificant in the larger picture. But even at the time of his own final illness Sol demanded assurance that full restitution was being made.

Howard Polk believes that "Sol became very jaded and
distrustful over time. He had built up a business on hand-
shakes and took any amount of shrinkage, although a fact of
life in the retail business, very personally." Sol carried his concern over theft to an extreme. Howard remembers a morning
in 1987 when Sol came through the headquarters store on
North Avenue and picked up a portable radio from a display.
Sol at that time had trouble walking due to a serious bone deterioration in his hip. Howard says,

> I saw Sol grab the radio and start walking with it.
> You could see that he was in pain. Twenty minutes
> later I get a call from him. He says, "Come out here.
> I'm in the warehouse, in the back." When I got
> there, Sol was bawling everybody out. He is saying
> that here he was, walking out of the store with that
> radio, and nobody stopped him. "Anyone could steal
> anything out of this joint," he was saying.
>
> Sol Polk owned the company. He could throw
> refrigerators off the back dock if he wanted to, and
> nobody would stop him. But he didn't see it that
> way. In his mind he was demonstrating how easy it
> would be for somebody to steal a radio.

*   *   *

Given the diversity of Polk's business interests, it may seem surprising that Sol, unlike other tycoons, appeared to have no dreams of empire — beyond that which the family could hold within its hands and directly control.

Sam Walton, the founder of the Wal-Mart chain, visited Polk Bros. in the 1960s, and very likely learned something from Polk Bros.' example about the volume discount business he was building. But the Polks did not follow Walton's example. Given its reputation as the nation's largest independent dealer in appliances and home electronics, and its solid relationships with brand-name manufacturers, Polk Bros. might easily have taken steps in the 1960s to establish a national chain built on the model of its enormously successful Chicago stores.

Polk Bros.' television advertising reached markets in Indiana, Michigan, and southern Wisconsin, and the company did incorporate the Polk Bros. name in those states. But the company made no serious moves to establish stores there. The registration of the Polk Bros. name was not the indicator of serious intent that it might appear to be. In anticipation of possible future diversification, Polk Bros. registered, but never activated, a number of other names, including such now familiar cognomens as "Century 21" and "Polks' Computerland."

Expansion of the Polk Bros. chain beyond the Chicago area was unlikely in any event. The culture of the business militated against it. Sol did not delegate well, and the company remained to the end zealously protective of its privacy. The establishment of a middle-management structure capable of administering a far-flung empire was not a possibility. Moreover, the Polks always saw themselves as a Chicago business. They were the neighborhood store. The folks down the street. The slogan they chose to mark the company's fiftieth anniversary in business was: "Born in Chicago, Raised in Chicago, and Proud of It."

* * *

The Polk brothers' philanthropies and charitable contributions were as widespread as their business activities. And often just as private. The company was particularly supportive of youth organizations such as the Chicago Boys and Girls Clubs; veterans' interests such as the VFW and the USO; schools and other educational programs; and groups that assisted seniors and the handicapped.

The Polks did not just give money to philanthropies. They gave time. Advertising executive Jack Leonard recalls Sol Polk's response when he was named chairman of the annual fund-raising drive for the Catholic Youth Organization (CYO), founded by Chicago Archbishop Bernard Shiel. The fund-raising event was to be a night of amateur boxing at the Chicago Stadium.

The position of chairman was largely honorary, but Sol did not take it that way. Sol set up an office downtown at the Congress Hotel, called on Polk Bros. suppliers to buy blocks of tickets, arranged with his friend Red Quinlan at WBKB-TV to have the event televised, and got sportscaster and one-time Polk Bros. spokesman Jack Drees to announce the events. He persuaded Mogen David Wines to buy the TV time.

As a backup, in case his suppliers did not produce the number of bodies needed to fill the empty seats in the stadium, Sol and Jack Leonard went to the main Chicago post office and passed out free tickets to Chicago postal workers. On the night of the event, the stadium was packed. The amount of money raised set a record. People continued to muse over the effort that a Jewish boy from the West Side had put into the Catholic fund-raising event. To commemorate the occasion, Sol gave his Irish-Catholic friend Jack Leonard a gold St. Christopher medal with a Star of David on the back.

* * *

The death of David Polk in 1955 set in motion a succession plan that eventuated in the present-day Polk Bros. Foundation. In the early years of the company, ownership was divided, in varying proportions, among the five brothers and their sister, Goldie. Sol had the largest, but not the controlling, interest in the company — about thirty-five percent. The remainder was divided, in descending order, among Sam, Morrie, Harry, David, and Goldie, who owned about twelve percent of the business. When David died, the company bought back his shares.

The surviving Polk siblings established the Polk Bros. Foundation. They also entered into a buy-sell agreement whereby the company would have the option to buy back from each member's estate their shares in Polk Bros. Inc. In concept, the plan was designed to assure that ownership of the company would not pass out of the hands of the immediate family. In practice, as the estate plan was formulated, the foundation ultimately would own all the stock in the company, and the company would be run through the foundation. At the time, it was legal for a charitable foundation to operate a for-profit business. Over the years, the laws changed but the plan did not.

*   *   *

On August 1, 1973, Goldie Bachmann Luftig suffered a severe and disabling stroke. She was then sixty-eight years old. The event was devastating to the family. The physicians held out little hope, but Goldie fought her way back. It was a long pull involving months, and then years, of physical therapy and speech therapy. Ultimately Goldie retained all her conceptual faculties, but never recovered the power of speech. And she was never able to return to her place in the store.

In June of 1982, Sam's wife Thelma died from complications that followed an attack of meningitis. The loss was a profound shock to Sam, who, his daughters say, lost his zest and perhaps also his will to live. Sam had a serious stroke in

the fall of 1982. He appeared to be recovering when he suffered another, fatal, stroke in May of 1983.

*   *   *

From the time it was established in the late 1950s, the
Polk Bros. Foundation had functioned as a small giving program operated more or less informally. The assets of the foundation grew with a donation from Harry's estate in 1969.
When Sam died, the assets of the foundation again significantly increased. In 1985 Sol and Morrie established a second
foundation, the Polk Bros. Senior Welfare Foundation. This
entity was funded by a grant from the original foundation and
became an active charitable arm of the business.

With Sam's death, Morrie Polk's responsibilities multiplied. Irv Weiner stayed with the company to help with management of the real estate operations and the investment
portfolios. But Morrie took over the larger part of the management of the financial side of the business, as well as continuing to oversee the operations of the warehouse.

In September of 1985 Morrie and Marion Polk took a
long-deferred vacation. They went on a cruise to the Bahamas
where, Marion hoped, the concerns of the business would not
follow them. While on the cruise, Morrie, too, suffered a
stroke. He died just three weeks later, on October 12, 1985.

Sol was now alone in the business. Goldie was present
but incapacitated. And Sol himself was becoming ill. But the
company was strong and its roots were deep. Sol, though increasingly absent, was still the captain of the ship.

*   *   *

The Polk brothers made a great deal of money for their
company. They gave away a great deal of money. But they
were reluctant to spend money on themselves. Sol carried
personal frugality to an extreme. He never owned a house,
and preferred not to own an automobile. In his last years, ac-

cording to one source, he bought his clothes at Sears. Goldie continued to take the bus to work right up to the time of her retirement from the business.

The brothers provided comfortable, middle-class lives for their families, but, as one family member put it, "They always lived well below their means." The Polk wives were careful money managers. Any ostentation or display of wealth was anathema. The relative simplicity of their personal lifestyles was not an accident nor was it an eccentricity, says Sandra Polk Guthman, who guided the Polk Bros. Foundation into a new and very active role in the 1990s.

18

Fire!

" 'I never saw a fire move that fast in my life,' said a fire fighter at the scene."

— Chicago Tribune
June 2, 1987

"Polk Bros. is in business, and we're here to stay."

— Lester Bachmann
June 2, 1987

On the evening of June 1, 1987, Polk Bros.' Melrose Park headquarters store and the company's massive warehouse were leveled by one of the largest structural fires in Chicagoland memory. The loss was overwhelming. The North Avenue store was the centerpiece of Polk Bros.' far-flung operations, and the 400,000 square-foot warehouse was the distribution center for all of the stores in the Polk chain. The morning after the fire a banner headline screamed, "Polk Bros is Gone." The newspaper was wrong. Polk Bros. was down but not out.

*   *   *

The fire began insidiously, as a smoldering ember lurking among the massive rolls of carpeting housed at the northeast end of the warehouse, right behind the sales floor. It was a quiet Monday evening, the tag-end of the drivers' Sunday-Monday weekend break. The warehouse was dark, manned by only a skeleton crew.

Polk Bros.' corporate counsel, Paul Fischer, was the executive on duty that night. Although he might not have been. The duty rotated among Fischer, operations manager Michael Crane, and merchandising manager Howard Polk. Monday was Howard's night on, but he had switched his schedule so he could attend the annual consumer electronics show at McCormick Place.

Fischer took a phone call at about 6:30 p.m. that evening from a customer who was awaiting delivery of a Sony console television set. After checking the order files and the manual card-and-line inventory on that Sony model and determining that it should be in stock, Fischer decided to walk back to the warehouse himself to make a visual check on the merchandise.

With the help of a warehouseman manning a small electric tractor, Fischer searched the huge area marked off for television storage — without success. He was not pleased to find that the model he was looking for was not in inventory. It was close to 7:20 p.m. when he headed back to the main offices. Taking a short-cut, Fischer walked due east past the long racks of carpet rolls stored on the north wall behind the employee cafeteria.

Paul was thinking hard about how to handle the inventory problem when out of the corner of his eye he sensed, rather than saw, a light flicker somewhere within the darkened forest of carpet rolls. He stopped, turned, and looked again. He remembers the moment:

A narrow pillar of flame suddenly shot up in one of the carpet aisles, going from floor to ceiling. "Holy

Cow!" I thought. I'm thinking, I'm here by myself in the warehouse. I headed for the nearest fire hose — the one just outside the doorway to the carpet department offices. I started running out the hose and yelling to people in the office to call the fire department and get people out of the store.

Major appliance buyer Jerry Unger had returned early from his 6:30 p.m. dinner break, anticipating meetings with sales representatives for the Roper company and General Electric. He was with them in his small office near the order department when he heard Fischer's calls from the warehouse.

I ran to the back and saw that Paul had unrolled the fire hose and was running back to turn on the valve. He yelled, "Unger, get on the back of the hose!" We hit the base of the flame with water. Julio Barra, a carpet salesman, was right behind me. He was helping us.

The heat-activated overhead sprinkler system kicked in at this point, drenching the men and burying the lick of flame in a cloak of black smoke. The warehouse alarm bells began to clang. Within minutes the first of three trucks dispatched from the Melrose Park Fire Department arrived and hooked a pumper to the hydrant on North Avenue. Fischer and Unger continued to man the hose in the warehouse.

All of a sudden the fire hose just went limp. There was no more water coming out. Jerry and I were like two of the three stooges, looking around like crazy and saying, "hey, who's stepping on the hose!" We had no idea what had happened.

What happened was that the entire system that supplied water to the Polk Bros. complex had failed. Activation of the overhead sprinkler system had made a sudden, heavy draw on the self-contained water system. The fire department's effort to back-pump at the North Avenue hydrant to build up pressure to feed their hoses stressed the buried pipes beyond their capacity. The main underground line burst.

Back in the warehouse, the sprinkler system sputtered and failed. Fischer watched helplessly as dense clouds of black smoke began to roll back through the warehouse.

> I was still thinking that it was going to be all right. Then, through all this smoke, Unger and I saw the same pillar of flame going right back up. We said, "Well, it's time to go. We have no water. The fire department is here. Let's adios." We went out through the order department. There were still some ladies there. We said, "Grab your purses. Grab anything. Don't hang around. It's time to get out of here."

*　　*　　*

The response within the store was calm. There was no smoke there, no sign of flames, no sense of alarm. Fischer's first warning had set in motion emergency procedures that had long been in place. An alert to clear the building had gone out over the public address system. Store manager Sam Falato had seen the few customers on the floor out the door. He then checked the second-floor offices to be sure that everyone was leaving. The cash registers were closed and locked and the safe was slammed shut. The atmosphere was that of a school fire drill. Fortunately, if that could be said, the fire occurred at the slowest point of the business day. There were very few people in the store. It was the dinner hour, the lull between the steady stream of daytime traffic and the arrival of after-dinner shoppers.

Warehouse supervisor Frank Genatempo was also on duty that night. Calls to the Melrose Park Fire Department went out almost simultaneously from front office staff who had been alerted by Fischer, and from the central security station in the back of the warehouse where the automatic warning system set off alarms on a master control panel.

Frank Genatempo drove an electric truck into the depths of the warehouse to locate the few warehousemen who were on duty that night. Working with this small crew, Genatempo began backing the first of forty-five delivery trucks up to the docks to load merchandise that had been staged there for the Tuesday morning deliveries. Even before they started it was already too late. Nineteen loads of furnishings already on the docks would go up in flames, along with everything else in the warehouse. Ultimately only the trucks were saved.

Some of the office staff did not immediately heed the warning to evacuate the building. Many, including credit manager Jim Boysen returned to their offices, hoping to gather up irreplaceable records. Paul Fischer himself was one of those. He headed for his upstairs office to get his briefcase and some legal papers. In a feeble gesture toward normalcy, Fischer, whose white dress shirt was blackened with oily smoke and water, took his suit coat from the back of a chair and slipped it on.

Employees clustered in small groups along the street in front of the store, asking one another what had happened. "Nobody really thought that the whole building could go," Fischer remembers. "We still had no idea the water main had broken — that the fire department had no way to fight this thing."

Abruptly, the atmosphere changed. The darkened warehouse came alive with light — as if a master switch somewhere had been thrown. The employees gathered on the street now could see flames racing, window by window, through the building, from the front to the back. "That's when people started crying," Fischer says.

> I remember Sam Falato pacing up and down the street and saying, "Oh, my god! I'm going to lose my store. How can this be happening? I'm losing my

store!" Then the glass panes started blowing out of the windows: "Bang! Bang! Bang!"

At that point, the fire ripped through the warehouse with the force of a high explosive bomb and the heat of a blast furnace. "I saw it when it was just a little flame and all of a sudden . . . the whole building was gone," one witness told a reporter for the *Chicago Tribune*.

"It was just literally a ball of fire," said another.

The speed with which the inferno moved was truly stupefying. The fire was driven by a violent draft that sucked the flames through the huge warehouse, creating what amounted to a tornado inside the building. The twisted steel that remained in the aftermath led investigators to estimate that the temperature inside the warehouse had reached as much as four thousand degrees.

More than a dozen suburban fire departments and hundreds of fire fighters responded to the five-alarm fire. Water was pumped from the Melrose Park and Elmwood Park substations and from a relay station on North Avenue. But the fire fighters could do little more than keep the flames, which were driven by a strong south wind, from spreading to nearby buildings and from leaping North Avenue to the Thatcher Woods Forest Preserve across from the store. Streets were condoned off for several blocks around the scene. Police and civil defense units struggled to hold back spectators. The *Chicago Sun-Times* estimated the crowd at over a thousand persons.

By 8 p.m. the spectacular blaze had lit up the western suburban skies. The smoke could be seen from Chicago lakefront highrises more than ten miles to the east of the scene. The Chicago fire department itself received dozens of calls reporting huge clouds of smoke blanketing the downtown area. "It looks like the whole city is going up," one Chicago dispatcher said.

Polk Bros. television announcer Bill Hamilton was a licensed pilot. He says that the phenomenon of the Polk Bros.

fire dominated not only the eastern and western skylines, but even the skies over Chicago itself:

> Polk Bros. headquarters store was right on the approach path for Runway 32-L at O'Hare International Airport. The fire was so large that it created what appeared to be a small rain storm on the radar at the field. Incoming flights had to be diverted because the controllers could not send them through this enormous plume of smoke.

At 10 p.m. the roof collapsed. The remaining walls fell inward like a tray of dominoes. The event was witnessed throughout Chicagoland, as the three major network stations broadcasted live from the scene: Bill Kurtis anchored the story at CBS; Linda Yu was on the scene for ABC; Art Norman reported the fire for NBC. Eerily, the giant Polk Bros./GE red-and-white neon sign standing in front of the store blazed on against the backdrop of the roaring inferno. The travelling white lights on the sign continued, throughout the night, to flash like a Broadway theater marquee, beckoning shoppers into the store.

*   *   *

Howard Polk had done a good day's business at the electronics show. He'd wrapped it up by joining several of Polk Bros.' regular vendors for dinner. He was headed home at nine o'clock. Swinging north on Lake Shore Drive, he flipped on his car radio: "Extra . . . alarm fire in Melrose Park . . . Polk Bros. warehouse engulfed in flames. . . ."

Howard could not believe the words. He made a sharp left turn through Lincoln Park and raced westward on North Avenue toward the store. Reaching the police barricades, he abandoned his car in the middle of the street and ran the remaining three blocks. "I don't even remember driving there," he said. "I was in a daze. It was total disbelief."

Even before the warehouse exploded in flames, Paul Fischer had found a pay phone at the McDonald's restaurant at the corner of North Avenue and First Street. He made two calls. The first was to his wife, Jennifer. The second call was to Lester Bachmann. Bachmann, recovering from a mild heart attack, was under doctor's orders to cut back on his fifteen-hour work days. Fischer reached him at his home in suburban Northbrook. The conversation was very brief.

> I said, "Lester, the warehouse is on fire." He didn't say anything. There was just silence. I was almost crying at that point. I said, "I think we're going to lose the whole building."
>
> He said, "Oh, my god." Then he hung up.

It took Bachmann half an hour to get back to Melrose Park, all the while monitoring early reports of the fire on his car radio. It took several minutes longer to persuade police to let him through the lines. Service department manager Gerry Bruns had seen the smoke from her home in nearby Stone Park and had rushed to the scene. She was horrified to see Bachmann running full out across the parking lot toward the burning building. His intention was to advise fire officials that there were two large propane gas tanks stored near the service building south of the warehouse. That done, he stopped to assess the situation.

> The whole building was in flames at that time. I was dumbstruck. Like everyone else, I just looked with disbelief. There were explosions everywhere. The tubes in the television sets were exploding. It was clear that nothing was going to be saved.

Bachmann thought at that moment of a conversation with his wife, Gail, earlier that day. "I told her that we had just had the biggest May in the history of the company."

It was the best and the worst. Bachmann would have been

acutely aware that on this night the warehouse was filled to absolute capacity. There were two periods in the year when Polk Bros. warehoused a far larger than usual inventory: late spring — as it then was — when air conditioners for summer sales were stocked by the tens of thousands, and fall, when Christmas-season merchandise began to arrive. Moreover, over the past week, end-of-the-month orders, a peak buying time for Polk Bros., had been arriving in the warehouse.

Sometime after 10 p.m. Michael Crane, Howard Polk, Paul Fischer, and a few others gathered at the Country Club motel, located on North Avenue just east of the burning warehouse. The motel buildings had been evacuated earlier in the evening, but, Jerry Unger remembers, "They opened the bar for us." At the same time Lester Bachmann and others were meeting at the nearby Denny's restaurant. Lester asked that all the managers, department heads, and buyers be notified that he was calling an 8:30 a.m. managers' meeting to be held at the old store at 2850 North Central Avenue. Both groups began making calls.

In a sense, at the time of the fire, the Polk Bros. executive staff was a legion with a fallen leader. Sol Polk — the company's founding spirit — was hospitalized, battling complications of diabetes and hypertension from which he would not recover. And the brothers now were gone. The decisions that were made that night and that would be made in the days to come would determine the future of the company.

By dawn the warehouse was leveled, and the 8311 North Avenue retail store and showrooms were in ruins. A television reporter on the scene pronounced the requiem: "Devastation. That is the only word I can use. It's just gone."

An aerial photograph taken that morning shows twenty acres of blackened rubble. Two huge snorkels were still playing water over the area, extinguishing hot spots and flare-ups. With the exception of the warehouse offices over the loading docks, not a wall was standing. The railroad tracks that ran through the warehouse had been contorted into a buckled tangle of iron. The skeleton of the landmark water tower can be seen in the photograph, standing impotently at the eastern edge of the property.

"The whole building just melted," Jerry Unger says. "It's hard to imagine metal appliances disappearing," Bruce Bachmann observed. "But that's what happened."

*   *   *

Early on the morning of June 2, Polk Bros. top staff gathered in the old Polk City headquarters offices on North Central Avenue to establish what they informally called their "Disaster Recovery Center." Even as they met, a storm moved in from the west, mercifully drenching the still smoldering ruins out on North Avenue with a heavy rain.

The assembled group — exhausted, anxious, and sleepless — knew immediately what the choice would be: Quit or keep going. There were perhaps fifty people at the meeting. Their number included the executives, store managers, department heads, merchandise managers, and other key staff people.

Lester Bachmann, acting in Sol Polk's absence as chief executive officer, opened the meeting, Howard Polk recalls, with a little pep talk. "It was as peppy as Lester can be," Howard remembers, adding that Bachmann's innate dignity and reserved manner was a calming presence in the room. Lester's message to the team was simple: "Polk Bros. is in business," he said. "And we're here to stay."

Bachmann would later tell a reporter: "We didn't have anything. But we did have the dedication of our employees, and they took the attitude that whatever had to be done, they would do."

For the next eighteen months, the company's leadership operated out of this temporary command center at 2850 North Central Avenue. Many who passed through these makeshift offices felt the nostalgic pull of the place: This, after all, was where it all began. Bachmann's office, a former storage room, was just a few feet from the cubicle he had shared with Sam Polk in the 1940s and 1950s. Beyond the old balcony — where Irv Lewis first met the five Polk brothers — the space now reclaimed for office cubicles had once been the Polk family bedrooms.

For months after the fire, the headquarters offices of this multi-million-dollar business still looked much the way it had in the first days of the emergency. The *Chicago Sun-Times*, in a gesture of support, donated a load of used furniture from their own offices.

Office manager Barbara Toomey and her staff worked four to a desk. Gerry Bruns' work space was a corner of another desk, where she sat wedged under a shelf. Her service department was run out of a cardboard carton stored under her chair. Business reporter Janet Kay, writing for the *Chicago Tribune* in mid-October, described the setting.

> The executive office is two desks pushed together in an old storage room, up a short flight of wooden stairs hidden among the washers, dryers and microwave ovens in the Polk Bros. store at 2850 N. Central Avenue. The executive conference room is up and down several more steps, among the dinette sets in the furniture department.

Within three days of the fire, a new central switchboard had been installed in the "Disaster Recovery Center" at the 2850 store, and every available hand was enlisted to answer customer calls. The first order of business was to meet the orders for merchandise already scheduled for delivery. Copies of customer orders from the remaining ten stores enabled the company to reconstruct business done on the day of the fire from all but the warehouse store. Wherever possible, these orders were filled with display models and other inventory available on the Polk Bros. sales floors and showrooms. Customers who had purchased merchandise at the warehouse store were asked to bring their original sales slips to any Polk Bros. store.

It was a stop-gap measure. Managers estimated that without the central warehouse, appliances in the stores would be sold out in less than a week. Polk's vendors — some who had done business with Polk Bros. for as long as fifty years — rushed to help, dispatching special shipments of merchandise directly to the remaining stores. In the crisis, some, such as Zenith, were able to deliver merchandise to retail customers directly out of their own facilities. Gerry Bruns remembers the first days after the fire.

> We had to reassure vendors that we had money, that we were here, that they were going to be taken care of. We wrote to every one, asking for copies of invoices and copies of purchase orders if they had them. Gradually you saw whole departments rebuilding out of nothing.

Polk Bros. also had to reassure customers not only that the company was still in business but also that it was doing business as usual. Polk's instinct for turning adversity to advantage was evident as soon as the second morning after the fire when the *Chicago Sun-Times* hit the streets with this headline: "Fire won't hurt retail business — Polk Bros."

Two weeks later Polk Bros. launched a media blitz. Full-page newspaper ads in the form of an "open letter to our valued customers" promised:

> Even though Polk Bros. has suffered a major fire at our warehouse and store in Melrose Park, we still have ten great Chicagoland locations **READY** to serve you! No matter what your furniture or appliance needs.
>
> As the ashes begin to cool, we at Polk Bros. are swinging into action, ordering trainloads of top quality brand name appliances, plus truckloads of furniture. For over 50 years, Chicago's own Polk Bros. has proudly served millions of Chicagoland

families, and we look forward to serving you and
your families in the years to come.

Radio ads were folksy — and masterful:

> The fire which leveled our Polk Bros. warehouse in
> Melrose Park has certainly caused a lot of inconve-
> nience, but little, or none, for Polk customers. . . .
> A terrible fire, such as that which destroyed our
> Polk Bros. warehouse in Melrose Park is, of course,
> deeply traumatic. But, as loyal Polk customers
> would expect, the fifty-two-year-old Polk philoso-
> phy is stronger than ever. The ten other Polk stores
> have picked up the slack and it's business as usual. . . .
> As you may have noticed, it takes more than a
> warehouse fire to diminish Polk Bros.' dedication to
> loyal Polk Chicagoland customers. . . .

True to form, the post-fire advertisements reinforced the
relationship between Polk Bros. and national brand-name
manufacturers. A radio ad for refrigerator-freezers led with
these words:

> Polk Bros. wants you to know how terrific General
> Electric has been in helping out after that destruc-
> tive fire which leveled our warehouse in Melrose
> Park. Not the least of which is generously making
> extra factory inventory available, for our Polk cus-
> tomers . . . superb people.

*　*　*

With inventory moving again, albeit haltingly, the company struggled to recover or recreate its financial records. Accounts receivable were of primary importance. On the day of
the fire, the credit department had run a backup of the company's short-term "net-ten" receivables. These were the print-

outs that Jim Boysen carried out of the building. In retrospect, it was an heroic action. The billings for these accounts alone, for which there was no other central record, totaled more than two million dollars.

The computer tape for Polk's revolving charge accounts had been stored in the office fireproof safe. The data survived but just barely. The plastic reel on which the tape was housed had melted into the tape itself. IBM laboratories in Tucson, Arizona, were able to recover most of the data, as well as a substantial body of the company's personnel records. While this work was in progress, the company resumed billings using records provided by the credit bureau where customer credit applications were filed. Simultaneously, Polk Bros.' outside accountant, Stan Weiss of Terrel, Weiss, & Sugar, began the long labor of recreating the company's general ledger book.

Reconstruction of other business records, including those related to the company's real estate and mortgage business, was a far more tedious undertaking. Paul Fischer began the process by requesting copies of files kept by lawyers who had represented the company at real estate closings. These were supplemented from title company records. Painstakingly, one by one, a thousand mortgage files were recreated.

While it appeared that every record, every memento of the company's fifty-year history, had been virtually vaporized in the tremendous heat of the fire, Fischer was reluctant to give in to the inevitability of total loss. For weeks after the fire he made a daily circuit of the ruins, wearing mechanic's coveralls and hiking boots. Carrying a walking stick, he poked and rummaged through the rubble searching for office safes, file cabinets, and strong boxes that might yield up charred papers and company memorabilia.

Fischer did find some of these materials, but the yield was disappointing. The contents of even the heaviest fireproof safes were seared by the sheer heat of the fire. Singed and brown, papers crumbled into brittle fragments at the slightest touch. With the help of a document restoration service, Olga Sarwas, who had been with the company since the 1940s, and

Paul Fischer worked for weeks separating the pages of records thought to be important with tweezers, and copying, wherever possible, patchworks of pieces to make up whole pages.

In other respects the search of the rubble assumed the character of an archeological dig. The smallest finds took on an exaggerated importance. There seemed to be some comfort, some sense of order, in putting things back as they were, however insignificant the act. A roll of stamps stored in a tin with petty cash was found fused together by the heat. The stamps were taken to the post office to be replaced. Small amounts of cash, soggy and burned beyond recognition, were sent to the federal reserve bank. Paul Fischer kept one souvenir from his searches: a mound of coins that had melted into a solid mass. He used it as a paperweight.

* * *

Long before Fischer began his search of the rubble, the official inquiry into the cause of the fire was underway. Investigators from the state fire marshal's office and the Alcohol, Tobacco and Firearms Bureau of the U.S. Treasury Department were on the scene by early Tuesday. Polk's insurers conducted an independent investigation, and the Melrose Park Fire Department contributed its own report. The results of all these investigations were disappointingly inconclusive.

The origin of the fire was readily traced to the carpeting section where Fischer first sighted the flames. But the cause was never determined. Analysis of debris samples conclusively ruled out arson. Polk employees speculated that a cigarette smoldering in trash removed that evening from the employee cafeteria might have been a contributing factor. Polk Bros.' insurers paid the maximum value of the policies. Refusing to disclose the extent of this coverage, tight-lipped Polk executives would say only that the amount was "adequate." "When you don't need it, you have too much; when you do need it, it's never enough," Howard Polk would later say.

Discussions of the failure of the water system would go

on for many more months. The property at 8311 North Avenue had been annexed by the Village of Melrose Park in 1985; Polk Bros. contributed more than a quarter of a million dollars annually to the town's tax revenues. But the complex was not connected to the municipal water system. Water from a deep well on the Polk property was pumped to a towering storage tank located on the southeast side of the building. The normal water needs of the complex were met from a second, ground-level tank.

The collapse of this on-site water system was a death knell to any hope that some part of the doomed building or its contents might have been saved. Precious, anxious minutes had ticked by as firemen raced to run hoses from auxiliary hydrants located blocks away and as tanker trucks from county departments were called to the scene. For a time, fire fighters had weighed the feasibility of running lines to the nearby Des Plaines River which ran through the forest preserve across from the store. Months later, as part of the rebuilding process, Polk Bros. committed a $500,000 loan to the village of Melrose Park for construction of a twelve-inch water main connecting the First and North Avenue site to the village pumping station.

* * *

The brave front that Polk Bros. presented to the world belied the very real emotional and physical devastation that the company experienced in the wake of the fire. Although Polk Bros. never released any figures, industry sources pegged losses at $35 million, offset by an estimated $20 million in insurance coverage. This was the tip of the iceberg. The drain on the company's cash flow was merciless as the price of recovery from the fire continued to rise.

The human costs were also high. No one was injured in the fire, but more than half Polk Bros.' work force of thirteen hundred men and women was displaced. Some two hundred warehouse and delivery workers lost their jobs altogether, leading to a lingering morass of union and legal problems that would consume the company's energy and sap its reserves for years to come.

As the summer wore on, the company's leadership realized that they had two choices: They could fold the old carnival tents and succumb to the mounting competitive challenges of the glitzy new superstores that were then seriously eroding Polk Bros.' hegemony in the Chicago market. Or they could rebuild and come back fighting.

Polk Bros. billboards that appeared around the city in the fall announced the decision: "We're Coming Back! Watch Us Grow. . . ."

19

Going Out in Style

*"Until the day God says 'Turn off the switch,'
I'll want to be associated with new products."*
— Sol Polk
Quoted in **Fortune**, 1955

*"I've been shopping at Polk Bros. for forty
years. . . . . It's like a part of life is gone."*
— Polk Bros. customers
Closing Sale, 1992

Polk Bros. did come back, as promised, and with a new look. In the spring of 1988 the company broke ground for a gleaming new flagship store and corporate headquarters, built on the site of the old, fire-ravaged warehouse. In the process of rebuilding, the small group of key executives made valiant efforts to modernize and restructure the business to meet the market challenges of the late 1980s and early 1990s. The problems were formidable. In January 1989 *Crain's Chicago Business* surveyed the terrain:

In the past 18 months, Polk Bros. has suffered the destruction of its warehouse, the influx of dozens of new superstore outlets, a legal battle among family members and the death of its founder, Sol Polk. Any one of those events could have dealt a knockout punch to the venerable electronics, appliance and furniture retailer that 55 years ago virtually invented the discount, name-brand hard-goods business. Yet the company has aggressively answered the bell for another round of retailing fisticuffs in what today is perhaps the most competitive arena in consumer goods.

By 1991, Polk Bros. was armed with an upscale image, three new state-of-the-art stores, renewal of television advertising campaigns, and plans to cut a new niche for itself in the suburban home furnishings market. For a time, it seemed that a turnaround was not only possible but might even be happening.

*   *   *

Sol Polk died on May 14, 1988. It was his seventy-first birthday. His death came just short of one year from the night of the fire that had consumed Polk's giant warehouse and plunged the family business into a fight for its life. He had been hospitalized at the time of the fire, and would remain so until his death. Although Sol was still titular head of the company, with the titles of Chairman and then Chairman Emeritus, the great engine had run down. He was unable to contribute more than a founder's spirit to the rebuilding effort.

Like his brother Harry, Sol was a diabetic. And, like others in the family, he suffered from a tendency toward severe hypertension. Similarly, he refused to acknowledge the existence of illness at any level — a common trait in the family. Sol was able, for the most part, to hide the extent to which his health was failing, until he developed a painful and increasingly debilitating deterioration of the bone in his hip. Even so, he treated the pain with ever-larger doses of over-the-counter medications, made valiant efforts to conceal his inability to stand or walk easily, and attributed the problem to "a touch of arthritis."

After Sol's first long hospitalization in the mid-1970s, he moved from his rented room at Chicago's Standard Club to the ground floor apartment in the two-flat building that Georgia Rice owned on Montrose Avenue. The arrangement was intended to be temporary, geared to his convalescence. He stayed ten years.

As mentioned earlier, Georgia did what she could to supervise Sol's diet and attend to his medical needs. For a time she chauffeured him to the places he needed to go. When his irascibility stretched the bounds of even Georgia's patience, others took over the driving. Morrie Polk did it up to the time of his own death in 1985. Michael Crane and Howard Polk took over from Morrie.

In late 1986 company executives made a decision without consulting Sol. During one of Sol's increasingly frequent hospitalizations they purchased a one-bedroom ranch-style house in River Forest, just east of the Melrose Park headquarters store. Irv Weiner, Michael Crane, and Howard Polk picked Sol up at the hospital shortly after Christmas and brought him to the new house, modestly furnished out of the Polk Bros. warehouse. An amiable Polish nurse was waiting. Sol was not pleased. Howard remembers the day:

> Sol said, "Hey! Where are we going!"
> I said, "We're going to take you to your house we bought." Well, you should have heard the roar of protest! He yelled at me to turn around and take him back, but I kept on driving. When we pulled up to the house, he refused to go in.

Ultimately, Sol loved the house. Clearly he had experienced frustration over his increasing dependence on others and over his inability to quell the infirmities that were robbing him of energy. When he moved into the house, with a paid caregiver, Sol seemed to recover a sense of autonomy and control. Howard remembers:

> The time that he was in the house — maybe four or five months — was the happiest that I had ever seen him. He was a changed man. He was almost emotional over it. He would say, ironically, "You know, this is the first time I ever owned a house." There was a period of a few months that he was just euphoric.

In the spring Sol went back into the hospital. He was there when he was told of the death of Georgia Rice, who had succumbed to a rapidly progressing brain tumor. As Sol's diabetic condition worsened, so did the bone infection. He never fully recovered consciousness following surgery on his hip in the fall of 1987. A shunt in his brain failed to relieve intracranial pressure. Measures to save him were heroic, protracted over a period of many months, and futile.

The account of memorial services published in *Crain's Chicago Business* bore the headline: "A royal sendoff for the discount king." The article noted, "It was no accident that the funeral procession for Chicago retailing legend Sol Polk wound past the Polk Bros. flagship store that's being rebuilt in Melrose Park." It continued:

> The 600 mourners who attended services at Oak Park Temple last week included the leading lights of the appliance and electronics industries, including top executives from General Electric Co., Whirlpool Corp., Maytag Co. and Zenith Electronics Corp. The [designated] pallbearers included such Chicago notables as W. Clement Stone, Sterling "Red" Quinlan and Irv Kupcinet. All agreed that Chicago is unlikely to ever see a merchant like Mr. Polk again.

*   *   *

As Sol became increasingly incapacitated, responsibility for running the company had fallen naturally to executive vice-president Lester Bachmann, who, more than any other, understood Sol's ways of doing business. Lester was backed up by two young executives, Michael Crane and Howard Polk, who had grown up within the family circle and in whom Sol had placed his confidence.

When it became apparent in early 1988 that Sol would not be able to resume his post as chairman, the three were appointed legal guardians, entitled to make business decisions for him. They would later become trustees of his estate and executors of his will. Shortly before Sol's death, Bachmann, Crane, and Howard Polk were formally elected chairman, vice-president of operations, and treasurer, respectively, of the corporation. Paul Fischer was elected secretary.

Michael Crane, the son of the Polk brothers' lifelong friend and personal attorney Ben Crane, had been an assistant state's attorney and was in private practice before coming to Polk Bros. in 1980. Howard Polk, Morrie's son, was an experienced buyer who had held key positions as the company moved into the highly competitive home electronics field. Fischer, an attorney with a background in corporate accounting, had been with Ben Crane's firm, Wisch and Crane, and had done legal work for Polk Bros. for a number of years before coming over to the company full-time in 1983.

*   *   *

Even before the rubble from the fire had been cleared, Polk Bros. had begun the long, hard process of rebuilding its flagship store in Melrose Park. At the same time, plans were being made to close out its less productive locations, including the Skokie store, the last of the non-furniture outlets. Space-starved and increasingly shabby Polk Bros. stores in the older Chicago neighborhoods would be the next to go.

The "Polk Plaza" development at the site of the old warehouse in Melrose Park was an ambitious undertaking. The effect at the November 1988 pre-Christmas opening, and the February 1989 Grand Opening, was dazzling. Designed by Belli & Belli Architects, the 110,000-square-foot sales floor included a hands-on diorama display of camcorders, more than one hundred separate furniture groupings, and a constellation of designer kitchens and bath shops. More drama was provided by a round, 1,600-square-foot, glass-enclosed sound booth used for demonstrations of stereo and home theater equipment.

The 60,000-square-foot office space on the second floor, reached by an impressive staircase overlooking the parking area, housed general offices, a large sales training center, and a showroom for Polk's premium division, Incentive Planners. Lester Bachmann described the facility as "the corporation's tribute to the founder of Polk Bros." The *Chicago Tribune*, covering the opening, remarked:

> The late Sol Polk, who founded Polk Bros. 54 years ago, would not recognize the chain's newest store at 8311 W. North Avenue, Melrose Park. That's just fine with his nephew, Howard Polk. "It's like nothing you've ever seen," he says. "It's very upscale."

Howard elaborated a long-standing company philosophy:

> The store will have the basic refrigerator and it will have the refrigerator for the person building a dream kitchen. We try to be what people say we can't be — all things to all people.

A second new store was opened at the same time, in a 45,000-square-foot leased space in the Iroquois Shopping Center in southwest suburban Naperville. The Naperville store replaced the small Glen Ellyn store that had previously served that area. A third store, built by Polk Bros. on the pattern of the flagship store, was opened in late 1989 in the growing northwest suburb of Mundelein.

For a time the sun seemed to be shining once again on Polk Bros. But there were clouds on the horizon. And there would be, as it turned out, no silver lining. The death of the company's founders and the fire had taken a heavy toll.

*   *   *

The dislocation caused by the fire resulted in a precipitous loss of market share, with sales dropping by some thirty percent from the company's peak of more than $150 million. Polk Bros.' gross profit margin had long been balanced on the economy of the Polk-owned and operated warehouse and delivery service. The loss of this facility dealt Polk Bros. a crippling blow.

For a time, the company leased warehouse space in suburban Des Plaines, but the measure was only temporary. These were the blackest days, when Polk Bros. was unable to maintain the standard of customer service that had been its trademark. A decision had to be made. The question was whether to make the financial commitment — and take the time needed — to rebuild the Melrose Park warehouse and re-establish delivery services, or go outside the company and hire a contractor to provide those services.

The concern over customer service prevailed. Over the summer of the fire Polk Bros. entered into a five-year contract with California-based Merchants Home Delivery Service, Inc. The costs of the contracted service turned out to be far higher than anticipated, both in terms of customer satisfaction and in real dollars. The Merchants Home contract, for a fixed figure, was based on pre-fire volume. It did not anticipate the dramatic loss in sales that followed the fire. Delivery costs, as a percentage of sales, rose accordingly.

But out-of-pocket costs would grow higher yet. Some two hundred drivers and warehouse workers, three-fourths of them union members, were laid off after the fire. When the company hired Merchants Home Delivery Service, the drivers' union, Chicago Truck Drivers, Helpers and Warehouse Workers, sued Polk Bros. They claimed Polk Bros. had violated the union contract. In late August the company learned that a labor arbitrator's binding judgment could force Polk Bros. to pay as much as five million dollars in back pay and other compensation to the unionized employees.

Polk's competitive edge was further eroded by the high price of its pre-existing union contracts. Polk Bros., unlike its competitors, had a unionized sales force. This was a double-edged sword. Polk salesmen were the best trained and most knowledgeable in the business but they were also the most expensive. While competitors could hire minimum-wage sales staff, Polk Bros. was locked into unionized commission rates and union work rules. A top salesman in the late 1980s could make upwards of fifty thousand dollars a year.

* * *

Polk Bros. was in a very tough spot. The cost of building and opening new stores, layered over recovery costs that were climbing inexorably, hit Polk's at precisely the time that price-competition in the red-hot Chicago appliance and consumer electronics market become more intense than ever before. Polk Bros. had just begun to regroup when the phenomenon of the discount electronic and appliance chains hit.

By the late 1980s the Detroit-based appliance giants, Highland Superstores Inc. and Fretter Inc., along with Philadelphia-based Silo, were breaking into the Chicago market in a big way. Sears, Roebuck and Co. and Montgomery Ward had become Polk Bros. imitators with the opening of their Brand Central and Electric City stores. The entrance of the Circuit City and Best Buy national chains was just around the corner. Polk Bros.' ability to compete in this overheated market was severely compromised by problems closer to home — and of far longer duration. Even before the fire, Polk

Bros. had fallen far behind other retailers in modernizing its operating procedures and installing computer systems. Howard Polk commented on this management dilemma:

> In the early 1980s the retail operations were still run the same way they were in the 'forties and 'fifties. This was the time when we should have been changing over to technology, but we weren't. We used the computer for our own credit card. We also used it to create reports, but these were thirty to forty days old by the time they were generated. We never acquired the on-line technology that was available for inventory control. We wrote up every sale in big order books until the end. We had customers come in to buy batteries, and we'd write up a three-page carbon-copy order form.

The lack of computerized systems reflected a management philosophy that dated from the beginning. At Polk Bros., sales were everything. Volume was what counted, the salesman was king, and the sales manager ran the store. By contrast, in the modern superstores entering the arena, systems and operations were everything. Wal-Mart Stores Inc., for example, is organized around the principle that the greatest efficiency yields the lowest operating cost. Polk Bros. was organized to produce the highest sales volume, with the expectation that all else would follow.

Mark Miller, writing in *Crain's Chicago Business* at the time the stores closed made this observation:

> [Sol] Polk's real insight was to give you the sense that you were as close as possible to the factory floor, and that you could cut your own best deal with him. Polk accomplished this as a matter of gut instinct and force of personality. Big, latter-day competitors like Highland, Fretter and Silo took that instinct and transformed it into a highly sophisticated, comput-

erized distribution and marketing system — a system Polk himself never developed. He didn't need
to, or so he thought.

Polk Bros. bought new computers after the fire, but used
them only to recreate the old systems. The company did not
seize this moment to install the modern management information system needed to take computerized controls to the
next level. Polk Bros. had pioneered the practice of just-in-
time buying, now standard in the industry, but even in its maturity, the company never moved beyond the concept of
manual inventory control.

Payroll and accounts receivable had been computerized
for a number of years, but accounts payable remained for the
most part a manual process. An inordinate amount of executive time was consumed by the check-signing ritual, but the
practice remained. That was the way Sol had done it. Over the
two years of the rebuilding process, some progress was made.
By 1990 the disbursement process had been converted to a
computer matching system — a significant step forward. In
late 1991 Howard Polk pushed to get point-of-purchase systems on line to eliminate the lengthy hand-written order system and achieve better control over inventory. By then it was
too late.

*   *   *

In common with many founders of family-run businesses, Sol had failed to build a professional management
team or provide for an orderly succession. He did not replace
people when they left; he loaded their duties onto the shoulders of the people who remained.

Moreover, Sol had let management talent, even within
the family slip, away. Bruce Bachmann spent ten years in the
management ranks but left the company in 1968 to go on to a
career in real estate development. "I grew up in it, I worked in
it, I left it," Bruce says. Irv Lewis, a family member by mar-

riage, was a top executive who lived the business day and night for twenty years. He left the company in 1978. Irv was acutely aware of the company's failure to adapt to the times. But there was little he could do to change the culture.

Four of the five founding brothers had died: David in 1955, Harry in 1969, Sam in 1983, and Morrie in 1985. In each case Sol did not bring in top-side management to fill the gap. He merely closed the circle a little tighter. By the time of Sol Polk's death in 1988, the company, in the words of one journalist, had become an anachronism. A veteran Polk Bros. salesman characterized the business, as Sol left it, as "just a big, dumb giant."

*   *   *

At the time of Sol's final hospitalization, ownership of the stock in the privately held company was divided among Sol Polk, his sister Goldie Luftig, and the company treasury, which had purchased each of the other brothers' shares when they died. On May 14, 1987, two weeks before the fire, Polk Bros. Inc. had privately initiated an action to buy back Goldie's shares as well.

Goldie challenged the move through her guardian, Bruce Bachmann. In August the company filed a lawsuit to compel Goldie to sell, claiming that her long-standing incapacity activated a buy-sell option in a 1959 stock agreement made among the five Polk siblings. Bachmann, on his mother's behalf, countersued. *Crain's Chicago Business*, in a November 1987 analysis of the circumstances, cast the action in a dramatic light:

> An internecine legal battle for control of privately held shares threatens to tear apart Polk Bros. Inc. The legal action pits master merchant Sol Polk — at 70, the youngest of six Polk siblings and the driving force behind the Polk Bros. company — against the oldest and only other surviving Polk sibling. Both are incapacitated due to illnesses.

The issue, as the negotiations proceeded, was not so much ownership of the stock but the value of it, and the value of any ancillary benefit that might have accrued to Goldie had she been able to remain active in the company. The 1959 agreement had divided four thousand three hundred shares among the four surviving brothers and Goldie at an original price of two thousand dollars a share, with the stipulation that the stock would be revalued from time to time as the company's book value increased. At the time the suits were filed, Polk Bros.' book value exceeded $150 million.

The lawsuits were resolved in a confidential settlement that allowed the company, through an employee stock ownership plan, to purchase Goldie's shares at an undisclosed price. The 1988 settlement resulted also in a restructuring of the Polk Bros. Foundation, severing the foundation from the corporate entity, Polk Bros. Inc. The settlement paved the way for the infusion, ultimately, of almost all of the company's assets into the Polk Bros. Foundation.

The settlement triggered a move within the company to activate an employee stock ownership plan (ESOP). The ESOP became the vehicle for the purchase of Goldie's shares. Some portion of Sol's shares also were sold to the ESOP to make up the legally required thirty percent. To make the purchase, the ESOP borrowed money. The loan was guaranteed by the company, Polk Bros. Inc., which also made the payments, charging them against the retail operations. This created debt expenses that the retail business had not had up to this time. The amount of red ink that retail ran in the last years of the business, perhaps coincidentally, was almost equal to the dollars being paid out in debt service.

Participation in the stock ownership plan was offered to all of Polk's six hundred employees, in lieu of future pension contributions. Union members, who included most of the sales staff, voted down the offer. The union vote, as it turned out, brought a double windfall to the non-union employees — executive, administrative, and support staff and those salesmen who were not in the union — who received the benefit of the full thirty percent when the company later liquidated.

*   *   *

Re-energized, but staggering from the impact of the 1990 to 1991 recession, the company proceeded with its plan to close the older and least productive stores. The decision would reduce the number of Polk Bros.' stores from ten to five. The first to go was the patriarch of the Polk Bros. chain: 2850 North Central Avenue, built by the five brothers on the site of the Polk family apartments in the years of feverish growth that followed World War II. The property was auctioned in late 1992; the building was razed a year later to make way for a supermarket.

The former reconditioning and surplus center at 3500 West Grand was the next to go, followed by the Near North store at 1048 West Belmont. That decision would have been made in any circumstances. Sol frequently closed non-producing stores and opened others in the peak years of the business. When these three Chicago Polk Bros. stores were closed, they looked very much as they had the day they opened. They were just thirty years older and that much more threadbare. Modernization was not a feasible option.

The Belmont Avenue store, for example, was housed in a century-old building that had never lent itself even to the installation of air-conditioning. The nineteenth-century tenant, a furniture dealership, had made deliveries by horse-drawn cart. When Polk Bros. bought the building, it still had a hay loft in the back and a horse trough on the alley.

The other stores targeted for closing were newer. The inclusion of their names on the list was a more telling indication of the extent of the company's problems. These were the Waukegan store, which had been open since the mid-1960s, and the Naperville store, which was then only two years old. Polk Bros.' decision to close half its stores was publicized as a "consolidation of retail operations," involving "a phase-out" of the five locations. Implicit was a promise that new stores would be opened at some indeterminate later date.

Rumors that Polk Bros. was facing bankruptcy circulated, but these were without foundation. If gross revenues can be taken as a measure, the retail business was, in fact, getting back on its feet at the time of the five store closings: Sales volume was improving. But the company was being squeezed. In the three years since the fire, competitive pressures had driven margins down, while at the same time the company's post-fire liabilities had driven operating costs up. There was very little meat left in the sandwich.

Burned by the rumors, but still optimistic, Polk Bros. hired a Chicago advertising agency, Smith, Badofsky and Raffel, to help pick up momentum. A new series of television ads, produced in late 1991, featured Polk employees and challenged the superstore chains by stressing the Chicago origins of the business. Howard Polk explained, "We are getting the message out that Polk Bros. is, was, and always will be a serious competitor with a hometown edge. We are not waiting for the recession to end to stimulate buying."

*   *   *

In the fall of 1990, Polk Bros. celebrated Lester Bachmann's fiftieth year with the company. In July 1991 Lester announced his plans to retire, with the action to be effective at the end of September. In early November the company hired a new president and chief executive officer, going outside the family circle for the first time in its fifty-seven-year history. Polk Bros.' choice was Arthur J. Landen, who at the time was serving as president and CEO of John M. Smyth Co.'s Homemakers, a well-known Chicago firm specializing in home furnishings.

While the appointment was characterized as another step in the expansion and modernization of the company, the appointment signalled Polk Bros.' concerns over its cash position. Landen, a CPA, had been with John M. Smyth for some thirty-eight years. He was a financial management specialist, characterized by a business writer as "a bean counter, a bottom-line, assets-and-liabilities kind of guy."

Commenting on the appointment, Howard Polk explained, "We knew we needed some expertise in the area of systems and financial, everything that Art Landen represents." Landen himself said, "It's like the modern world at Polk Bros. started with the fire." He added, "This business has come a long way in the last few years toward modern times and becoming state-of-the-art, but they're a long way from being there."

Landen was able to confirm what the principals already knew. The retail operation was bleeding out. Millions would have to be spent to refurbish physical plants, bring the computer system into the 1990s, recover control of warehousing and delivery operations, and renegotiate contracts. The choices were these: Spend what would be needed to get the retail operation back on its feet; sell the stores; or liquidate the company, turning the assets over to the foundation. Anyone who knew Sol knew that he would never have sold one square inch of Polk Bros.

*　*　*

In March of 1992 the newly formed Polk Bros. Inc. board of directors sat down to face the facts. The business decision was clear. The company could not in good conscience continue to underwrite the money-losing retail operations. The emotional component of the decision was no less clear, but much more difficult. The time had come to let the venerable business die a natural and honorable death. Polk Bros., as Chicago had known it, had reached the end of its life cycle. It was a hard choice and a sad choice. "This was the decision no one wanted to have to make," Howard Polk remembers.

On Thursday morning, April 2, Polk Bros.' four hundred fifty employees were told that the company was closing. It was an emotional meeting. "I thought there would be a lot of anger and frustration," Howard Polk said. "But people were simply crying. It was, as many said, like a death in the family."

The reason given was straight-forward and true. Polk Bros. was closing its retail operations because, as Howard Polk told the *Tribune*, "Our bills are current and we have ample cash reserves. However, the Polk stores have not operated profitably in recent years, and the board could not let this situation continue any longer."

Many older employees attributed the closings to the loss of the company's founders. "When Sol Polk died, something left that was irreplaceable," said retail consultant George Rosenbaum. A sentiment voiced among the salesmen was: "If Sol were alive, none of this would have happened." In a sense, they were right. As Howard points out, "If Sol and Sam and my dad had still been around, they would have underwritten the retail business forever, no matter what it cost. They loved it."

Chicagoans were stunned to read the news. The front-page banner headline in the *Chicago Tribune* on the morning of April 3 announced, "End of an era: Polk Bros. to close doors." The *Chicago Sun-Times* headline read: "Polk Bros. shutting for good." A later headline in the Pioneer Press chain of community newspapers declared simply: "Polk Brothers — rest in peace."

The passing of Polk Bros. was an inevitability, but the company's departure was by no means a rout. It was a dignified leave-taking. The corporation was solvent. Every supplier and every bill was paid in full. Employees were offered outplacement assistance and given severance pay based on their time in service with the company. With ESOP benefits, the package for many employees amounted to as much or more than a year's pay. There would be no phony going-out-of-business sales — just an orderly liquidation at honest prices of inventory already in stock. Salesman John Beyer remembers the sense of loss among the veteran sales force: "It was sad seeing these great old stores sold down to nothing. In the end, well, there just was nothing left to sell."

The Chicago store at 85th and Cottage Grove Avenue — the first store to be built by the brothers from the ground up and the only Polk Bros. store remaining within the Chicago city limits — was the first to go. The next closings were the suburban Schaumburg, Mundelein, and Burbank stores. The Melrose Park headquarters store held the final going-out-of-business sale over the weekend of June 17, 1992. At the end of the last day, Howard brought out a case of champagne which was shared among the sales staff and the customers remaining in the store. "I don't know whether it was an Irish wake or auld lang syne," Howard said. "It just seemed we had to do something to mark the moment."

The Polk family itself was overwhelmed by the outpouring of sentiment that accompanied both the announcement that Polk's would close, and the subsequent "farewell sales" held over a three-month period as the stores were phased out. Columnists in the major newspapers and business periodicals reminisced in pieces with titles such as: "A store of memories from N. Central Avenue" and "In Polk Bros.' demise, Chicago lost a legacy."

Hundreds of emotional calls, letters, and telegrams poured into the company lamenting the decision. One customer started a petition drive in the hope of keeping the business going. "It just heightens the sadness of it all," Howard told a reporter for the *Daily Herald*. "Customers are calling like crazy saying, 'This is where I bought my first refrigerator.'"

As the *Chicago Tribune* recognized, the families who came to the sales did regard the demise of Polk Bros. as the "end of an era" and the passing of an institution that had been part of their own lives for decades. Chicago resident Ruby Greb, interviewed by the *Franklin Park Herald-Journal*, said,

> You just can't find service like this anywhere else. I bought my first furniture at Polk Bros. many years ago. I never bought my appliances from Sears or

Montgomery Ward, only Polk Bros. I came to say
goodbye. They will be missed.

In July the company held the sale to end all of Polk Bros.'
fabulous sales. The three-day auction of the remaining store
equipment would be Polk Bros.' last hurrah. *Chicago Tribune*
columnist Eric Zorn painted a poignant picture for his readers:

> Used typewriters, desks, phones and calculators
> from the corporate offices were among the first of
> 7,000 items up on the block. Next came appliance
> dollies, fire extinguishers, the massive model train
> diorama once used to show off various models of
> camcorders and even the actual mold for the famous
> Polk plastic santas.
>
> "This is the saddest day in the world," said
> Carol Lenardi, a factory worker from Elmhurst
> who took the day off to prowl the Melrose Park
> store for leftover dining room sets and desks. "I've
> been shopping at Polk Bros. for 40 years. I bought
> my first Beatles album here. I saw the flowers on the
> desks upstairs and I thought, 'This is like being at a
> wake.' " . . .
>
> "It's sad. Unbelievable. Depressing," said ac-
> counting supervisor Mariann Dragojlovic, a thirty-
> three-year employee who watched the auction with
> moist eyes. "I came down here to try to buy my old
> typewriter, but I was too late. They'd already sold
> it."

Zorn stopped by to see Howard Polk in his second floor
office of the flagship store, which had been opened with much
bravado and optimism just three years earlier. He wrote,

> Up in his office, Howard Polk, 40, the last of the
> Polks still involved in the day-to-day operation,

chewed a stick of red licorice (not for sale) and looked out a window at hundreds of cars belonging to those who were even then cleaning the bones of his dead store. "These last few weeks have been tough," he said. "But I tell you, it sure feels great to have the parking lot full and people in the store again."

* * *

Polk Bros. was by no means alone in 1992 in its response to a genuine upheaval in the retail industries. Retail failures were occurring at an unheard-of rate in this period. Shortly after Polk Bros. closed, a chief competitor, Highland Superstores, abandoned the Chicago market. Soon after that, Sears, whose troubles had been known for years, divested itself of its financial businesses and refocused attention on healing its merchandise groups. Kmart was in trouble and was, like Polk Bros., struggling to bring outdated systems and aging physical facilities into the 1990s.

From the day the closing was announced, Howard Polk set about the business of putting the company out of business. Only the retail operations were closing. Polk Bros. Inc. still ran the mortgage company and had substantial holdings in real estate, including the store properties themselves. Howard, who had assumed the presidency of the corporation, was in charge of the liquidation process, which included the multitude of transactions involving the company's real estate, the fulfillment of employee benefit plans, and the business of closing the books on some $20 million in customer accounts receivable.

For five months Howard Polk, Paul Fischer, and general managers Barbara Toomey and Gerry Bruns worked out of the denuded and echoing headquarters building. Gerry, who had worked six days a week for twenty-five years, said, "I'm having a hard time getting used to the shorter hours. Forty hours a week at Polk Bros. is a part-time job." As the dog days of summer wore on, the men doffed their conservative business suits and ties and began coming to work in sports shirts. Howard grew a beard.

Barbara and Gerry with a small and loyal staff completed the job of packing and sending to dead storage such memorabilia and small pieces of history that remained. These included cartons of correspondence files, salvaged by Paul Fischer from the smoldering ruins of the old warehouse. The charred and sodden contents had been reduced by age to blackened blocks of papier-mache. Howard and Paul carried the boxes out to the dumpster behind the building.

The "move downtown" was accomplished in October when an even smaller group, made up of Howard, Paul, Barbara and a small staff carried their files, an antiquated copying machine, and their desktop computers to offices next door to the offices of the Polk Bros. Foundation. Over the next two years they would complete the liquidation process and oversee the transfer of the company's assets to the foundation.

By a turn of fate, if not by design, Sol's Polk's succession plan had kicked in. Sol established the Polk Bros. Foundation to run the business. And ultimately the business returned to the foundation. Polk Bros. didn't close its doors in the traditional sense. It became another entity. Even as the corporation was winding down its business, the foundation was gearing up its work of "giving back to Chicago."

20

Giving Back to Chicago

"Polk brothers' giving outlasts their selling."
— ***Chicago Tribune*** headline
September 27, 1992

"The focus of the foundation is Chicago. This is where our parents earned their money — in the Chicago area — and this is where they wanted it to go back."
— Sandra Polk Guthman
President
Polk Bros. Foundation

The stores were gone, the lights were out, the parking lots were empty. A work force that at one time numbered more than fifteen hundred men and women had dwindled to six. Polk Bros., as three generations of Chicagoans had known it, was now a memory.

But the Polk brothers left an unexpected legacy. The entire assets of the corporation, totaling at that time some $170

333

million, together with the personal donations from each of the brothers' estates, would be transferred to the Polk Bros. Foundation, re-energized under family leadership and committed to supporting Chicago educational and community programs. The heirs of the company's founders claimed no inheritance.

Sol Polk was not one to do things in a small way. As the business of liquidating the company's assets proceeded, the true size of Polk Bros.' endowment began to emerge. It was greater than anyone had anticipated. Within two years of the day the stores closed, the Polk Bros. Foundation was recognized as the single largest private foundation dedicated to giving to Chicago, and the sixth largest foundation in the state of Illinois. The extent of the Polk Bros. Foundation's outreach into Chicago neighborhoods and communities came to involve hundreds and then many hundreds of educational and social programs, health services, and cultural activities — and as foundation support for many of Chicago's most cherished institutions, in the form of capital grants for building programs and the establishment of educational centers, became visible.

As mentioned earlier, the 1988 settlement of the lawsuits over the disposition of Goldie's shares severed the foundation from Polk Bros. Inc. That same year, Sol Polk died, which precipitated a formal restructuring of the foundation. Sol, who died without direct descendants, bequeathed his entire estate to the foundation. The assets of the foundation swelled significantly at this time, and decisions regarding stewardship of those assets assumed a greater importance and urgency.

The reorganization of the foundation brought outside directors to work along with Polk family members for the first time. J. Ira Harris, senior partner of the Lazard Freres & Co. investment banking firm; Raymond F. Simon, president of the Helen V. Brach Foundation; Gordon Prussian, chairman emeritus of General Parking Corporation; and Sidney Epstein, chairman of A. Epstein & Sons, took positions as outside directors. The three family seats were held by Sandra Polk Guthman, who was elected president of the board; Bruce Bachmann and Roberta Lewis, who shared the second family seat; and Howard Polk, who held the third. Together they brought a depth of talent and experience in finance, business, civic affairs, and law to the planning and policy-making process.

* * *

The demise of the retail organization, and the complete liquidation of the Polk Bros. empire, which would occur four years later, could not have been foreseen at the time of the restructuring. But when the decision to close the stores and liquidate the company's assets was made in the spring of 1992, no time was lost. The foundation was prepared to move forward, with a vision for the use of the endowment that was clear from the beginning. The course had been set by the five brothers during their lifetimes, and continued by their sister Goldie through her own private donations.

The causes that Polk Bros. had supported over its fifty-seven-year history were many, including sponsorship of the nation's first fund-raising telethon on behalf of cerebral palsy. But the family's particular interests had clustered around activities that improved educational opportunities, provided for the health and well-being of children and the elderly, and encouraged pride and participation in the cultural resources of the city. The Polk Bros. Foundation, the directors determined, would perpetuate these goals.

One of the great strengths of the Polk Bros. stores lay with the family's ability, no matter how large the business grew, to remain close to the neighborhoods and the people they served. Accordingly, it was decided that the foundation would focus its support on programs that served community-based organizations providing direct service to their constituencies — programs that promised to have a tangible and immediate impact on the lives of people throughout Chicago.

In 1983, as Polk Bros. approached its fiftieth year in business, the company sponsored a twelve-page supplement to the

Chicago Tribune, entitled "Chicago — Second to None." The occasion was the commemoration of the city's one hundred fiftieth anniversary, and the supplement celebrated Chicago's history, its museums and cultural institutions, its architecture, its unique lakefront, and the contributions the city had made to the American economy. "Chicago — Second to None" received enormous circulation through the newspaper, but the demand was even greater. Polk Bros. reprinted one million additional copies and distributed these, as a public service, to Chicagoland schools, businesses, visitors' bureaus, and to Polk's own mailing list.

The foundation honored the Chicago-oriented sentiment expressed in "Chicago — Second to None" by adopting this motto: "The Polk Bros. Foundation: A Chicago Concern."

*   *   *

As the foundation refined its goals, it laid out four program areas around which grant-giving would be structured: social service, education, culture, and health care. These reflected the priorities to which the Polk brothers and Goldie, in their own charitable activities, had directed their money and their time. The foundation's first major grant, however, acknowledged retailing, the area of enterprise in which Polk Bros. had made its greatest contribution and which was the source of the wealth that would support the foundation's future giving. The foundation endowed the Polk Bros. Chair in Retailing at the J. L. Kellogg Graduate School of Management at Northwestern University.

From the first year of the reorganized board, family members demonstrated their commitment to hands-on involvement in achieving the goals of the foundation. In 1989 the Bachmann and Lewis families made a personal pledge to the national "I Have a Dream" program by volunteering their time and energies to shepherding a group of fifty-five sixth-grade students from an inner-city neighborhood through high school and into college. It was a ten-year commitment supported by a grant from the foundation to the Association House of Chicago, a social services agency that serves a primarily Hispanic community on the city's West Side.

In their role as sponsors, Ann and Bruce Bachmann and Roberta and Irv Lewis became mentors, tutors, cheerleaders, and friends to their family of "Dreamers." Irv Lewis, who was accustomed to the fourteen-hour days that he had put in as vice-president of operations at Polk Bros., committed as much time, if not more, to the task of helping some thirty teenage "dreamers" build a play lot for the younger children in their neighborhood.

Working from dawn to dusk in the summer of 1992, and continuing in 1993, Irv Lewis and project coordinator Eduardo Anguiano taught the youngsters — who came in shifts scheduled around summer school classes — about carpentry, landscaping, project planning, teamwork, and pride in a job well done. The dedication of the play lot in September 1992 was celebrated by community leaders, officials of city and state government, and even a former governor of the State of New Mexico.

* * *

By 1991 the Polk Bros. Foundation was approaching the level of maturity and the scope of outreach envisioned when the board began its work in 1988. With a fund balance of $143 million, the foundation made a grant distribution in 1991 of nearly $3.1 million to more than two hundred Chicago organizations. More than half of this funding was directed to critical needs such as services for disabled people, drug and child abuse prevention, shelter for the homeless, and job training and counseling, reflecting the foundation's 1991 theme: "Innovative Response to Community Needs."

In 1992 the foundation's assets grew to $178 million. Taking as its theme, "Working Neighborhood by Neighborhood," the foundation directed the largest portion of program funding to social services and support for neighborhood and community-based programs, particularly those serving the needs of Chicago children. Grants to these programs totaled $1.7 million.

That same year, the foundation's long-range plan to increase support for arts in the schools and for the city's cultural institutions began to bear fruit. Grants in support of educational outreach programs were made to cultural institutions that included the Adler Planetarium, the Brookfield Zoo, the Chicago Historical Society, the DuSable Museum of African American History, the Field Museum, and the Museum of Science and Industry.

In addition, in 1992 the Polk Bros. Foundation major commitments included a five-year one-million-dollar grant creating the Polk Bros. Educational Endowment Fund at the Museum of Contemporary Art. Two years later the foundation made a similar one-million-dollar gift to Chicago's Lincoln Park Zoo for the establishment of the Polk Bros. Foundation Educational Institute.

The year 1993 marked the Polk Bros. Foundation's thirty-seventh year of operation; it also marked Sandra Guthman's fifth year as the president of the board of directors and the foundation's guiding spirit. That fall Sandra increased her personal commitment by leaving behind a twenty-eight-year career as a top IBM executive to devote all of her energies to the Polk Bros. Foundation. She became the president and chief executive officer of the foundation.

*　　*　　*

Sandra's move coincided with the culmination of the activities related to the liquidation of Polk Bros. Inc., the corporate entity under which the stores and the subsidiaries of the business had operated. The greatest part of this work involved disposition of the company's real estate holdings. In January 1994, Polk Bros. Inc. ceased to exist; a trust was set up within the foundation to carry on remaining business, such as the administration of employee pensions. Rand Investment, the mortgage company, continued to operate under the trust as an asset of the foundation. At this point, the foundation's fund balance reached $218 million.

By 1994 the Polk Bros. Foundation had total assets exceeding $220 million and a 1994 grant distribution totaling almost $10 million, providing support to three hundred forty community organizations and institutions.

* * *

Even before the reorganization of the board, the Polk family charities extended beyond the work of the original foundation. In the mid-1980s, after the death of Sam Polk, Sol and Morrie Polk created the Polk Bros. Senior Welfare Foundation, funding it with a grant from the larger foundation. The mission of Senior Welfare (the name later became Fifty-five Plus) was very specific: To help schools, churches and other organizations establish meal programs for elderly neighbors.

The Senior Welfare goal was to provide more than a simple nutrition program. The intent was to feed the spirit as well, by creating opportunities where older adults, who might be living alone, could meet over a meal and socialize with their peers. Polk Bros. helped with the organization of neighborhood programs and funded the meal service, which often was catered. In the five years that the program operated, the Senior Welfare Foundation served more than three hundred thousand meals to Chicagoland seniors.

In December of 1992 the eleven surviving sons and daughters of the original family came together in Chicago for the annual meeting of what was then the Polk Bros. Senior Welfare Foundation, the first meeting since the closing of the stores. At that time, it was decided that this foundation would be perpetuated as the Polk Family Charitable Fund. The Senior Welfare Foundation thus became a small grant-making

foundation within the rubric of the larger operating foundation, with the eleven cousins serving as directors of the fund.

In the same period of time Goldie, with the assistance of
her family, was proceeding with her own work of "Giving
Back to Chicago." In 1991 the Goldie Bachmann Luftig
Health Center was opened at the Ark, a social service agency
for the indigent funded in part through the Jewish Federation
of Metropolitan Chicago and the Jewish United Fund.

Subsequently, Goldie endowed a building in Skokie as a
center for the services of affiliate agencies of the Jewish Federation: Jewish Children's Bureau, Jewish Family and Community Service, and Jewish Vocational Services. The Goldie
Bachmann Luftig Building was dedicated on December 15,
1994 — Goldie's ninetieth birthday.

*   *   *

In 1986 Sol Polk had launched what would be his last
grand promotion. The occasion was the celebration of the
one-hundredth anniversary of the dedication of the Statue of
Liberty in New York Harbor. For the event Polk Bros. purchased a precisely scaled model of the Statue of Liberty from
a European-born sculptor. The Liberty replica, standing fifteen inches high, was distributed by Polk Bros., together with
a thirty-minute cassette tape relating the history and meaning
of the monument.

The meaning that the Liberty promotion held for Sol
was profound, and speaks to the spirit that animates the Polk
Bros. Foundation in the work it does today. The five brothers
and their sister were born into an eastern European immigrant family that found refuge in Chicago at the turn of the
century. They worked hard, and America was good to them.

Sol Polk regarded the Liberty replica as a tangible link
between that first generation of bold and hopeful immigrants
and the second and third generations of children born to these
families. To him, the statue was a living symbol of the free-
doms and ideals that made it possible for an immigrant family

to build a company in America. He noted at the time of the promotion that many of the hundreds of "products for good living" carried in Polk Bros. stores had been "created by the fertile minds and craftsmanship of folks whose first glimpse of this great land was the lamp in Lady Liberty's up-raised hand." The legacy to be protected and communicated to succeeding generations, he urged, was the singularly American spirit of hard work, free enterprise, and shared prosperity that had made a business like Polk Bros. possible.

Sol's intention was expressed in a story told at the time:

> We know of one elderly customer, an immigrant who has served his new homeland valiantly, who gathered his grandchildren around him, played for them the inspirational tape recording that comes with the statue, and used those moments together to help them understand a little better why they must never forget what Lady Liberty symbolizes. He then presented them with his Statue of Liberty. A gift infinitely more important than merely the marble and bronze statue. The very idea that Polk Bros could have been a silent partner in that gentleman's expression of love for his country is overwhelming.

The immigrant Pokovitz family realized their American dream. The Polk Bros. Foundation is the successor to that dream, and "expression of love" and gratitude to the country and the city that made it possible.

Index

Q-R

Y-Z